SHARE the Music

MACMILLAN/McGRAW-HILL

AUTHORS

Judy Bond,
Coordinating Author

René Boyer-Alexander

Margaret Campbelle-Holman

Marilyn Copeland Davidson,
Coordinating Author

Robert de Frece

Mary Goetze,
Coordinating Author

Doug Goodkin

Betsy M. Henderson

Michael Jothen

Carol King

Vincent P. Lawrence,
Coordinating Author

Nancy L.T. Miller

Ivy Rawlins

Susan Snyder,
Coordinating Author

Janet McMillion,
Contributing Writer

Mc Graw Hill Macmillan McGraw-Hill

New York   Farmington

HAL•LEONARD®

Acknowledgments

Grateful acknowledgment is given to the following authors, composers, and publishers. Every effort has been made to trace the ownership of all copyrighted material and to secure the necessary permissions to reprint these selections. In the case of some selections for which acknowledgment is not given, extensive research has failed to locate the copyright holders.

Fran Smartt Addicott for *Let Music Surround You.*

Allyn and Bacon, Inc. for *The Wabash Cannonball* by William Kindt.

American Folklore Society for *Stone Pounding*, edited by T. Grame. Reprinted by permission of the American Folklore Society.

Argus Magazine for *I Wonder How It Feels to Fly* by Earl Thompson. Courtesy of Argus Magazine, Seattle, WA.

Association for Childhood Education International for *I Wish (aka The Shiny Little House)* from SUNG UNDER THE SILVER UMBRELLA by Nancy M. Hayes. Reprinted by permission of the Association for Childhood Education International, 11141 Georgia Avenue, Suite 200, Wheaton, MD 20902. Copyright © 1935 by the Association.

Irving Berlin for *It's a Lovely Day Today.*

Boosey & Hawkes, Inc. for *The Derby Ram* by Peter Erdei from 150 AMERICAN FOLK SONGS. Copyright © 1974 by Boosey & Hawkes, Inc. Reprinted by permission. For *Dormi, Dormi*, arranged by Mary Goetze. Copyright © 1984 by Boosey & Hawkes, Inc. This arrangement is made with the permission of Boosey & Hawkes, Inc. Reprinted by permission. For *The Path to the Moon* by Eric H. Thiman and Madeline C. Thomas. For *A Tragic Story* from FRIDAY AFTERNOONS by Benjamin Britten. © 1936 by Boosey & Co., Ltd.; Copyright renewed. Reprinted by permission of Boosey & Hawkes, Inc. For *Troika* from LIEUTENANT KIJE by S. Prokofiev. © 1936 by Edition A. Guthiel. Copyright assigned to Boosey & Hawkes, Inc.; Copyright Renewed. Reprinted by permission.

Marie Brown Associates for *Nathaniel's Rap* by Eloise Greenfield. Reprinted by permission of MARIE BROWN ASSOCIATES; © 1988 by Eloise Greenfield.

Margaret Campbelle-Holman for *Allundé, Alluia.* Arranged by Margaret Campbelle-Holman. For *And Where Is Home?* by Margaret Campbelle-Holman.

Canadian Museum of Civilization for *Feller from Fortune (Lots of Fish in Bonavist' Harbour)* from SONGS ON THE NEWFOUNDLAND OUTPORTS by Kenneth Peacock. National Museum of Canada, Bulletin 197, Anthropological Series 65, vol. 1, Ottawa 1965.

Cherry Lane Music Publishing Company, Inc. for *Calypso* by John Denver. © 1975 Cherry Lane Music Publishing Company, Inc. This Arrangement © 1994 Cherry Lane Music Publishing Company, Inc. All Rights Reserved. Used By Permission. For *Garden Song* by David Mallet. © Copyright 1975 Cherry Lane Music Publishing Company, Inc. This Arrangement © Copyright 1994 Cherry Lane Music Publishing Company, Inc. For *Take Me Home, Country Roads.* Words and music by Bill Danoff, Taffy Nivert, and John Denver.

Choristers Guild for *Come and Sing Together* from CANONS, SONGS AND BLESSINGS by Helen and John Kemp. Copyright © 1990 Choristers Guild. Used by permission.

Vernon Clark for *Martin's Cry* by Vernon Clark. © 1991 Vernon Clark.

continued on page 401

Macmillan McGraw-Hill

Published by Macmillan/McGraw-Hill, of McGraw-Hill Education, a division of The McGraw-Hill Companies, Inc., Two Penn Plaza, New York, New York 10121.

ISBN 0-02-295566-6 /4

4 5 6 7 8 9 058 04 03

SPECIAL CONTRIBUTORS

Contributing Writer
Janet McMillion

Consultant Writers
Teri Burdette, Signing
Brian Burnett, Movement
Robert Duke, Assessment
Joan Gregoryk, Vocal Development/
  Choral
Judith Jellison, Special Learners/
  Assessment
Jacque Schrader, Movement
Kathy B. Sorensen, International Phonetic
  Alphabet
Mollie Tower, Listening

Consultants
Lisa DeLorenzo, Critical Thinking
Nancy Ferguson, Jazz/Improvisation
Judith Nayer, Poetry
Marta Sanchez, Dalcroze
Mollie Tower, Reviewer
Robyn Turner, Fine Arts

Multicultural Consultants
Judith Cook Tucker
JaFran Jones
Oscar Muñoz
Marta Sanchez
Edwin J. Schupman, Jr., of ORBIS
  Associates
Mary Shamrock
Kathy B. Sorensen

Multicultural Advisors
Shailaja Akkapeddi (Hindi), Edna Alba
(Ladino), Gregory Amobi (Ibu), Thomas
Appiah (Ga, Twi, Fanti), Deven Asay
(Russian), Vera Auman (Russian, Ukrainian),
David Azman (Hebrew), Lissa Bangeter
(Portuguese), Britt Marie Barnes (Swedish),
Dr. Mark Bell (French), Brad Ahawanrathe
Bonaparte (Mohawk), Chhanda Chakroborti
(Hindi), Ninthalangsonk Chanthasen
(Laotian), Julius Chavez (Navajo), Lin-Rong
Chen (Mandarin), Anna Cheng (Mandarin),
Rushen Chi (Mandarin), T. L. Chi (Mandarin),
Michelle Chingwa (Ottowa), Hoon Choi
(Korean), James Comarell (Greek), Lynn
DePaula (Portuguese), Ketan Dholakia
(Gujarati), Richard O. Effiong (Nigerian),
Nayereh Fallahi (Persian), Angela Fields
(Hopi, Chemehuevi), Gary Fields (Lakota,

Cree), Siri Veslemoy Fluge (Norwegian),
Katalin Forrai (Hungarian), Renee Galagos
(Swedish), Linda Goodman, Judith A. Gray,
Savyasachi Gupta (Marati), Elizabeth Haile
(Shinnecock), Mary Harouny (Persian),
Charlotte Heth (Cherokee), Tim Hunt
(Vietnamese), Marcela Janko (Czech), Raili
Jeffrey (Finnish), Rita Jensen (Danish), Teddy
Kaiahura (Swahili), Gueen Kalaw (Tagalog),
Merehau Kamai (Tahitian), Richard Keeling,
Masanori Kimura (Japanese), Chikahide
Komura (Japanese), Saul Korewa (Hebrew),
Jagadishwar Kota (Tamil), Sokun Koy
(Cambodian), Craig Kurumada (Balkan),
Cindy Trong Le (Vietnamese), Dongchoon Lee
(Korean), Young-Jing Lee (Korean), Nomi Lob
(Hebrew), Sam Loeng (Mandarin, Malay),
Georgia Magpie (Comanche), Mladen Marič
(Croatian), Kuinise Matagi (Samoan), Hiromi
Matsushita (Japanese), Jackie Maynard
(Hawaiian), David McAllester, Mike
Kanathohare McDonald (Mohawk),
Khumbulani Mdlefshe (Zulu), Martin Mkize
(Xhosa), David Montgomery (Turkish), Kazadi
Big Musungayi (Swahili), Professor Akiya
Nakamara (Japanese), Edwin Napia (Maori),
Hang Nguyen (Vietnamese), Richard Nielsen
(Danish), Wil Numkena (Hopi), Eva Ochoa
(Spanish), Drora Oren (Hebrew), Jackie
Osherow (Yiddish), Mavis Oswald (Russian),
Dr. Dil Parkinson (Arabic), Kenny Tahawisoren
Perkins (Mohawk), Alvin Petersen (Sotho),
Phay Phan (Cambodian), Charlie Phim
(Cambodian), Aroha Price (Maori), Marg Puiri
(Samoan), John Rainer (Taos Pueblo, Creek),
Lillian Rainer (Taos Pueblo, Creek, Apache),
Winton Ria (Maori), Arnold Richardson
(Haliwa-Saponi), Thea Roscher (German),
Dr. Wayne Sabey (Japanese), Regine Saintil
(Bamboula Creole), Luci Scherzer (German),
Ken Sekaquaptewa (Hopi), Samouen Seng
(Cambodian), Pei Shin (Mandarin), Dr. Larry
Shumway (Japanese), Gwen Shunatona
(Pawnee, Otoe, Potawatomi), Ernest Siva
(Cahuilla, Serrano [Maringa´]), Ben Snowball
(Inuit), Dr. Michelle Stott (German), Keiko
Tanefuji (Japanese), James Taylor
(Portuguese), Shiu-wai Tong (Mandarin),
Tom Toronto (Lao, Thai), Lynn Tran
(Vietnamese), Gulavadee Vaz (Thai), Chen
Ying Wang (Taiwanese), Masakazu Watabe
(Japanese), Freddy Wheeler (Navajo), Keith
Yackeyonny (Comanche), Liming Yang
(Mandarin), Edgar Zurita (Andean)

CONTENTS

Time for Singing! . . . . **viii**

Time for Singing!

Once you start this song, it may not stop just because you finish singing it. Some songs are like that. You may find yourself hearing or singing them the rest of the day.

DON'T LET THE MUSIC STOP

Words and Music
by Eugene Butler

Don't let the mu - sic stop,__ let's keep it firm and strong;

Don't let the mu - sic stop,__ let's sing the whole day long.

Don't let the mu - sic stop,__ don't let it ev - er cease, 'Cause the

mu - sic that I sing makes the world go round,__ It brings

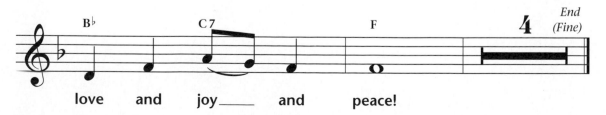

love and joy__ and peace!

I hear_____ A-mer-i-ca sing-ing, I hear her sing-ing,

Var - ied car - ols I hear._____

I hear_____ A-mer-i-ca sing-ing, I hear her sing-ing,

Go back to **A** *and sing to end*
(Da Capo al Fine)

Var - ied car - ols I hear._____

A famous American poet, Walt Whitman, wrote the words that inspired this song over 100 years ago. You'll find other "varied carols" or songs that Americans love to sing on the pages that follow.

Were you ever so excited that you could not sit still? The enslaved African Americans who created "Oh, Won't You Sit Down?" sang about heaven because their lives on earth were difficult. Joyful songs like this one gave them hope.

OH, WON'T YOU SIT DOWN?

African American Spiritual

Freely Refrain

Oh, won't you sit down?— Lord, I can't sit down.—

Oh, won't you sit down?— Lord, I can't sit down.—

Oh, won't you sit down?— Lord, I can't sit down.—

'Cause I just got to Heav-en, gon-na look a-round.—

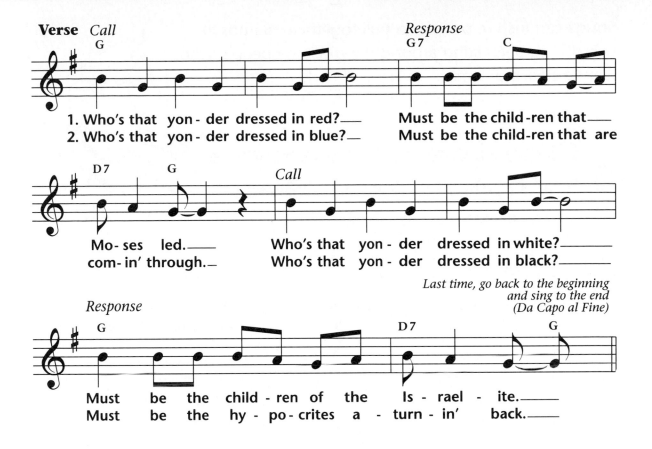

Verse *Call*

G

G7 *Response*

C

1. Who's that yon-der dressed in red?— Must be the child-ren that—
2. Who's that yon-der dressed in blue?— Must be the child-ren that are

D7 G *Call*

Mo-ses led.— Who's that yon-der dressed in white?_____
com-in' through.— Who's that yon-der dressed in black?_____

Last time, go back to the beginning and sing to the end (Da Capo al Fine)

Response

G

D7

G

Must be the child-ren of the Is-rael-ite._____
Must be the hy-po-crites a-turn-in' back._____

After you have learned the song below, you can sing it as a round. When your class sings all of the phrases at one time, music really will surround you!

LET MUSIC SURROUND YOU

Words and Music
by Fran Addicott

1
G F 3 G

2
G F G

do

Let mu-sic sur-round you. Let it fill your heart.

3
G F G 3

G F G

Those who sing in har-mon-y.— Nev-er grow a-part.

Songs can inspire people to pull together. "Somos el barco" has been sung around the globe by people who want a peaceful world.

Somos el barco
We Are the Boat

Words and Music by Lorre Wyatt

A **Refrain**

Spanish: So - mos el bar - co,_____ So - mos el mar.
Pronunciation: °°so mos el baɾ ko so mos el maɾ

Yo na - ve - go_____ en ti, Tu na - ve - gas_____ en mí.
yo na βe go en ti tu na βe gas en mi

We are the boat, We are the sea.

Last time only: repeat this line

I sail in you, you sail in me.

1. B **Verse**

1. The stream sings_____ it to the riv - er,_____ The

riv - er sings it to the sea. The sea sings it

4

to the __ boat that car - ries you __ and me. ____ So - mos el

so mos el

2. – 4. C **Verse**

2.   The   boat   we   are ____ sail - ing   in ____ was
3. With our   hopes   we   raise   the   sails ____ to
4.   The   voy - age   has   been ____ long   and   hard ____ and

built   by   man - y ____ hands,   The   sea   we   are ____
face   the   wind   once __ more,   With our   hearts _____ we
yet   we're   sail - ing __ still,   With   a   song   to   help   us ____

Go back to the sign

D.S. 𝄋

sail - ing   on _____   Touch - es   ev' - ry __ sand. ____
chart   the   wa - ters   Nev - er   sailed   be - fore. ____   } So - mos el
pull   to - geth - er   If   we   on - ly __ will. ____   *so mos el*

The Wabash Cannonball was a famous train running between large cities in the midwest beginning in 1851. But originally this song was about an imaginary train that went all over North America. The more the song was sung, the more fantastic the train became.

The Wabash Cannonball

Words and Music
by William Kindt

1. From the great At - lan - tic O - cean to the wide Pa - cif - ic shore, To the green old flow- 'ring moun - tains to ice - bound Lab - ra - dor, She's long and tall and hand - some and known quite well to all, She's the mod - ern com - bin - a - tion called the Wa - bash Can - non - ball.

Refrain: So_____ lis - ten to the jin - gle, the_____ jum - ble and the roar, As she glides a - long the wood - lands through the hills and by the shore. Hear the might - y rush of the en - gine and the lone - some ho - boes squall, While_____ rid - ing through the jun - gle on the Wa - bash Can - non - ball.

2. Now she came in from Birmingham on a cold and frosty day,
   As she rolled into the station you could hear the people say,
   "There's a gal out there from Tennessee, she's long, boy, and tall,
   She's the modern combination called the Wabash Cannonball."
   Refrain

3. Now the Eastern states are dandy, so all the people say,
   From New York to Saint Louis and Chicago by the way,
   From the lakes of Minnesota where the rippling waters fall,
   No change in standard gauging on the Wabash Cannonball.
   Refrain

Words like these take on even greater meaning when they are set to such powerful music. Think of what makes you proud to be an American as you sing this song.

This Is My Country

Music by Al Jacobs
Words by Don Raye

1.–2. This is my coun-try! Land of my { birth. / choice.

This is my coun-try! { Grand - est on earth. / Hear my proud voice.

I pledge thee my al - le - giance, A - mer - i-ca the bold, for

This is my coun-try, to have and to hold!

VOICES OF THE WORLD

There is music
in the hearts of people—
the music of joy
turned into song—
a roundelay of happiness—
lifting all voices
in one choir
of the world.

There is a dance-step
to the heart-beat of people—
a timing of gladness—
of nimble feet
and clapping hands—
widening around
the magic circle
of the world.

There is music
in the gypsy-tune
of violins—
a piper's flute—
the roll of an organ chord—
a tinkling chime—
the drum-beat
of a town-band on parade. . .
Music is the sound of life awakening
The voices of the world!

—*Stefi Samuelson*

WHERE IN THE WORLD?

In cultures throughout the world, people enjoy expressing their thoughts and feelings through music. A song's origin can often be identified by the way the melody and rhythms sound, the instruments used, and the words.

Duke Ellington

Sir Duke

Words and Music by
Stevie Wonder

1. Mu - sic is a world with - in it - self
2. Mu - sic knows it is and al - ways will be

with a lan - guage we all un - der - stand,
one of the things that life just won't quit.

with an e - qual op - por - tu - ni - ty
But here are some of mu - sic's pi - o - neers,

for all to sing dance and clap their hands
that time will not al - low us to for - get

but just be-cause a re-cord has a groove don't make it in the groove
for there's_ Ba-sie, Mil-ler, Satch-mo,_ and the king of all, Sir Duke,

but you can tell right a - way at let - ter A_ when the
and with a voice like_ El - la's ring - in' out,_ there's no

Refrain

peo -ple start to move. They⎫ can feel it all_ o - ver._
way the band can lose. You⎭

They⎫ can feel it all_ o - ver,_ peo -ple._ ⎰They⎱ can feel it all_
You⎭ ⎱You⎰

o - ver._ ⎰They⎱ can feel it all_ o - ver,_ peo - ple, go!
⎱You⎰

Is there anyone you look up to? Stevie Wonder expresses his admiration for some of his heroes in "Sir Duke."

Ella Fitzgerald

Louis Armstrong

A MUSICAL WORLD

Take Me Home, Country Roads

Words and Music
by Bill Danoff, Taffy Nivert,
and John Denver

Verse

Al - most heav - en,_____ West Vir - gin - ia,_____

Blue Ridge Moun - tains,_____ Shen - an - do - ah

Riv - er._____ Life is old there,_____

old - er than the trees, young - er than the

moun - tains_____ grow - in' like a breeze._____

Refrain

Coun - try roads,_____ take_ me home_____ to the

place_____ I be - long:_____ West Vir - gin - ia,_____

When you tap your foot to a song, you're tapping to the **beat**, or the steady pulse that you feel.

The long and short sounds and silences that occur when you sing the words are called the rhythm of the words.

BOGGED DOWN BY BEATS?

Here's part of an Irish folk song, "Hi! Ho! The Rattlin' Bog."
Bogs are swampy areas where mosses float on top of plants.
A bog shakes or "rattles" when somebody steps on it.

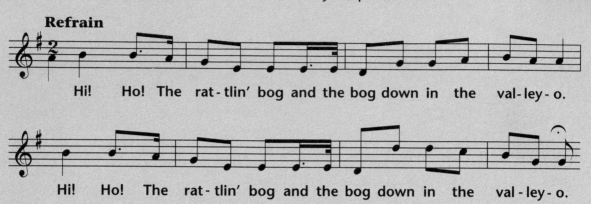

Refrain

Hi! Ho! The rat-tlin' bog and the bog down in the val-ley-o.

Hi! Ho! The rat-tlin' bog and the bog down in the val-ley-o.

SING "Hi! Ho! The Rattlin' Bog," patting with the beats that feel stronger and clapping quietly with the other beats.

How are the strong and weak beats grouped?

The **meter signature** of a song shows how many beats are in each set. A song that has *one* strong and *one* weak beat in each set could have a meter signature with a 2 on the top.

Sets of beats can be felt differently. These patterns show beats that feel strong and weak.

Here's a folk song from the islands of Trinidad and Tobago.
As you listen, see if you can feel the beat.

I Let Her Go, Go

Folk Song from
Trinidad and Tobago
Adapted by Carol King

I let her go, go, Ee ay I let her go, go,

Ee ay I let her go ——— I let her go, go, go.

FIND the pattern on page 14 that shows
the set of beats used in this song. What
is the meter signature?

Musical Ideas Are Everywhere

Have you ever read a story without words? Try this one! Each picture stands for one idea. When all the ideas are put together, they tell a story.

Music is also made up of ideas. A complete musical idea is called a **phrase.** A phrase is made of high and low sounds, or **pitches.** When phrases are put together, they make up a song or a **melody.**

In a **call-and-response** song, call phrases are sung
by a leader and response phrases are sung by the group.
Find the phrases as you listen to this song.

'Way Down Yonder in the Brickyard

Traditional African
American Game Song
As Performed by the
Georgia Sea Island Singers

A *Call* **Freely** *Response*

'Way down yon-der in the brick-yard, Re-mem-ber me.

Call

'Way down yon-der in the brick-yard, Re-mem-ber me.

B *Call* *Response*

Oh, step it, step it, step it down.—— Re-mem-ber me.

Call

Oh, step it, step it, step it down.—— Re-mem-ber me.

C *Call* *Response*

Oh, swing your la-dy, turn her a-round,—— Re-mem-ber me.

Call

Oh, swing your la-dy, turn her a-round,—— Re-mem-ber me.

A SONG FROM INNER MONGOLIA

Inner Mongolia is part of China. Some people live by herding animals, and the children help by watching over their families' sheep. The children may sing or play flutes to calm the flocks, just as you'd sing a lullaby to comfort a baby.

CHINESE MIRROR PAINTING

This mirror was painted when Qian-long was emperor of China (1735–1796). One woman plays a traditional flute, the other a frame drum and wooden clappers.

MOVE your arm in an arch to show each phrase you hear in "Mongolian Night Song." Then sing the song.

Mongolian Night Song

Traditional Inner Mongolian Song
Collected and Translated by Gloria Kiester

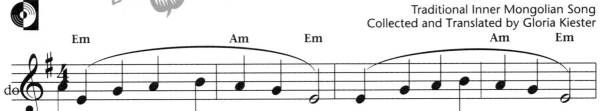

1. Lit - tle girl who tends the sheep, Brings them to the fold to sleep.
2. In the moon-light's gold - en glow, Soft the wind be - gins to blow.

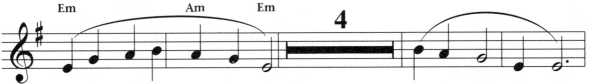

Lit - tle lambs are bounc - ing by to their moth - er's bleat - ing cry,
Lit - tle lambs are fast a - sleep, ly - ing by the oth - er sheep.

Un - der-neath a star - lit sky. ⎫
Still a si - lent watch she keeps. ⎬ All a - lone she waits.

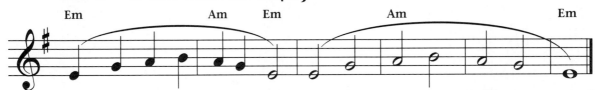

"In the dark I'm not a - fraid. I've a lamp to light the way."
"When I'm tend - ing all a - lone, All I think a - bout is home."

Unit 1 *Where in the World?* **19**

CHOICES WITH VOICES

Have you ever disguised your voice or tried to sound like somebody you know? Then you know you can change the sound of your speaking and singing voice.

 LISTENING

Mañana Iguana

by Bobby McFerrin

Bobby McFerrin uses his voice to make all sorts of interesting sounds. What are some things he does to change his voice?

One way to change your voice is to change the register. The **lighter register** is quieter and generally higher in pitch. The **heavier register** is usually louder, fuller, and lower in pitch.

20

I Wish

Nancy M. Hayes
Adapted by Carol King

1   **2**

I   wish,   how I   wish,   that I   had a   lit - tle   house,

With a   mat   for   the cat   and a   hole   for   the mouse,

And a   clock   go - ing "tock"   in   the cor - ner of   the room

And a   ket - tle, and a cup - board, and a big   birch   broom.

In a **canon,** all parts perform the same song or poem, but start at different times. Change the sound of the poem by speaking in canon. One group speaks in the heavier register, the other in the lighter register.

SING HIGH! SING LOW!

Using different registers, you change the **tone color** of your sound. You can sing different styles and make singing some pitches easier.

Compare two melodies. Most of the notes in "I Let Her Go, Go" are on the lower part of the staff. The lower pitches are probably easier to sing in the heavier register.

I let her go, go,

Now look at the second melody. Are these notes mostly higher or lower than the ones in "I Let Her Go, Go"? Which register will you probably use to sing this part of "Hi! Ho! The Rattlin' Bog"?

Verse

Now in this bog there was a tree, a rare tree, a rat-tlin' tree;

"Hi! Ho! The Rattlin' Bog" song is called a **cumulative** song because each verse adds to the story. Have a rattlin' good time!

Hi! Ho! The Rattlin' Bog

Irish
Folk Song

Refrain

Hi! Ho! The rat-tlin' bog and the bog down in the val-ley-o.

End here, last time

Hi! Ho! The rat-tlin' bog and the bog down in the val-ley-o.

Verse

1. Now in this bog there was a tree, a rare tree, a
2. Now on this tree there was a limb, a rare limb, a
3. Now on this limb there was a branch, a rare branch, a
4. Now on this branch there was a nest, a rare nest, a
5. Now in this nest there was an egg, a rare egg, a
6. Now in this egg there was a bird, a rare bird, a

Add a repeat with each verse

rat - tlin'	tree;	The		
rat - tlin'	limb;	The	limb on the tree and the
rat - tlin'	branch;	The	branch on the limb and the
rat - tlin'	nest;	The	nest on the branch and the
rat - tlin'	egg;	The	egg in the nest and the
rat - tlin'	bird;	The	bird in the egg and the

(Skip this measure for verse 1)

1.-6. tree in the bog and the bog down in the val-ley-o.

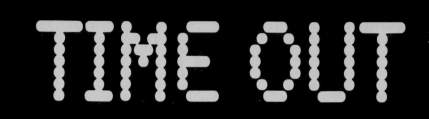
TIME OUT

Playing and resting are part of both sports and music.

Musical sounds have different lengths. Musicians know how long to play or sing by following written music. Look at the chart to see how musical sounds can be written when a quarter note gets the beat.

♩	**quarter note**	one sound to a beat
♫	two **eighth notes**	two sounds to a beat
♪	**half note**	sound lasting two beats
𝄽	**quarter rest**	silence the length of a beat

PAT each quarter note, snap the eighth notes, and brush your hands for each half note.

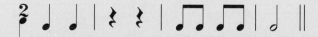

FOR RHYTHMS

THINK IT THROUGH

What are some movements you can make to show 𝄽 ?
Why did you choose those movements?

A **coda** is a special ending for a song or poem.

CREATE a coda for "I Wish" by performing the pattern on page 24 two times after you speak the poem.

STILL MUSIC

This painting shows a stage after a rehearsal or concert. Why do you think the artist, Ben Shahn, called it "Still Music"?

To see how sets of beats are felt in a song, look at the meter signature. The top number tells how many beats are in a set. The **bar lines** divide the notes into sets, or **measures**, based on the top number.

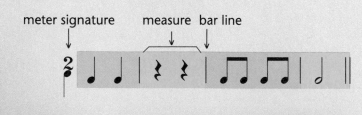

You can write $\frac{2}{\downarrow}$ as $\frac{2}{4}$. The lower number tells what note lasts one beat. When there are three quarter notes in each measure, the meter signature can be written as $\frac{3}{4}$. What could you write if there were four quarter notes in each measure?

LISTEN for the sets of beats in "Mongolian Night Song." Decide where the missing bar lines go.

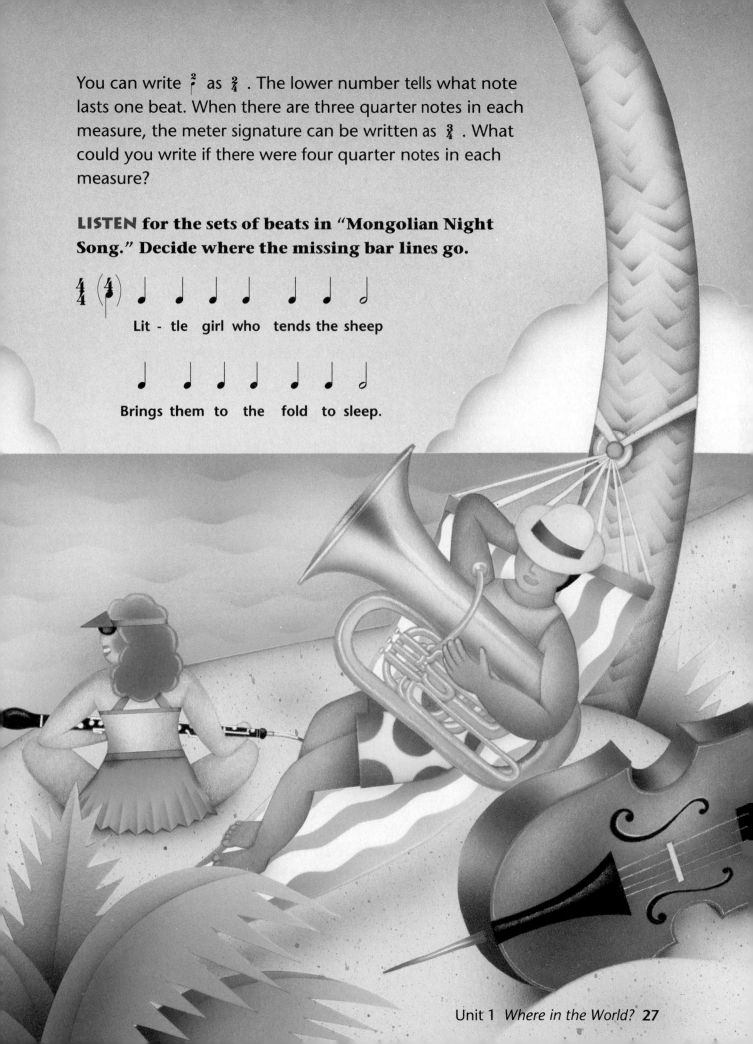

Lit - tle girl who tends the sheep

Brings them to the fold to sleep.

MELODIES TAKE SHAPE

Look at the shapes of three phrases from
" 'Way Down Yonder in the Brickyard."
The phrases use **pitch syllables** named
do re mi so.

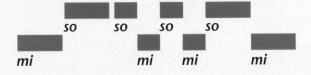

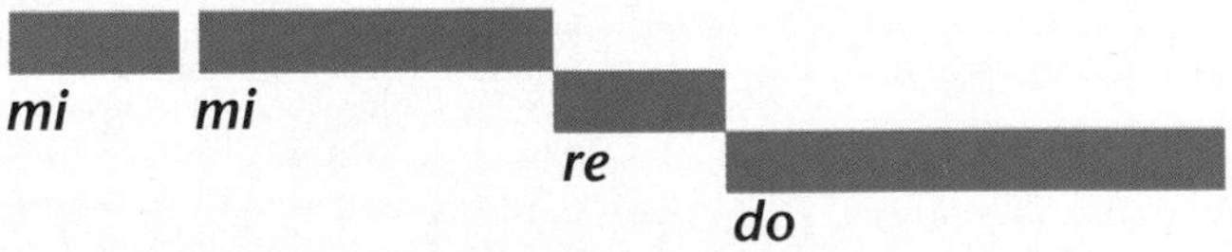

so   so   so   so

mi   mi   mi   mi

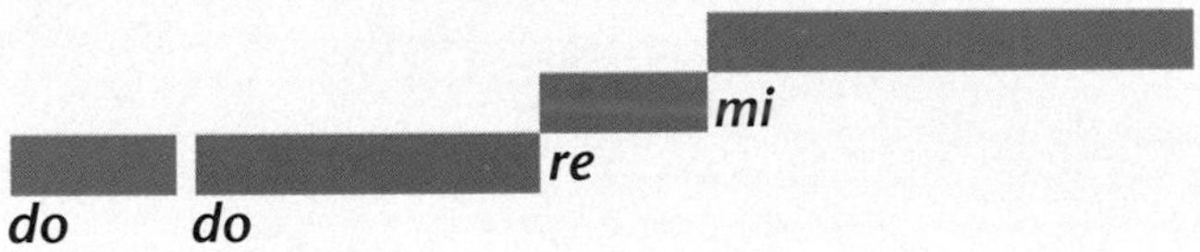

mi

re
do

do   do

re

mi   mi

re
do

SING each phrase of " 'Way
Down Yonder in the Brick-
yard." Find the pattern with
the same shape.

Melodies can be written on a **staff** of five lines and four spaces. In " 'Way Down Yonder in the Brickyard," *do re mi so* look like this.

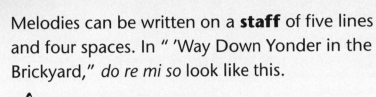

do   re   mi   so

Because *do* is below the staff, an extra line called a **ledger line** is used.

'Way down yon-der in the brick-yard,

Re - mem - ber   me.

'Way down yon-der in the brick-yard,

Re - mem - ber   me.

MATCH these phrases with the patterns on page 28.

MOVING ON

You often hear *do* at the beginning and end of a song. *Do* can be written on any line or in any space of the staff. If *do* moves, the other pitches also move.

do   re   mi   so

do   re   mi   so

do   re   mi   so

When *do* is on a line, where are *mi* and *so*? When *do* is in a space, where are *mi* and *so*?

LISTEN to some melodies. Which set of pitches do you hear?

do   do
     do   re   mi   mi   so

People traditionally gathered to share folk songs, learning them from family and friends. Playing along on instruments, which were sometimes made at home, added to the fun.

Fed My Horse

Southern Appalachian Folk Song

Fed my horse in a pop-lar trough, Fed my horse in a pop-lar trough,

Fed my horse in a pop-lar trough, Then she caught the whoop-ing cough.

Coy ma-lin-do Kill-ko, kill-ko; Coy ma-lin-do Kill-ko me.

Which pitch sounded just right to end on?
Find the pitch in this song that is <u>not</u> *do re mi* or *so*.
The name of that pitch is *la*.

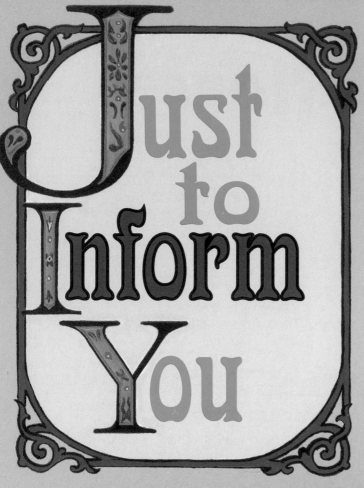

Just to Inform You

When you look at the shape or outline of something, you see its **form.** The form can be made up of one large shape or many smaller shapes.

DESCRIBE the forms in this building.

Music has form, too. You can hear the form of a song by listening to the order of its phrases or sections.

The order of a song's phrases is called its phrase form. To describe the form when two phrases are the same, use a a. When two phrases are different, use a b.

LISTEN to two phrases from a piece of music called "Troika."

Model of St. Basil's
Cathedral, Moscow

SPOTLIGHT ON
SERGEI PROKOFIEV

Sergei Prokofiev (1891–1953) was a renowned Russian pianist, conductor, and composer. His first piano teacher was his mother. He began composing when he was five, and tried to write an opera when he was nine. Prokofiev became a very good pianist, and once won a piano in a competition.

Prokofiev loved theater, and composed operas, ballets, and film music. He also wrote symphonies and concertos. Unusual stories attracted him. For example, he wrote music for Lieutenant Kijé, a movie about an imaginary man.

Prokofiev's music was criticized at first because people were not used to his modern harmonies and rhythms. However, others found his music brilliant and appealing, and he received many invitations to compose. Now he is remembered as one of the greatest modern composers.

LISTENING

Troika (excerpt) from *Lieutenant Kijé Suite*

by *Sergei Prokofiev*

Prokofiev wrote "Troika" as part of the music for the movie Lieutenant Kijé. A troika is a Russian sleigh or carriage pulled by three horses.

LISTENING MAP *Raise your hand when the first two phrases (a and b) return in "Troika."*

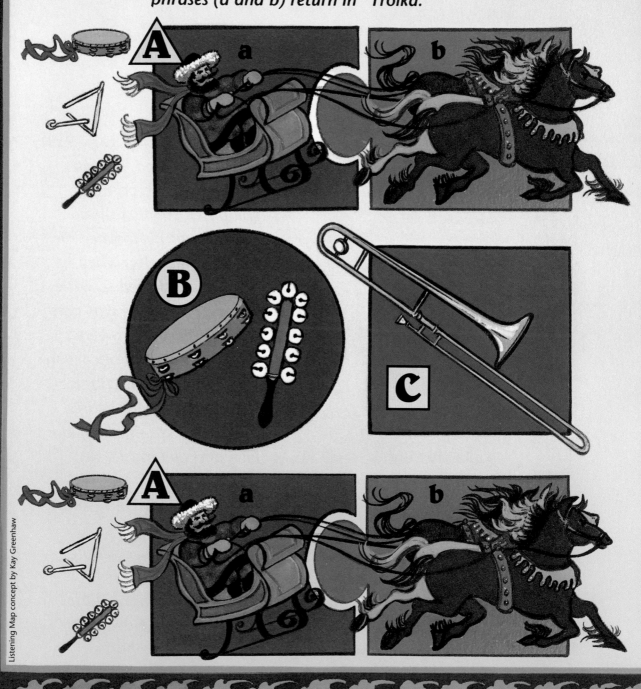

Listening Map concept by Kay Greenhaw

SIMILAR PHRASES

These snowflakes are similar, but not the same.
How are they different from one another?

Sometimes musical phrases are almost the
same, or similar.

When you describe a form that has similar
phrases, add a mark (ꞌ) called a prime to the
letter for the similar phrase. The form can be
called a aꞌ or b bꞌ.

Is the phrase form a aꞌ or a b in the first two
lines of "Hi! Ho! The Rattlin' Bog"? Where
does the difference occur?

IT'S A PITCH PUZZLE!

Are you ready for a puzzle? The first four phrases of " 'Way Down Yonder in the Brickyard" are all mixed up.

SING each phrase with pitch syllables.

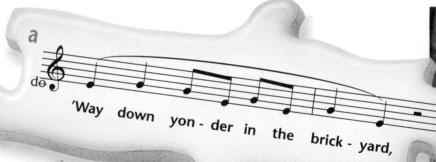

a

'Way down yon - der in the brick - yard,

b¹

Re - mem - ber me.

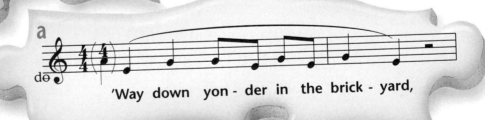

a

'Way down yon - der in the brick - yard,

What is the correct order for the phrases, a b b¹ a or a b a b¹?

b

Re - mem - ber me.

NAME THOSE PITCHES!

You are listening to the radio, and you decide to join in the "Name Those Pitches" game. You try to recognize the mystery melody. It could be a melody with *mi so la* or one with *do re mi*.

How will you figure out the winning pitches? Listen carefully!

FROM POETRY TO PITCHES

Have you ever tried to set a poem to music? That's what songwriters do all the time! This activity may give you some ideas.

CREATE a melody for "I Wish."

Use the pitches shown with the lines of the poem. Match them by color.

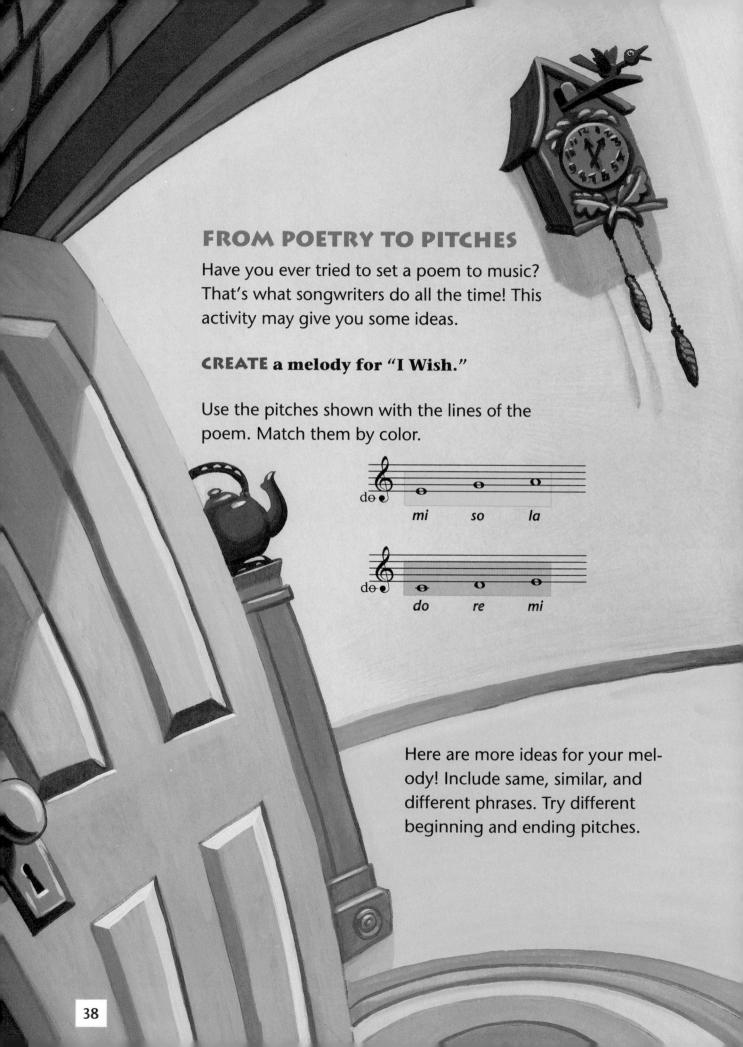

do   mi   so   la

do   do   re   mi

Here are more ideas for your melody! Include same, similar, and different phrases. Try different beginning and ending pitches.

Create an accompaniment for your melody with the instruments shown, or make your own special sounds on the words that have instrument pictures.

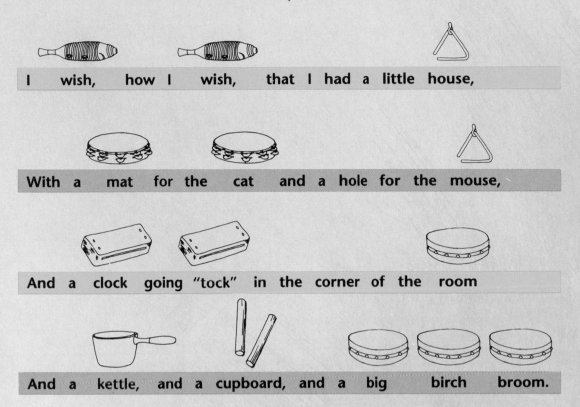

I wish, how I wish, that I had a little house,

With a mat for the cat and a hole for the mouse,

And a clock going "tock" in the corner of the room

And a kettle, and a cupboard, and a big birch broom.

THINK IT THROUGH

If you want to play your melody with a friend tomorrow, what are some ways you can remember it? Which way would work best for you?

Rhythms that Repeat

If you have a melody in mind, why not add some rhythms? Try an **ostinato,** a pattern that repeats many times.

CREATE a rhythm ostinato by repeating this pattern. Snap the eighth notes and brush your hands for the half notes.

Two instruments can also share the ostinato.

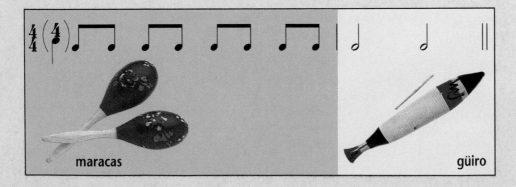

maracas

güiro

PERFORM the ostinato with the instrumental section of "I Let Her Go, Go."

OSTINATO "TO GO"

You can add a playful movement ostinato to "I Let Her Go, Go."

FOLLOW the pictures to find out what to do each time you sing *go*.

1

I let her go, go,

2

Ee ay I let her go, go,

3

Ee ay I let her go

4

I let her go, go, go.

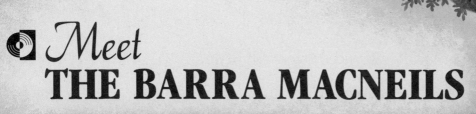

Meet
THE BARRA MACNEILS

The Barra MacNeils are from Nova Scotia, Canada. They perform traditional Celtic and Canadian music and write their own songs as well.

LISTEN to the Barra MacNeils discuss their music.

LISTENING

The Foxhunter's from
Flower Basket Medley

Arranged by Sheumas, Kyle, Stewart, and Lucy MacNeil

Listen for the mouth music in "The Foxhunter's." Mouth music is created by singing very fast rhythms with nonsense syllables. It can be dance music when no instruments are handy. Try this mouth music.

die od-dle dee-dle i-dle did-dle-y i-dle dee-dle dum

Can you keep up with "The Foxhunter's"?

RHYTHMS HIT THE ROAD!

CREATE a dance of movement ostinatos. First, choose a pattern to perform with your feet.

Find a partner and teach one another your steps. Together, create an ostinato using both patterns. How many beats long is it?

PERFORM your ostinato to "The Foxhunter's."

Music Is a World Within Itself

People all over the world enjoy music. The songs in this unit come from near and far.

Name each song pictured on the map, then name the country from which each song comes. Plan a travel route that includes all the orange countries.

SING the songs that come from these countries as you visit around the musical world.

Which songs are in $\frac{2}{4}$ meter? In $\frac{4}{4}$?

Which songs have phrases of different lengths? The same length?

CHECK IT OUT

1. How many phrases do you hear?

   a. two   **b.** three   **c.** four

2. Locate the rhythm pattern that is played. Which measure has the wrong number of beats?

   a. Measure 1   **b.** Measure 2   **c.** Measure 3   **d.** Measure 4

   Pattern 1

   Pattern 2

   Pattern 3

   Pattern 4

3. Which rhythm do you hear?

   a.

   b.

   c.

   d.

4. Which melody do you hear?

   a.    **c.**

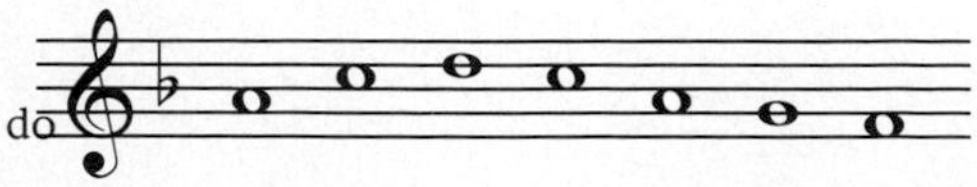

   b.   **d.**

CREATE

Introduction in Eight

CREATE a melody. Use the pitches F G A C' D'. Use this eight-beat rhythm pattern.

On a piece of paper, write your melody with the letters you find on the bells you chose.

The bell with the letter F sounds like *do*. Write your melody with pitch syllables, too.

If the meter signature of this rhythm pattern is ²/₄ , where do the bar lines go?

Play your melody as an introduction to "Fed My Horse."

Write

Stevie Wonder wrote "Sir Duke" in honor of jazz musician Duke Ellington. Think of a musician you admire.

Write a poem telling who the person is and why you look up to that person.

The California Song

American Folk Song

Verse

1. We've formed our band and we are all well manned
2. Oh, the gold in thar most an - y - whar,
3. Oh don't you cry or heave a sigh,
4. We ex - pect our share of the coars - est fare,

To jour - ney a - far to the pro - mised land,
They dig it out with an i - ron bar,
For we'll come back a - gain bye and bye,
And some - times sleep in the o - pen air,

Where the gold - en ore is thick in store
And where it's thick with a spade and pick,
Don't have fear or shed a tear,
Up - on the cold ground we will sleep sound,

On the banks of the Sac - ra - men - to shore,
They've ta-ken out lumps as big as a brick.
But pa-tient - ly wait for a - bout two year.
Ex - cept when the wolves come howl - ing round.

Refrain

Then ho, boys, ho! to Cal - i - for - nia go,

for the moun - tains bold are cov - ered with gold on the

banks of the Sac - ra - men - to,

Heigh, ho a - way we go,

Dig - ging up gold in Fris - co.

ENCORE
Carnival Time in Puerto Rico

Costumes, food, parades, and music are the most important ingredients of Carnival in Puerto Rico.

Since 1858, men and boys have dressed up as *Vejigantes*, masked pranksters. The Vejigantes travel the streets, teasing children with good-natured pranks. They wear colorful costumes with wings.

The Vejigantes wear handmade papier-mâché masks with many horns. They use *vejigas*, balloon-like cow bladders, to surprise the children.

Vejigantes

In Puerto Rico, not only is music an important part of Carnival time, but also of everyday life.

Typical Puerto Rican instruments include from left to right: rasp, pandereta (flat drum), maraca, bomba drum, güiro (snake-shaped gourd), and cuatro.

Bomba is one of the oldest forms of Puerto Rican music. It combines dance, singing, and percussion. The percussion usually features a single maraca and three differently pitched drums made from barrels. There are two kinds of calls and responses in bomba: the solo singer and chorus respond to one another, and the drummers and dancer respond to one another. They challenge each other in a lively competition. It's very exciting!

LISTENING

Campo *Puerto Rican bomba*

The singer tells of his sad, hard life. He wants to be free to dance to the bomba, hoping it will help him to be happy.

Los Pleneros de la 21 performing a bomba.

El Marunguey

*by Angel Luis Medina
and José Rivera*

"El Marunguey" tells of going to the mangroves to catch crabs, fish, and eels. It is a type of music called *plena*. Plena is an exciting and joyful type of Caribbean music. It is often called *el periodico*, or "the sung newspaper," because daily events are described in improvised music. Plena combines both African and Spanish musical traditions. It usually consists of calls and responses between soloist and chorus.

Children playing a pandereta and güiro with rasp.

Plena instruments include a güiro, made from a gourd, and three or more hand-held frame drums, each of a different size, called *panderetas*. Each pandereta plays a different rhythm.

STEP and play this rhythm to the plena "El Marunguey."

right   left   right   left   right   left   right   left   right   left

TRAVELING ON

Roads Go Ever Ever On

Roads go ever ever on,
    Over rock and under tree,
By caves where never sun has shone,
    By streams that never find the sea;
Over snow by winter sown,
    And through the merry flowers of June,
Over grass and over stone,
    And under mountains in the moon.

Roads go ever ever on
    Under cloud and under star,
Yet feet that wandering have gone
    Turn at last to home afar.
Eyes that fire and sword have seen
    And horror in the halls of stone
Look at last on meadows green
    And trees and hills they long have known.

—*J. R. R. Tolkien*

City of New Orleans

Words and Music
by Steve Goodman

Freely

1. Rid - in' on___ the Cit-y of___ New Or - leans,

Il - li - nois___ Cen - tral Mon - day morn - in' rail.___

Fif - teen cars___ and fif - teen rest - less rid - ers,

three con - duc - tors and twen - ty - five sacks of mail.___

And the sons of old___ men por - ters and the

sons of en - gi - neers___ Ride their fa - thers'___ ma - gic car -

- pets___ made of steel.___

Am

Moth - ers with____ their babes____ a - sleep____ are

Em

rock - in'____ to the gen - tle beat____ and the

G   G 7   C

rhy - thm of____ the rails is____ all they feel.____

F   G 7   C

Good morn - ing A - mer - i - ca,____ how are____ you?

Am   F   C

Say don't you know__ me, I'm your na - tive son.

G 7 G 9 C   G   Am   Am7

I'm the train they call the Cit - y of____ New Or - leans.

D 7   E♭   F   G   G 9   C

I'll be gone____ five hun - dred miles__ when the day__ is done.

2. Night time on the City of New Orleans,
   Changin' cars in Memphis, Tennessee.
   Halfway home, we'll be there by mornin'
   through the Mississippi darkness rollin' down to the sea.
   But all the towns and people seem to fade into a bad dream
   and the steel rail still ain't heard the news.
   The conductor sings his songs again
   the passengers will please refrain
   this train's got the disappearin' railroad blues.
   Good night America, how are you?
   Say don't you know me, I'm your native son.
   I'm the train they call the City of New Orleans.
   I'll be gone five hundred miles when the day is done.

HOME, SWEET HOME

Do you sing with your family or friends to pass the time on a trip? Cowboys sang on long cattle drives. They also sang at night to calm the herds, to keep away wild animals, and to ease loneliness.

SING "Trail to Mexico." Move your arm to show the shape of the melody.

TRAIL to MEXICO

American Cowboy Song
Music Adapted by Carol King

1. I made up my mind _____ in the ear - ly morn _____
2. 'Twas in the — year _____ of — eight - y - three _____
3. 'Twas in the— spring - time— of the year

To leave the home _____ where — I was born, _____
That A. J. Stin - son— hired _____ me.
I vol - un - teered_____ to— drive the steers. _____

To leave my na - tive home for a while, _____
He said, "Young man, _____ I want you to go,
I'll tell you, boys,_____ 'twas a long— hard go, _____

And trav - el— west _____ for — man-y a mile. _____
And fol - low my herd _____ to— Mex - i - co."
As the trail rolled— on_____ in - to Mex - i - co.

When you take a trip, your last stop is probably your home.
Usually, the last pitch of a melody is a note called the home
tone or **tonal center.** Ending on this note makes the melody
sound finished.

ON YOUR WAY HOME

Children often make up their own words as they play a clapping game with this song. The words don't have to make much sense!

LISTEN to the song, then hum the tonal center.

Caribbean Folk Song
Collected by Lois Choksy

Four white hors-es on the riv-er, Hey, hey,— hey,—

up to-mor-row, Up to-mor-row is a rain-y day.

Come on up— to the shal-low bay. Shal-low bay— is a

ripe ba-nan-a, Up to-mor-row is a rain-y day.

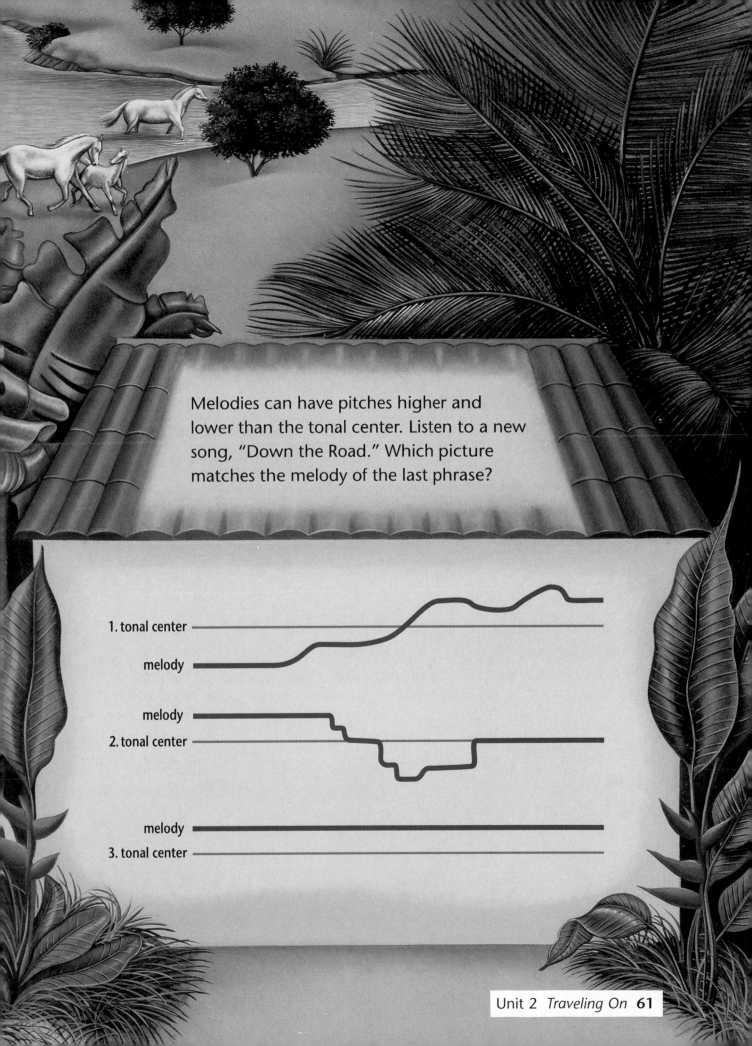

Melodies can have pitches higher and lower than the tonal center. Listen to a new song, "Down the Road." Which picture matches the melody of the last phrase?

1. tonal center

melody

melody

2. tonal center

melody

3. tonal center

A Story

Before radio and television were popular, songs like "The Old Carrion Crow" were passed from person to person. As you sing, see how the clear story, repeated melodies, and funny nonsense syllables could make this song easy to remember.

The Old Carrion Crow

Nova Scotian Folk Song

Verse *mf*

1. Oh, the old car-rion crow was sit-ting on an oak,
2. Hur-ry now bring me my cross and my bow,
3. Oh, the tai - lor shot and missed his mark,
4. The old sow died and the bells did toll,
5. Oh, now the old sow's dead and gone,

Fol the rid - dle, all the rid - dle hey ding

(1.) doh,
(2.) doh,
(3.) doh, And he
(4.) doh, And the
(5.) doh, And the

62

in a Song

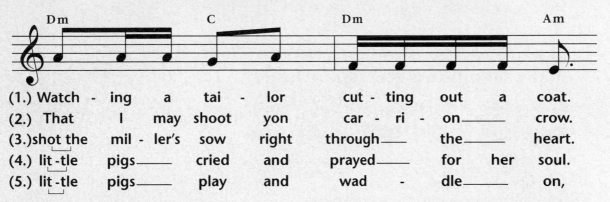

(1.) Watch - ing a tai - lor cut - ting out a coat.
(2.) That I may shoot yon car - ri - on crow.
(3.) shot the mil - ler's sow right through the heart.
(4.) lit -tle pigs cried and prayed for her soul.
(5.) lit -tle pigs play and wad - dle on,

Sing he, sing ho, the old car - rion crow, Fol the rid -dle, all the rid -dle

Refrain

hey ding doh. Ki - me -lea - ro kill my kea -ro, ki - me -lea - ro ki - mo,

To me bump, bump, bump, jump Pol -ly wol -ly lee, Lin - ko kil -ly cum ki - mo.

FOL-THE-RIDDLE RHYTHMS

Here's a chance to practice some new rhythms.

CLAP the beat and pat each rhythm. How many sounds to a beat do you hear?

fol the rid - dle   kil - ly cum   cum kil - ly

hey   ding   doh

PERFORM a new rhythmic phrase by reading this pattern.

kil - ly cum   kil - ly cum   kil - ly cum   doh

fol the rid - dle cum   kil - ly   hey   ding   doh

Karşi Bar *Turkish Dance*

LISTENING

LISTEN for the rhythmic phrase shown above. Then dance to the music.

SING and pat the rhythm for
each instrument.

piti, piti, piti, el pitío

ton, ton, ton, el tambor

tara, tara, tara, la guitarra

Which word patterns in the song
match these rhythms?

lin, lin, lin, el violín

THINK IT THROUGH

What are some ways you could use the rhythm patterns
or parts of the patterns to create other rhythm patterns?

MEET THE
INSTRUMENTS

You might see musical instruments among the odds and ends for sale at a flea market or fair. You will name quite a collection of instruments by singing this cumulative song!

En la feria de San Juan
In the Market of San Juan

Puerto Rican Folk Song
English Version by MMH

Verse

Spanish: En la fe - ria de San Juan, yo com - pré un pi -
Pronunciation: en la fe ɾya ðe san xwan yo kom pɾe un pi
English: In the mar - ket of San Juan, I— bought my - self a

Repeat this section, adding an instrument vocally each time

tí - o, pi - ti, pi - ti, pi - ti, el pi - tí - o.
ti o pi ti pi ti pi ti el pi ti o
whis - tle, *(whistle the melody)*— the whis - tle.

Refrain

Ven - ga u - sted, ven - ga u - sted, a la fe - ria de San Juan,
ßeng gau steð ßeng gau steð a la fe ɾya ðe san xwan
Come with me, come with me, to the mar - ket of San Juan.

Ven - ga u - sted, ven - ga u - sted, a la fe - ria de San Juan.
ßeng gau steð ßeng gau steð a la fe ɾya ðe san xwan
Come with me, come with me, to the mar - ket of San Juan.

66

2. En la feria de San Juan
   yo compré un tambor.
   Ton, ton, ton, el tambor, . . .

   en la fe ɾya ðe san xwan
   yo kom pɾe un tam boɾ
   ton ton ton el tam boɾ . . .

   In the market of San Juan
   I bought myself a drum.
   Tum, tum, tum, tum, the drum . . .

3. yo compré una guitarra,
   tara, tara, tara, la guitarra . . .

   yo kom pɾe una gi ta ɾa
   ta ɾa ta ɾa ta ɾa la gi ta ɾa . . .

   I bought a guitar,
   tara, tara, tara, the guitar . . .

4. yo compré un violín,
   Lin, lin, lin, el violín, . . .

   yo kom pɾe un βyo lin
   lin lin lin el βyo lin . . .

   I bought a violin,
   Lin, lin, lin, the violin, . . .

FAMILIES OF INSTRUMENTS

When you see a family picture, you might enjoy comparing the faces you see. Look at the **orchestral** families below. How are the instruments in each picture alike?

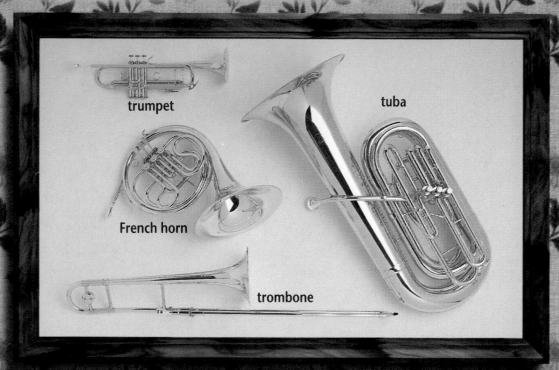

trumpet

tuba

French horn

trombone

BRASS FAMILY

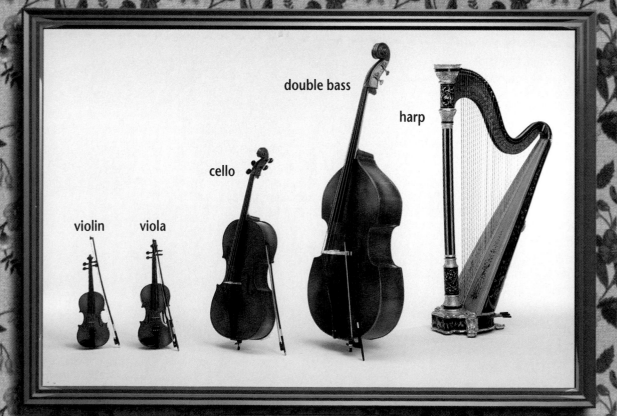

double bass

harp

cello

violin

viola

STRING FAMILY

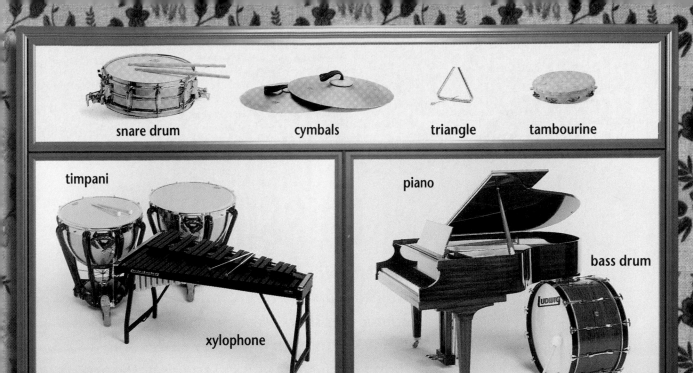

snare drum

cymbals

triangle

tambourine

timpani

piano

bass drum

xylophone

PERCUSSION FAMILY

piccolo

flute

clarinet

alto saxophone

bassoon

English horn

oboe

WOODWIND FAMILY

69

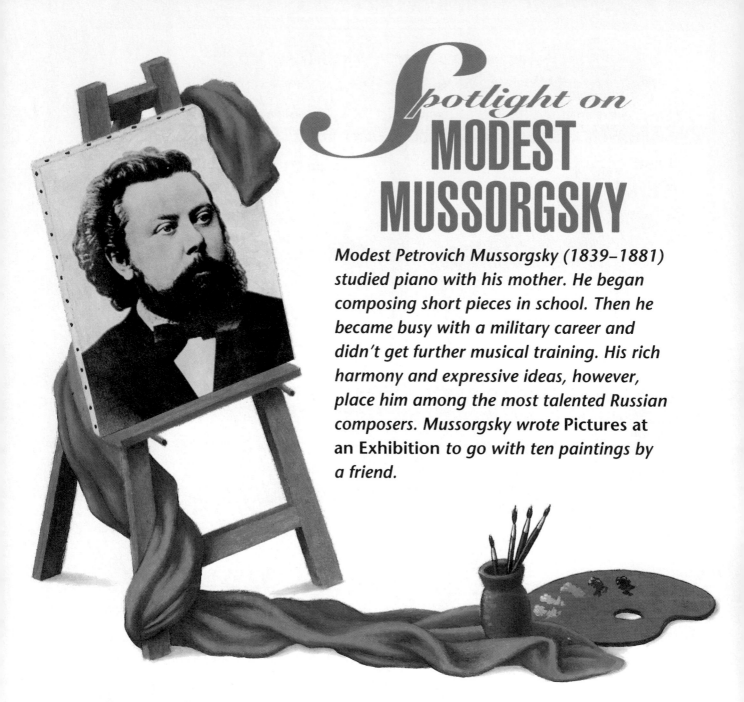

Spotlight on MODEST MUSSORGSKY

Modest Petrovich Mussorgsky (1839–1881) studied piano with his mother. He began composing short pieces in school. Then he became busy with a military career and didn't get further musical training. His rich harmony and expressive ideas, however, place him among the most talented Russian composers. Mussorgsky wrote **Pictures at an Exhibition** *to go with ten paintings by a friend.*

LISTENING

Promenade

from *Pictures at an Exhibition*

by Modest Mussorgsky

An art exhibition is a display of art. As you listen to Promenade, *imagine that you are walking and looking at paintings.*

LISTEN for the instrument families that play this melody.

LISTENING MAP *Tap each footprint as you listen for the entrance of each instrument family.*

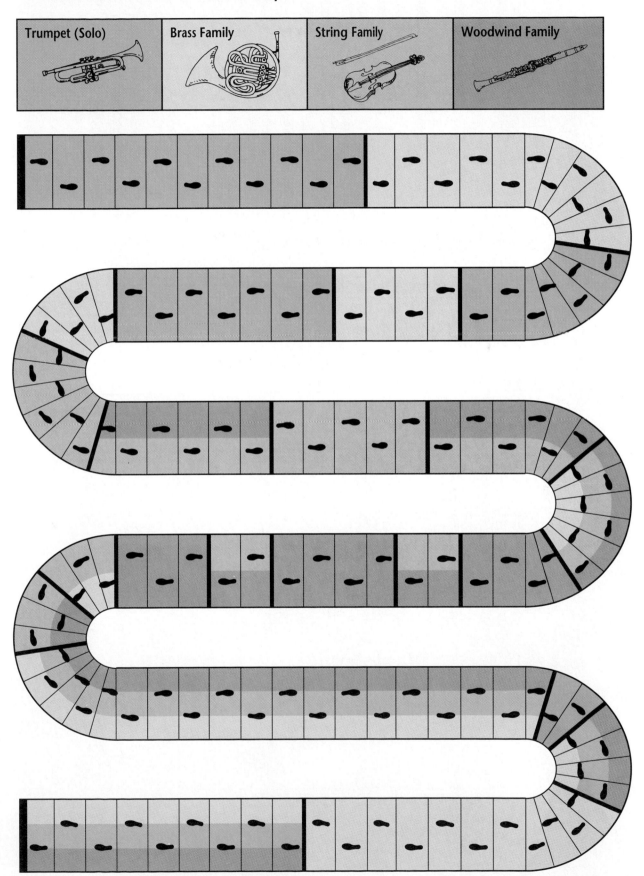

Trumpet (Solo)

Brass Family

String Family

Woodwind Family

Listening Map concept by Melody A. Long

Symbols and Cymbals

The musical symbols for four equal sounds to a beat can be written with four **sixteenth notes** (♪♪♪♪).

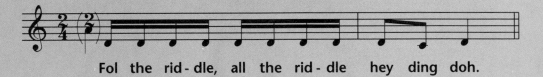

Fol the rid-dle, all the rid-dle hey ding doh.

Three unequal sounds to a beat can be written with two sixteenth notes and one eighth note (♪♪♪ or ♪♪♪).

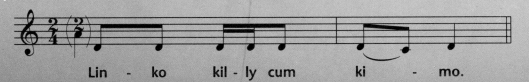

Lin - ko kil-ly cum ki - mo.

MAKE UP words with three unequal sounds to a beat.

Listen for beats with three or four sounds in "Karşi Bar."

Look at the notes below. Part of the rhythmic phrase from "Karşi Bar" is missing.

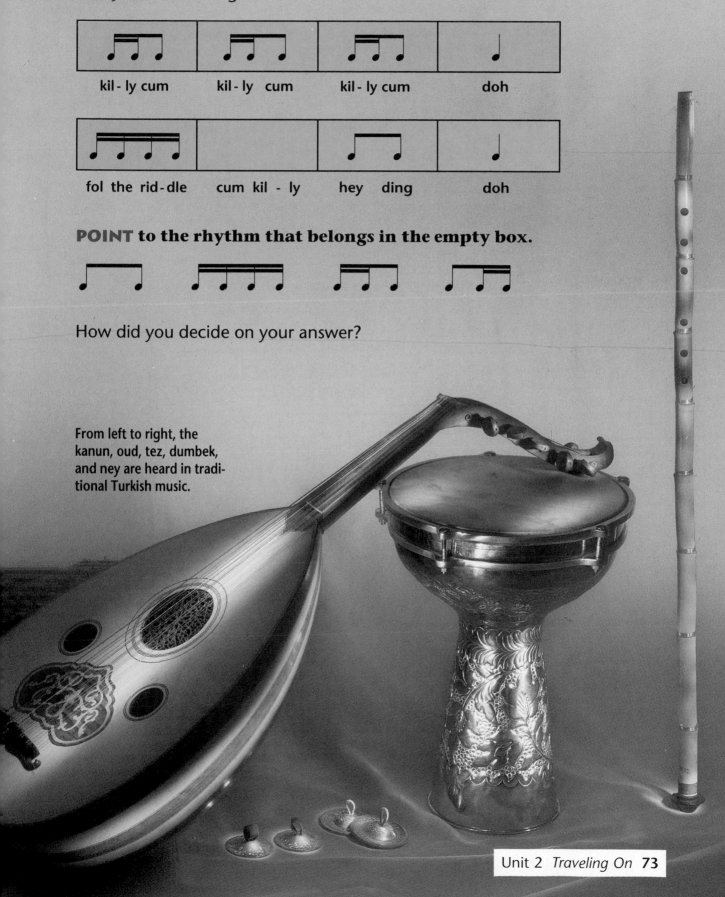

kil - ly cum   kil - ly cum   kil - ly cum   doh

fol the rid - dle   cum kil - ly   hey   ding   doh

POINT to the rhythm that belongs in the empty box.

How did you decide on your answer?

From left to right, the kanun, oud, tez, dumbek, and ney are heard in traditional Turkish music.

PAT the rhythm of the green line. Then sing the line
as an ostinato.

American
Cowboy Song
Music Adapted by
Carol King

1. I made up my mind _____ in the ear - ly
2. 'Twas in the __ year _____ of __ eight - y -
3. 'Twas in the __ spring - time __ of the

Vocal Ostinato

Rid - in' on the West - ern Trail.

morn _____ To leave the
three _____ That A. J.
year _____ I vol - un -

Up in the sad - dle all day.

home _____ where _ I was born, _____ To leave my
Stin - son - hired __ me. _____ He said, "Young
teered _____ to _ drive the steers. _____ I'll tell you,

Rid - in' on the West - ern Trail.   Up in the sad - dle all day.

Music that begins *before* the first beat of a measure begins on an **upbeat.** Look before the first bar line. When a song starts with an upbeat, there are fewer beats before the first bar line than are shown in the meter signature. Which part of "Trail to Mexico" begins with an upbeat, the melody or the ostinato?

MOVING

This song may bring some bounce to your steps! As you sing the melody, notice how it moves down to pitches below *do*.

DOWN THE ROAD

American Folk Song

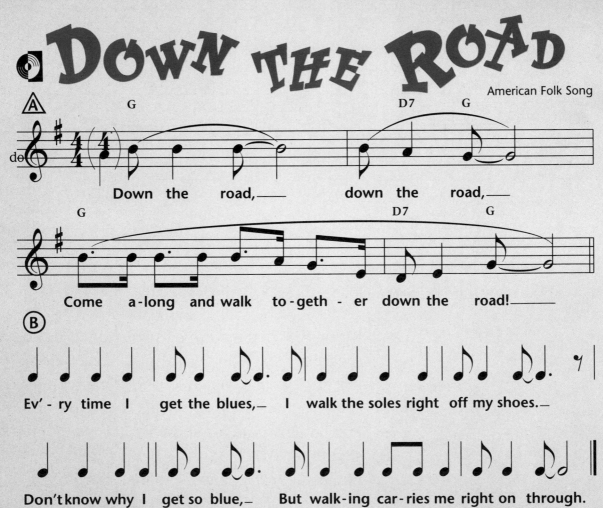

Down the road,_____ down the road,_____

Come a-long and walk to-geth-er down the road!_____

Ev'-ry time I get the blues,— I walk the soles right off my shoes.—

Don't know why I get so blue,— But walk-ing car-ries me right on through.

ON

In "Down the Road," you sang two pitches that are "down the road" from *do.*

FIND *do re mi.* Do is the tonal center of this song. Where are the new pitches?

The new pitches are called *low so* and *low la.* Recall the pitch syllables you have learned.

la
so
mi
re
do
la₁
so₁

The introductions are not yet over! Each pitch has a letter name as well as a pitch syllable name.

The letter names of the pitches in "Down the Road" are D E G A B.

SING "Down the Road" with letter names.

The **treble clef** is shaped like an old-fashioned letter G. It circles the second staff line, and a note on that line is called G.

HIT THE TRAIL

Now you can sing this ostinato three different ways.

SING it with pitch syllables, letter names, and words.

Vocal Ostinato

Rid-in' on the West-ern Trail.   Up in the sad-dle all day.

THINK IT THROUGH

Listen to "Trail to Mexico" with and without the ostinato. How does the ostinato change the song? Why would a composer add an ostinato to a song?

SING AND CLAP A PATTERN

Clap own hands.

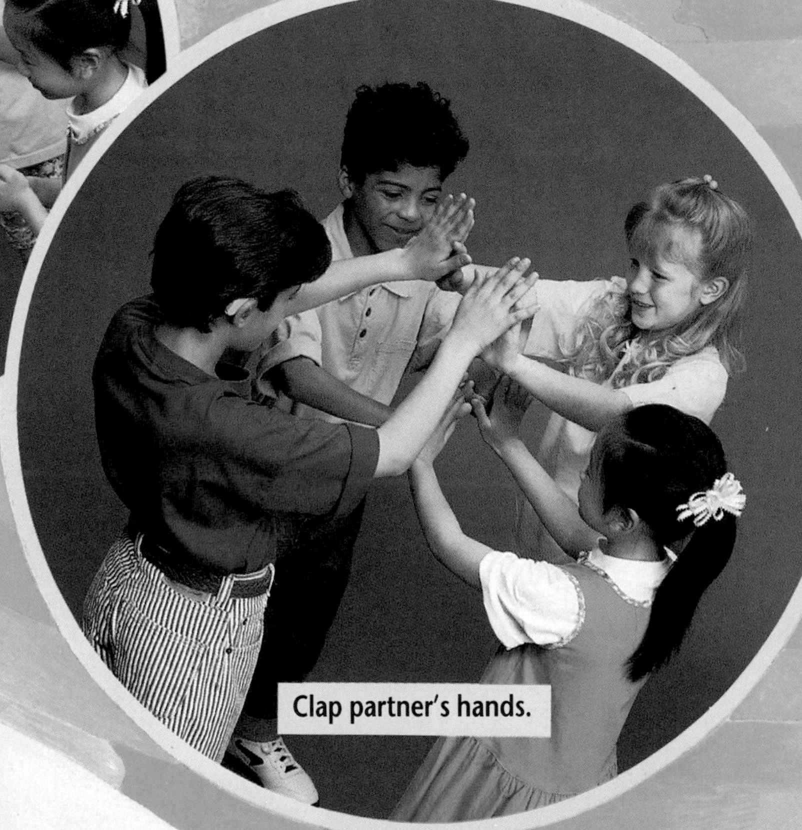

Clap partner's hands.

Review a song you know.

RAISE your hand when you hear this pattern in "Four White Horses."

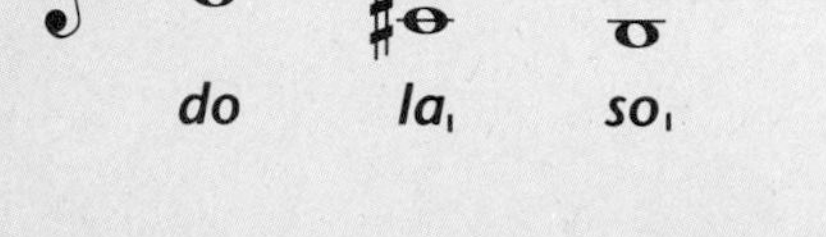

do   la,   so,

Play the game in groups of four.

Clap own hands.

Clap side partner's hands.

SWITCH TO SWAPPING

What does "swap" mean to you? In this song, the swapping goes on and on!

LISTEN to the song and find all the items that are swapped along the way.

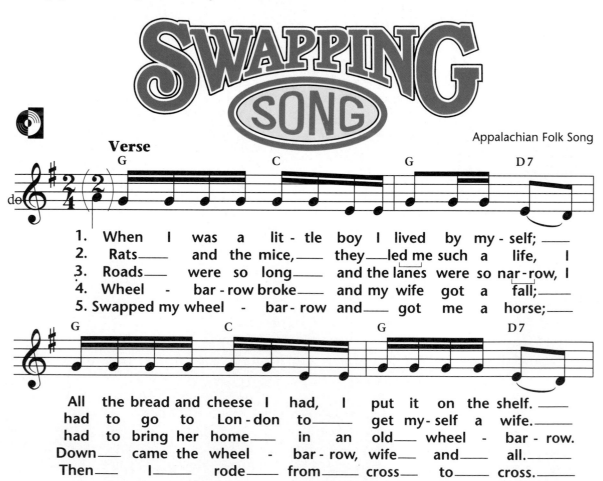

SWAPPING SONG

Appalachian Folk Song

Verse

1. When I was a lit-tle boy I lived by my-self; All the bread and cheese I had, I put it on the shelf.
2. Rats and the mice, they led me such a life, I had to go to Lon-don to get my-self a wife.
3. Roads were so long and the lanes were so nar-row, I had to bring her home in an old wheel-bar-row.
4. Wheel-bar-row broke and my wife got a fall; Down came the wheel-bar-row, wife and all.
5. Swapped my wheel-bar-row and got me a horse; Then I rode from cross to cross.

Refrain

G · C · Bm · Em

Wing wong wad-dle, to my Jack straw strad-dle, To my

Am · D7 · G · D7 · G

John-nie fair fad-dle, to my long ways home.

6. Swapped my horse and got me a mare;
Then I rode from fair to fair.

7. Swapped my mare and got me a mule;
Then I rode like a doggone fool.

8. Swapped my mule and got me a goat;
When I got on him, he wouldn't tote.

9. Swapped my goat and got me a sheep;
Then I rode myself to sleep.

10. Swapped my sheep and got me a cow;
And in that trade I just learned how.

11. Swapped my cow and got me a calf;
In that trade I just lost half.

12. Swapped my calf and got me a hen;
Oh what a pretty thing I had then.

13. Swapped my hen and got me a rat;
Put it on the haystack away from the cat.

14. Swapped my rat and got me a mouse;
Its tail caught afire and burned up my house.

NAME and point to the tonal center of this song.

You can read *all* the pitches and rhythms in this song!

Return to Rhythms

Can you remember the missing phrases of
"The Old Carrion Crow"?

Oh, the old carrion crow was sitting on an oak,

_____,
Watching a tailor cutting out a coat.
Sing he, sing ho, the old carrion crow,

_____.
Kimelearo kill my kearo, kimelearo kimo,
To me bump, bump, bump, jump Polly wolly lee,

_____.

Add a personal touch to this folk song! Replace the
traditional nonsense words with these rhythm patterns.

PERFORM a different pattern with each verse.

A scene from a performance of *Carmen* at the San Francisco Opera.

LISTENING **Prelude** (excerpt) from *Carmen*
by **Georges Bizet**

*An **overture**, or prelude, is an instrumental piece that begins an opera or other large musical work. The overture settles the audience and may introduce musical ideas that will be heard.*

TAP the coins on the beat from left to right as you listen to the prelude to *Carmen*.

How many beats are in each phrase? How many phrases did you hear?

*Each phrase of this prelude begins with a rhythmic **motive**. A motive is a short pattern used often in a piece of music. Which pattern shows the motive?*

1. ♪♪♪♪♪ ♩   2. ♩ ♪♪♩ ♪♪♪♪♪   3. ♩ ♪♪♪

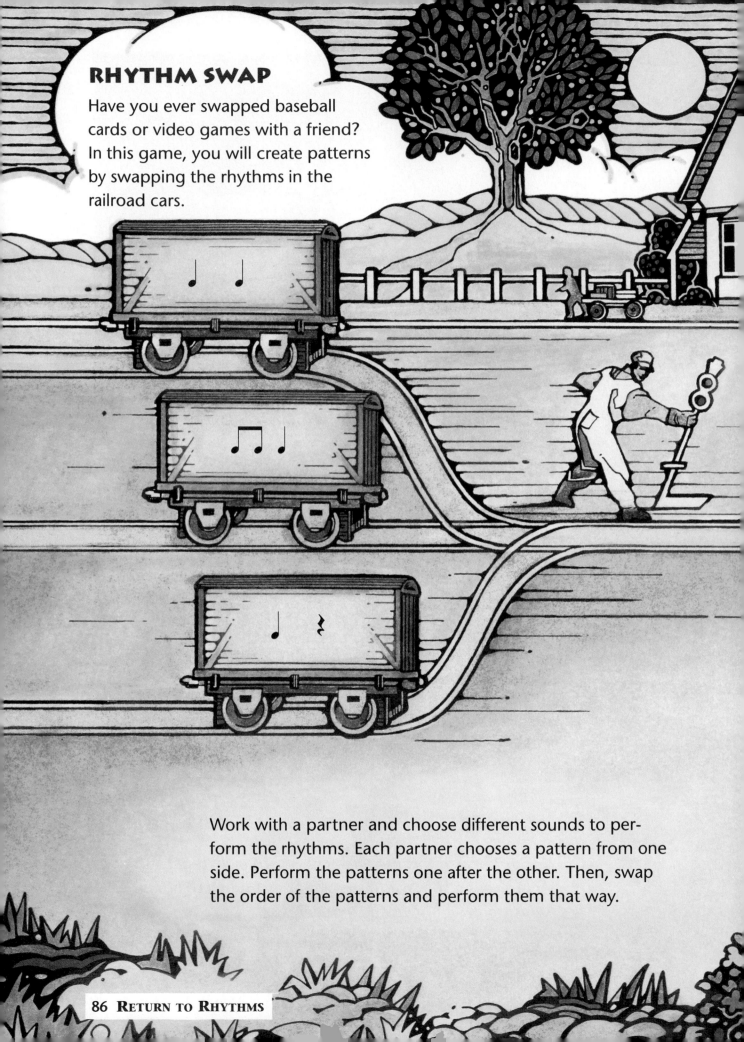

RHYTHM SWAP

Have you ever swapped baseball cards or video games with a friend? In this game, you will create patterns by swapping the rhythms in the railroad cars.

Work with a partner and choose different sounds to perform the rhythms. Each partner chooses a pattern from one side. Perform the patterns one after the other. Then, swap the order of the patterns and perform them that way.

An **interlude** is a short musical connection between sections or verses of a longer musical piece.

PERFORM your two patterns as an interlude between two verses of "Swapping Song."

FIND

Here's a song you know. How can you figure out what song it is without hearing it?

SING the song when you recognize it.

THE FORM

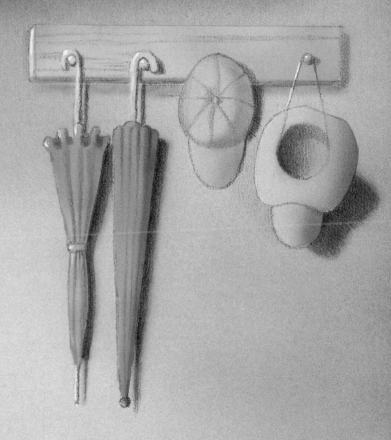

In music, you hear repetition and contrast. Some phrases are the same. Some are different. This is also true of larger parts of musical works.

Some music is made up of two or more sections. Songs with two sections that sound the same have a form called A A. Songs with two different-sounding sections have a form called A B.

NAME the form of the song "Down the Road." Why did you choose your answer?

In a Mountain Path

Traditional Chinese Song Arranged by Han Kuo-huang

"In a Mountain Path" is a Chinese song played by a modern Chinese orchestra. The modern Chinese orchestra is divided into bowed strings, plucked strings, woodwinds, and percussion. How are these families different from the families of the symphony orchestra?

Music from China, a modern ensemble, playing typical Chinese instruments.

What are some things you hear in this song?

RAISE your hand when the A section returns. Then improvise a dance to the music.

Unusual limestone hills near the city of Kuei-lin in southern China.

LANDSCAPE IN THE STYLE OF DONG BEIYUAN

This Chinese scroll was painted in the time of the Ming Dynasty (1368–1644). The word *Ming* means "bright" in Chinese. Can you see how the artist, Dong Qichang, used contrasts to make his ink painting interesting and dramatic?

GETTING THERE IS HALF THE FUN

Do you like sending postcards? Think of the song shown on one of these cards. Describe what you might see if you went to the place in the song. Then sing the song.

Choose your favorite card and write a message on a piece of paper to friends "back home." Tell them about the rhythm, pitches, or game that goes with the song on the postcard.

CHECK IT OUT

1. Which rhythm do you hear?

2. Which rhythm do you hear?

3. Which pitches do you hear?

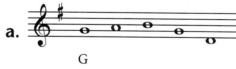

a.

G

c.

G

b.

G

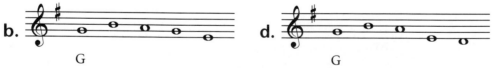

d.

G

4. Which pitches do you hear?

a.

G

c.

G

b.

B

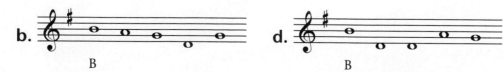

d.

B

CREATE

Pair Up for ABA

CREATE a melody with a partner. Use the pitches
D E G A B and one of the rhythm patterns below.

PERFORM your melody as part
of a B section between the
verses of "Trail to Mexico."

Write

The journey to a place can be as
interesting as the place you visit.

Write words for a song describing
your trip to the Market of San Juan
or on a cattle drive to Mexico.
Describe what you see, what you
think, who you meet, and what
surprises or difficulties occur along
the way.

When I Was a Lad

Music by Arthur S. Sullivan
Words by William S. Gilbert

1. When I was a lad I served a term As
2. As of-fice boy I made such a mark That they
3. Now, lands-men all, who-ev-er you may be, If you

of - fice boy to an at - tor - ney's firm; I
gave me the post of a jun - ior clerk; I
want to rise to the top of the tree, If your

cleaned the win-dows and I swept the floor, And I
served the writs with a smile so bland, And I
soul is-n't fet-tered to an of - fice stool, Be

pol-ished up the han-dle of the big front door. He
cop-ied all the let-ters in a big round hand; He
care-ful to be guid-ed by this gold-en rule: Be

pol-ished up the han-dle of the big front door. I
cop-ied all the let-ters in a big round hand; I
care-ful to be guid-ed by this gold-en rule: Stick

pol-ished up the han-dle so care-ful-lee That
cop-ied all the let-ters in a hand so free That
close—— to your desks,—— and nev-er go to sea, And you

now I am the rul-er of the Queen's Na-vee. He
now I am the rul-er of the Queen's Na-vee. He
all—— may be rul-ers of the Queen's Na-vee. Stick

pol-ished up the han-dle so care-ful-lee That
cop-ied all the let-ters in a hand so free That
close—— to your desks—— and nev-er go to sea, And you

now he is the rul-er of the Queen's Na-vee.
now he is the rul-er of the Queen's Na-vee.
all—— may be rul-ers of the Queen's Na-vee.

Orchestra Song

Austrian Round

1. **do** The vi - o - lin's ring - ing like
2. **do** The clar - i - net, the clar - i - net plays
3. **do** The trum - pet is sound - ing ta ta ta

love - ly ___ sing - ing, The vi - o - lin's
doo - dle, doo - dle, doo - dle, doo - dle det, The clar - i - net, the
ta ta ta ta ta ta ta ta ta ta, The trum - pet is

ring - ing   like   love - ly ——— song.

clar - i - net   plays   doo-dle,   doo-dle, doo-dle det.

sound - ing ta   ta   ta   ta   ta ta ta   ta   ta   ta   ta.

Add these parts to the first three.

4   de   The   horn,   the horn   a - wakes   me   at   morn.

5   de   The   drum's   play - ing two tones and   al - ways the same tones,

Five,   one,   one,   five,   five,   five,   five, five,   one.

Encore
BLUE SKIES

Songs, poems, and stories about rain are found in cultures all over the world. What feeling does this song express about rain? How do you feel when it rains?

SINGIN' in the RAIN

Music by Nacio Herb Brown
Words by Arthur Freed

I'm sing - in' in the rain, just sing - in' in the rain;

What a glo - ri - ous feel - ing, I'm hap - py a - gain!

I'm laugh - ing at clouds so dark up a - bove.

The sun's in my heart and I'm read - y for love.

GRAY SKIES

Gene Kelly, an American actor and dancer, made the song "Singin' in the Rain" famous in the movie of the same name.

Let the storm - y clouds chase ev' - ry - one—— from the place;

Come on—— with the rain, I've a smile—— on my face!

I'll walk down the lane with a hap - py re - frain,

And sing - in',—— just sing - in' in—— the rain!——

A FOLKTALE FROM KENYA

In the plains of Kenya, in Africa, where the land is dry, herders are always hoping for rain. Without it, the people and animals cannot survive. The Nandi people of Kenya tell the following tale.

Once there was a young cowherd who was very skilled with the bow and arrow. One summer there had been no rain, and the weather was very hot and dry. The cows had no water to drink. The cows also had nothing to eat because the grass had shriveled up and died.

One day the cowherd saw an eagle flying high above. As the eagle flew over him, a beautiful feather fell at his feet. The cowherd eagerly picked up the feather and saw that it would make a fine addition to his arrow.

The cowherd shot the arrow into a large cloud that was gathering above the plain. Suddenly, there was light-ning and thunder. The cloud burst and rain poured down. The long drought had ended. The cows were no longer thirsty, and the grass grew high and green again.

CHOOSE instrument sounds for each part of the story. Tell the story with sounds.

SING the following vocal call as an introduction and coda to the story.

Call *Response* 3

Please bring us, please bring us, bring us some rain.

Rainfall *by Linda Worsley*

People have dreamed of controlling the weather for thousands of years. Inventors have tried to make artificial rain. People living in dry areas held rain dances in the hope of rainfall.

MOVE to music that sounds like rain.

Cleo Parker Robinson, an American dancer, created her own rain dance.

Members of Cleo Parker Robinson's troupe rehearse "Raindance."

Meet CLEO PARKER ROBINSON

Cleo Parker Robinson has made her career as a choreographer, a person who creates dances. She trained in both modern dance and ballet. Robinson formed her own dance school while she was a college student. She has traveled with her dancers around the world and has received many awards for her teaching and community service. One of her goals is to make the experience of dance available to all.

LISTEN to Cleo Parker Robinson talk about her experiences performing her rain dance.

Just Imagine

I Wonder

I wonder how it feels to fly
high in the sky . . .
    like a bird.
I wonder how it feels to sit
on a nest . . .
    like a bird.
I wonder how it feels to catch
a worm in the morning . . .
    like a bird.
I feel funny . . .
maybe he is wondering
    how it feels to be like a man.

—*Earl Thompson (Yakima)*

Have you ever read about Pecos Bill, Paul Bunyan, or John Henry? They are all characters in traditional American stories called "tall tales." These stories stretch the truth just for fun. In a similar way, the composer used his imagination to make this song entertaining.

OH, SUSANNA

Words and Music by Stephen Foster

Verse

1. I___ come from Al - a - bam - a with my ban - jo on my knee.
2. I___ had a dream the oth - er night, when ev' - ry - thing was still.

I'm___ going to Loui - si - an - a, my___ true love for to see.
I___ thought I saw Su - san - na a - com - ing down the hill.

It___ rained all night the day I left, the weath - er it was dry,
The___ buck - wheat cake was in her mouth, the tear was in her eye.

The___ sun so hot I froze to death, Su - san - na, don't you cry.
Says___ I, "I'm com - ing from the South, Su - san - na, don't you cry."

Refrain

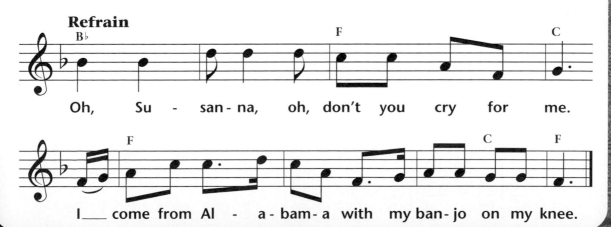

Oh, Su - san - na, oh, don't you cry for me.

I___ come from Al - a - bam - a with my ban - jo on my knee.

MOVING MELODIES

How do you feel when it rains?

TRACE the shape of the melody in the air while you sing the song.

I Don't Care If the Rain Comes Down

American Folk Song

A C   G7

I don't care if the rain comes down, I'm gon-na dance all day,

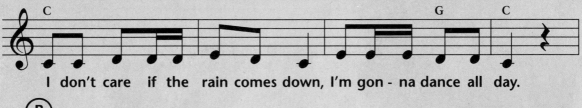

C   G   C

I don't care if the rain comes down, I'm gon-na dance all day.

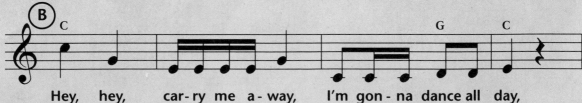

B C   G   C

Hey, hey, car-ry me a-way, I'm gon-na dance all day,

C   G   C

Hey, hey, car-ry me a-way, I'm gon-na dance all day.

Melodies can move in three ways.

Some move with **repeated notes,** using one pitch that is repeated.

I   don't   care   if   the   rain   comes   down

They can move by **steps.** Each note is followed by a pitch just above or below it.

I   don't   care   if   the   rain   comes   down

When a melody moves by **skips,** each note is followed by a pitch two or more steps away.

I   don't   care   if   the   rain   comes   down

MOVE to the repeated notes, steps, and skips in these melodies.

Listen for repeated notes, steps, and skips in the melody of this song.

La pájara pinta
THE SPECKLED BIRD

Mexican Folk Song
English Version
by MMH

Spanish: Y es - ta - ba la pá - ja - ra pin - ta sen - ta - da en su ver - de li -
Pronunciation: yes ta βa la pa xa ɾa pin ta sen ta ðaen su βeɾ ðe li
English: A bright speck - led bird — was sit - ting up - on a green lem - on

món. — Con el pi - co re - co - ge las flo - res, Con el
mon kon el pi ko ɾe ko xe las flo ɾes kon el
branch. — With her beak — she gath - ered flow - ers, with her

pi - co re - co - ge el a - mor. — Ay, ay, ay, ay! — ¿En
pi ko ɾe ko xel a moɾ ai ai ai ai en
beak — she gath - ered love, — Ay, ay, ay, ay Then

dón - de la en - cuen - tro yo? — Con el pi - co re - co - ge las
don de laen kwen tɾo yo kon el pi ko ɾe ko xe las
tell me where will it be? — With her beak — she gath - ered

flo - res, Con el pi - co re - co - ge el a - mor. —
flo ɾes kon el pi ko ɾe ko xel a moɾ
flow - ers, with her beak — she gath - ered love. —

This song is about the workers who load cargo onto ships. Sometimes, ship captains treated these workers unfairly.

SIGNAL to show how the melody moves. Does it move mostly by repeated notes, steps, or skips?

PAY ME MY MONEY DOWN

African American Work Song
from the Georgia Sea Islands
Collected and Adapted by Lydia A. Parrish

Verse
Call

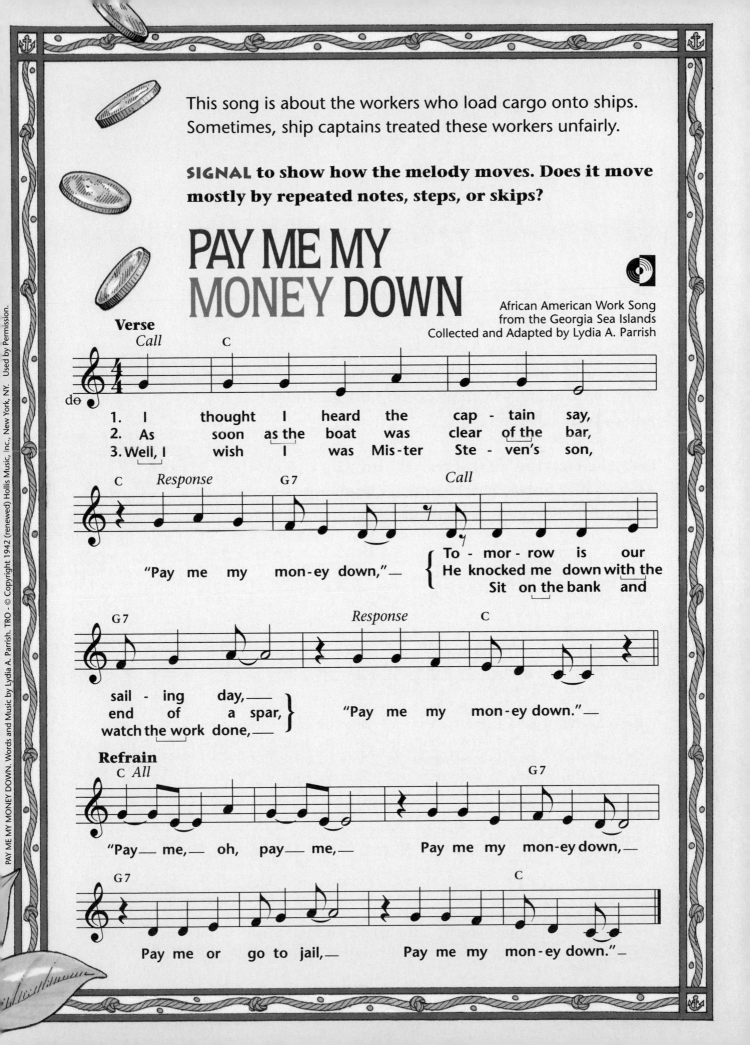

1. I thought I heard the cap-tain say,
2. As soon as the boat was clear of the bar,
3. Well, I wish I was Mis-ter Ste-ven's son,

Response

"Pay me my mon-ey down,"—

Call

To-mor-row is our
He knocked me down with the
Sit on the bank and

sail-ing day,—
end of a spar,
watch the work done,—

Response

"Pay me my mon-ey down."—

Refrain
All

"Pay— me,— oh, pay— me,— Pay me my mon-ey down,—

Pay me or go to jail,— Pay me my mon-ey down."—

AN OLD STORY

This song is based on a Biblical story. Noah saves some animals from a flood by loading them onto a boat called an ark.

PAT the rhythm of the words and sing the motive *There's one more river to cross.* Then sing the whole song and create more verses.

ONE MORE RIVER

Nineteenth Century
College Song

1. Old No-ah, he built him-self an ark;
2. The an - i - mals went in one by one;
3. The an - i - mals went in two by two;
4. The an - i - mals went in three by three;
5. The an - i - mals went in four by four;

There's one more riv-er to cross.

He built it out of hick' - ry bark;
The el - e - phant chew-ing a car-a - way bun;
The rhi - no - cer - os and the kang - a - roo;
The bear, the bug, and the bum - ble - bee;
The hip - po - po-ta - mus stuck in the door;

There's

one more riv-er to cross. There's one more riv-er, And

that wide riv-er is Jor-dan, There's one more

riv-er, There's one more riv-er to cross.———

6. The animals went in five by five;
   There's one more river to cross.
   "It's raining," said Noah, "so look alive!"
   There's one more river to cross.
   Refrain

7. The animals went in six by six; . . .
   The monkeys were up to monkey tricks; . . .
   Refrain

8. The animals went in sev'n by sev'n; . . .
   The rabbit said, "I wish I had driv'n.". . .
   Refrain

9. The animals went in eight by eight; . . .
   "That's 'nuff," said Noah, and slammed
      the gate! . . .
   Refrain

10. And as they talked of this and that; . . .
    The ark, it bumped on Ararat; . . .
    Refrain

DISCOVER BEAT DIVISIONS

Clap this motive while you walk with the beat. How many sounds are there to each beat?

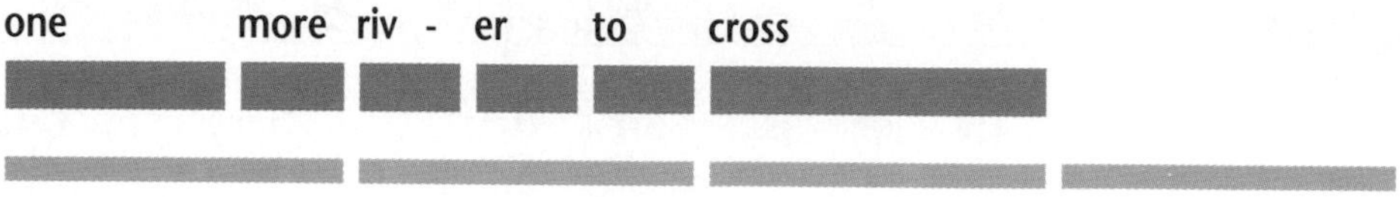

one   more   riv -   er   to   cross

The arks show the number of sounds to each beat.

MATCH each row to one of the beats shown above.

no sound to the beat	
one sound to the beat	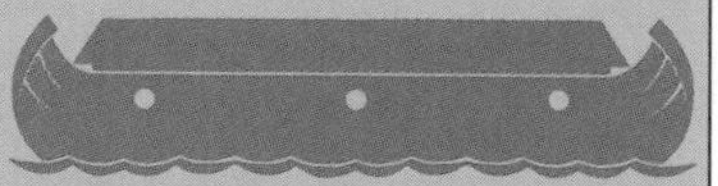
two unequal sounds to the beat	
three equal sounds to the beat	

CLAP the rhythms of these words. Then match them with the patterns of arks.

caraway bun

stuck in the door

kangaroo

one by one

Many beats in "Come and Sing Together" are divided into two parts.

LISTEN to discover if the beats are divided equally or unequally.

COME AND SING TOGETHER

Hungarian Melody

If you'd dance then you must have boots of shin-ing leath - er,

Mon - ey in your pock - et - book, in your hat a feath - er.

But if you would sing with me,

you don't need a cent, you see, so come and sing to-geth - er!

If you'd dance then you must have boots of shin-ing leath - er!

SPOTLIGHT ON

Maria Teresa
✦ Carreño ✦

Maria Teresa Carreño (1853–1917) was a child prodigy. Some people even called her another Mozart. She was born in Caracas, Venezuela, and gave her first piano concert in New York City when she was eight years old. When she was about ten, "Teresita" played for President Abraham Lincoln and his family.

Carreño was best known as a concert pianist. As an adult, she also directed and sang in operas, composed, and conducted. Her energy and enthusiasm were amazing.

LISTENING

Scherzo (excerpt) from String Quartet in B Minor
by Teresa Carreño

When do you hear three equal sounds to a beat? Two equal sounds to a beat?

In this photograph of a string quartet, which instruments of the string family do you see? Are they producing sound by bowing or plucking the strings?

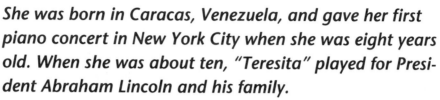

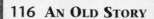

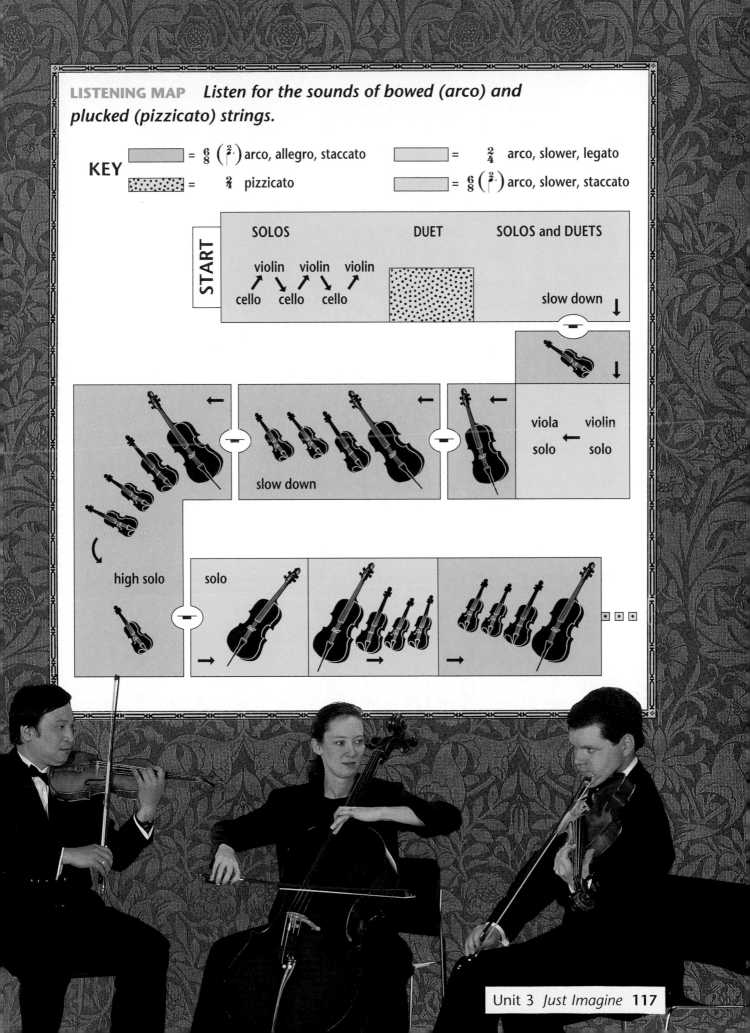

LISTENING MAP *Listen for the sounds of bowed (arco) and plucked (pizzicato) strings.*

KEY

= 6/8 (♪. = ♪.) arco, allegro, staccato

= 2/4 arco, slower, legato

= 2/4 pizzicato

= 6/8 (♪. = ♪.) arco, slower, staccato

START

SOLOS

violin → violin → violin
cello   cello   cello

DUET

SOLOS and DUETS

slow down ↓

↓

viola ← violin
solo   solo

←   ←   ←

slow down

high solo

solo

→   →   →

Flying with the Eagles

What do you think of when you see an eagle fly?

Dynamics are the levels of loudness and softness of the performance. How do the dynamics in this song help express feelings?

THE EAGLE

Music by Hap Palmer
Words by Martha Cheney

cresc. v.2 only

mf 1. Born   for a   west-ern sky, ___   sweep-ing   a   cir-cle
mp 2. Brave   and a   hunt-er's son, ___   *f* the land was his 'til he
p 3. There   on a   moun-tain high, ___   wound-ed ___   ea-gle
mf 4. Dream-ing of   days gone by, ___   when lit-tle chil-dren

as   he flies. ___
met   a gun. ___
wants   to die. ___   } He was free ___   when they let him be. ___
watched him fly. ___

SING the song with dynamics that are different from the recording. Find another way to express the feelings of the words.

Among many Native American cultures, the eagle is admired for its beauty, grace, and strength. The eagle is also a spiritual figure to many Native Americans, serving as a messenger between people and the Creator. The eagle has the sharpest eyes, flies the highest, and carries prayers on its feathers up to the Creator.

MEET JULIUS CHAVEZ

Julius Chavez is a Native American of the Navajo nation in Arizona and New Mexico. He has spent many years learning songs and dances of the Navajo people. He is also interested in learning and teaching the music of other Native American groups.

The songs and dances are passed on from performer to performer and from parents to children. One must listen carefully to learn the songs, because they are not written down. Mr. Chavez learned much of what he knows from his grandparents.

LISTEN as Julius Chavez explains the meaning of "A'tsah Biyiin Sin."

A'tsah Biyiin Sin

Traditional Laguna Melody
Words by Julius Chavez

In "A'tsah Biyiin Sin," (The Song that Belongs to the Eagle) Julius Chavez uses the melody from the traditional Laguna Eagle Dance Song with his own words in Navajo. The dance shows scenes in the eagle's life, which may teach people about their own lives.

LISTEN to "A'tsah Biyiin Sin."

YOUR TURN WITH DYNAMICS

Have you ever watched a fire in a fireplace, or a campfire? Fire is a very powerful natural force. Poets have written about fire as if it had a personality and feelings. This poem was written by a thirteen-year-old girl from England.

READ the poem. What is fire's enemy?

FIRE

I am fire. You know me
For my warmth and light
For my crackling, leaping
Colored light
Which comforts all.
I am fire. You know me
For my endless moving,
Burning, destroying hunger
Which eats all.
I am fire. I have one foe
Who conquers my might,
Who quenches my thirst,
Who swallows my light.

— Pat Taylor

THINK IT THROUGH

How could you use sound and movement to show a fire? How could you show the fire growing? Dying down?

CHOOSE the dynamics and movement you feel would best express the meaning of the poem. Speak the poem with dynamics and perform your movement.

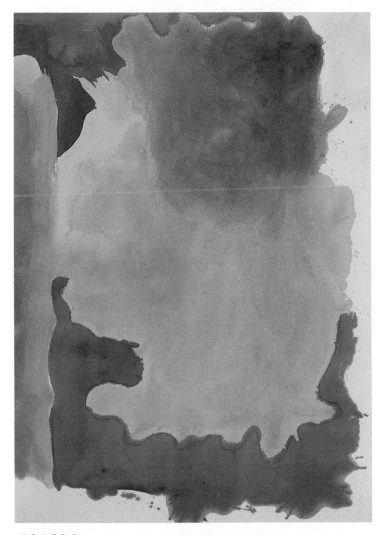

CANAL
The American artist Helen Frankenthaler often paints shapes of color that let each viewer see something different in them. What do you see in this painting?

Look closely at the pitches of "I Don't Care If the Rain Comes Down." Where is the new pitch?

I don't care if the rain comes down, I'm gon-na sing all day,

I don't care if the rain comes down, I'm gon-na sing all day.

Fa is the pitch syllable between *mi* and *so.* Name these syllables from low to high, then sing the verse with pitch syllables.

so, la, do re mi fa so la

SING the two melodic motives on the next page. Try the motions!

124

Motive 1

Touch shoulders.

Touch head.

Shake hands overhead.

Motive 2

Touch shoulders.

Touch waist.

Touch knees.

Volte *by Michael Praetorius*

The volte was a popular dance in European courts in the early 1600s. What kind of movement does this music make you want to do?

MOVE to the motives as you listen to "Volte." Then play each motive on resonator bells. C and F are the new letter names.

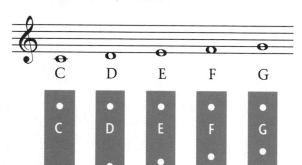

CONCERT CHAMPÊTRE

Musicians of Praetorius' time enjoyed playing various combinations of instruments. This painting shows early keyboard, string, and wind instruments.

Spotlight on
MICHAEL PRAETORIUS

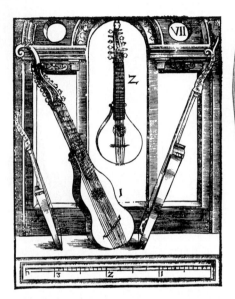

Michael Praetorius (1571–1621) was a scholar and a musician. He wrote many important books on church music, composition, performance, and musical instruments.

Praetorius' woodcut illustrations of Renaissance instruments were very detailed. Many historical instruments could be rebuilt much later by using his pictures as guides. His pictures include the string instruments above and the organ at right.

Praetorius worked as an organist for most of his life. He made collections of his own pieces and arrangements. His work made him a rich man, and when he died he left all his money to the poor.

Step to the Ark!

In the song "One More River," the animals did the walking. Now you can "step to the ark"! Before you move, look at the notation for each rhythm.

CLAP the rhythm of each word several times.

cross

hip - po

el - e - phant

BY TWO OR BY SIX?

The meter signature of "One More River" can be written in two ways, $\frac{2}{\cdot}$ and $\frac{6}{8}$. Although these two meter signatures look different, each measure lasts as long as two **dotted quarter notes** (♩. ♩.) or **six eighth notes** (♫ ♫).

FIND the meter signature and ♫ pattern in "One More River" on page 112. Learn the dance.

Form arches; first couple walks under.

Each couple follows the first couple.

CLAP and speak the rhythm pattern below. Say *cross*, *hippo*, and *elephant* for the three rhythms.

U.S. Marine Band

LISTENING

Over the Hills and Far Away (excerpt)

by Percy Grainger

This march was written by Percy Grainger for a military concert band in 1918. Unlike the orchestra, the concert band has only three families of instruments: woodwinds, brass, and percussion. Which family of instruments is not in a concert band?

LISTEN for the rhythms above in the march.

SPOTLIGHT ON
Percy Grainger

*P*ercy Aldridge Grainger (1882–1961) was an Australian composer and pianist. His mother gave him his first piano lessons, and he began his concert career at the age of ten.

One of Grainger's favorite foods was brown-sugar sandwiches. Because he didn't like carrying things, he tied his pens, pencils, and papers to his jacket with string. He also planned his own museum, including the donation of his own skeleton!

Grainger was known as a fine pianist. He also became an important scholar of English folk music, researching and collecting English songs, many of which he wove into his own new compositions.

ADD A LITTLE HARMONY

In this song the b'y, or boy, is a busy young fisherman from Newfoundland, an island off the east coast of Canada.

I's the B'y

Newfoundland Folk Song

Verse

1. I's the b'y that builds the boat, And I's the b'y that sails her!
2. Sods and rinds to cov-er your flake,— Cakes and tea for sup-per,
3. I don't want your mag-got-y fish,— That's no good for win-ter,

I's the b'y that catch-es the fish, And brings them home to Liz-er.
Cod-fish in the spring o' the year,— Fried in mag-got-y but-ter.
I could buy as good— as that— Down in Bon-a-vis-ta.

Refrain

Hip your part-ner, Sal-ly Tib-bo, Hip your part-ner, Sal-ly Brown!

Fo-go, Twil-lin-gate, Mor-ton's Har-bour, All a-round the cir-cle.

132

In "I's the B'y," *do* appears in the first space. What is the letter name for *do*?

The **key signature** comes before the meter signature at the beginning of a song. When *do* is F, the key signature has a **flat** (♭) on the third line.

Harmony is created when two or more different pitches are sung or played at the same time. Try singing *do* in harmony with "I's the B'y."

CREATE another harmony by singing this pattern with the song. Clap lightly with each *do*, pat with each low *so*.

THINK IT THROUGH

Which do you prefer for this song, harmony with pitches that stay the same or harmony with pitches that change? Why?

♫ **La raspa** *Mexican Folk Music*

LISTENING

"La raspa" (The Rasp) is a popular Mexican folk dance.

MATCH the harmonic pattern you hear in this dance with one of the patterns below.

HEARING HARMONY

Find your favorite harmony for "Pay Me My Money Down."
As you hear harmony that stays on the same pitch, predict
where harmony changes would sound better.

COMPARE these harmony changes with your
predictions.

How many times would you need to play this harmonic
pattern to accompany the song? Which other piece in this
lesson has similar harmony changes?

Dancers of the
Ballet Folklórico
of Mexico City.

THE DRAMA OF DYNAMICS

What does the word *dynamic* mean to you? It can mean constant activity and change.

In music, the dynamics are the changes in loudness and softness. Here are some common dynamic markings found in music.

f	**forte**	loud
mf	**mezzo forte**	medium loud
mp	**mezzo piano**	medium soft
p	**piano**	soft
<	**crescendo**	gradually get louder
>	**decrescendo**	gradually get softer

A DYNAMIC BAND

A wide range of dynamics is possible with a concert band. Not only can each instrument be played loudly or softly, but also different combinations of instruments can sound louder or softer.

LISTENING MAP *Listen for the dynamics in "Over the Hills and Far Away." The markings show you what to expect.*

THINK IT THROUGH

If *f* (forte) means loud, what do you think *ff* and *fff* mean? How do the dynamic changes affect the way you feel?

SINGING WITH DYNAMICS

"Come and Sing Together" tells of folk dancing in Hungary, a country in Europe where such songs and dances have been passed down for generations. Today, dances are seen at village celebrations of holidays and weddings, accompanied by live music and singing.

SING the first part of the song and follow the dynamic markings. Try singing it in two parts. Can you still hear the dynamic changes?

COME AND SING Together

Hungarian Melody

If you'd dance then you must have boots of shin-ing leath - er,

If you'd dance then you must have boots of shin-ing

Mon - ey in your pock - et - book, in your hat a feath - er.

leath - er, Mon - ey in your pock - et - book, in your hat a

A METER MYSTERY

The meter signature is missing from the music below.

LISTEN and follow the music. Think about how you can tell what the meter signature should be.

The rhythm has many clues. Clues: How many beats do you feel in a set, or measure? How many sounds to each beat do you hear? Are the beats divided equally or unequally?

What is the meter signature of this song?

WHICH RHYTHM?

"La raspa" has rhythms made for dancing! The music shifts back and forth between two sections, A and B. In each section you hear one rhythmic motive more than any other.

In which section do you hear ♩♪♪♩ many times? In which do you hear ♩ ♪ ? Try the motions to each motive, then listen for them again.

BAILE EN TEHUANTEPEC

When Mexican artist Diego Rivera traveled to the Tehuantepec region of Mexico, he sketched hundreds of scenes, some of which he turned into paintings years later. In this painting, the people are dancing to lively Mexican folk music.

Los Angeles County Museum of Art

DANCE TO LA RASPA!

La raspa means "the rasp," a tool used to smooth the rough places on metal. In the dance for "La raspa," the hands and feet move back and forth like a rasp. The dance is sometimes known as the Mexican Hat Dance because it can be danced around a hat placed on the floor.

1 Find a partner.

2 Move to the music.

④ Skip, gallop, or slide and find a new partner.

③ Swing your partner.

EXPRESSIVE **M**OMENTS

Music can express the way a singer or song-writer feels about something, from calm to angry, from amused to serious.

What are some feelings expressed by the songs pictured here?

SING your favorite song from the unit. Sing it expressively.

1. How does this melody move?

    a. steps and skips   **c.** repeated notes, steps, and skips

    b. mostly skips   **d.** repeated notes and steps

2. Which example do you hear?

a.    **c.**

b.    **d.**

3. Which melody do you hear?

a.    **c.**

b.    **d.**

4. Which rhythm do you hear?

146

CREATE

Snappy Interludes

CREATE an eight-beat pattern. Use each word and rhythm at least once. On a piece of paper, write your pattern.

cross

hip - po

el - e- phant

The boxes below will help you plan your patterns.

$\frac{6}{8}$ | | | | | | | | cross |

PERFORM the pattern twice through as an interlude between the verses of "One More River."

Write

Choose a person, bird, or animal from one of the songs in this unit.

Write a diary entry describing how the person, bird, or animal you chose feels about what happens in the song.

When I First Came to This Land

Words and Music by Oscar Brand

Verse

1.–5. When I first came to this land, I was not a wealth-y man.

Then I built my-self a shack.
Then I bought my-self a cow.
Then I bought my-self a horse. } I did what I could.
Then I got my-self a wife.
Then I got my-self a son.

Repeat these four measures for additional lines in verses 2-5

I { called my shack *Break - my - back.*
called my cow *No - milk - now,*
called my horse *Lame - of - course,* } I
called my wife *Joy - of - my - life.*
told my son *My work's done.*

Refrain

Still the land was sweet and good, I did what I could.

Over the Sea to Skye

Music by Annie MacLeod
Words by Sir Harold Boulton

Refrain

"Speed, bon - nie boat, like a bird on the wing:
"Car - ry the lad that's born to be king

On - ward! the sail - ors cry! Skye!"
O - ver the sea to

Verse

1. Loud the winds howl, loud the waves roar,
2. Tho the waves leap, soft shall ye sleep,
3. Man - y's the lad fought on that day,
4. Burned are our homes, ex - ile and death

Thun - der clouds rend the air; Baf - fled our foes,
O - cean's a roy - al bed; Rocked in the deep,
Well the clay more could wield, When the night came,
Scat - ter the loy - al men; Yet ere the sword

*Last time, go back to
the beginning and sing to the end
(Da Capo al Fine)*

stand on the shore, Fol - low they will not dare.
flo - ra will keep Watch by your wea - ry head.
si - lent - ly lay Dead on Cul - lo - den's field.
cool in the sheath, Char - lie will come a - gain.

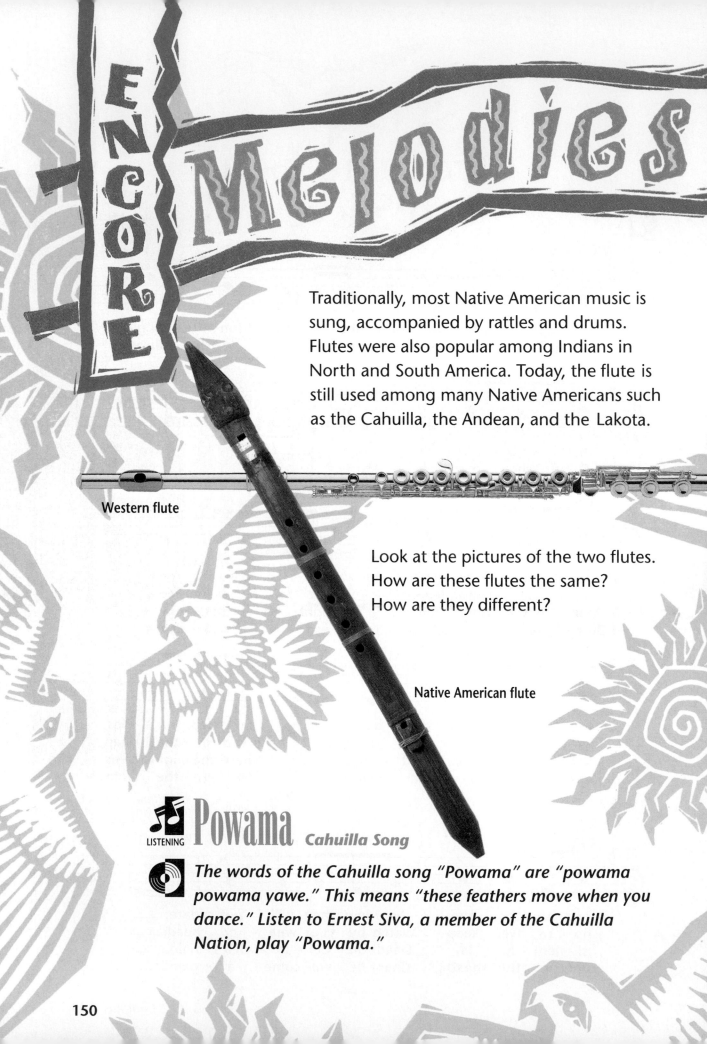

ENCORE Melodies

Traditionally, most Native American music is sung, accompanied by rattles and drums. Flutes were also popular among Indians in North and South America. Today, the flute is still used among many Native Americans such as the Cahuilla, the Andean, and the Lakota.

Western flute

Look at the pictures of the two flutes. How are these flutes the same? How are they different?

Native American flute

LISTENING Powama *Cahuilla Song*

The words of the Cahuilla song "Powama" are "powama powama yawe." This means "these feathers move when you dance." Listen to Ernest Siva, a member of the Cahuilla Nation, play "Powama."

in Flight

🎵 **El condor pasa** *Andean Song*

LISTENING

The Indians of South America also have flute songs about birds. "El condor pasa" is a popular folk song which describes the majesty of the condor as it flies over the Andes mountains.

Edgar Zurita playing the quena.

Among many Native Americans, the flute was the instrument that a young man used to court a young woman. Each day, he played beautiful melodies for her. According to Lakota legend, the first flute was created to win the heart of an important chieftain's daughter. Here is the story:

During a time when food was difficult to find, a young man from a certain village goes hunting. As he is walking, he spots some elk tracks. He begins to follow the tracks and soon loses his way in the forest. Because it is too dark to return home, he decides to spend the night there. He begins to make his bed for the night, but he is stopped by a strange sound. He listens more closely. After a time, he falls asleep. He dreams. In his dream, he meets a red-headed woodpecker, "woknooka."

The next morning, the young man wakes up to the sight of the woodpecker sitting in a tree. As the bird flies from tree to tree, the young man follows him. Finally, the bird lands on a hollow branch. The wind blows through the branch. Suddenly, the young man remembers the sound of the wind blowing through the branch as the strange sound he heard the night before. He takes the branch and returns to his home.

Once he is back, he tries to make the beautiful sound he remembers. Nothing happens. After many failures, he goes back out to the forest by himself. Once again, he falls asleep. In his dream, the woodpecker reappears as a man who shows him how to make a flute from the hollow branch. When the young man wakes up, he goes home. Once there, he makes a flute. When he learns about the chieftain's daughter who will not fall in love with anyone, he decides that he will win her heart by making up special flute songs for her.

 LISTEN to Gary Fields, a member of the Lakota and Cree Nations, tell the story about the first flute.

This poem expresses the importance of flutes in Native American cultures.

FOR THE FLUTE PLAYERS

Theirs is the sound of wood
whispering Creator's breath
through branches hollowed
with sacred instruction

Theirs is the sound of breezes
dancing timeless songs
of passionate hearts
in circles around the Earth

Theirs is the sound of birds
sending meadow voices
on feathered wings
to all directions

Theirs is the sound of echoes
shaping red rock walls
in long canyon spaces
that remember forever

—Edwin Schupman
Muscogee (Creek)

CONNEC

Finding A Way

I'd like you for a friend.
I'd like to find the way
Of asking you to be my friend.
I don't know what to say.

What would you like to hear?
What is it I can do?
There has to be some word, some look
Connecting me to you.

—*Myra Cohn Livingston*

TIONS

It's a Lovely Day Today

Words and Music
by Irving Berlin

It's a love-ly day to-day.____ So what-ev-er you've got to do,____ you've got a love-ly day to do it in,___ that's true.____ And I hope what-ev-er you've got to do is some-thing that can be done by two. For I'd real-ly like to stay.____ It's a love-ly day to-day.____ And what-ev-er you've got to do____ I'd be so hap-py to be

RHYTHM ALL AROUND

This song from southern Africa is about letting fire burn the bush, or wilderness area. Fire naturally clears the land of old shrub and allows space and sunlight for new growth. *Watsha* means "burn," and the song says "We are the burning fire; we burn, we burn."

SING this call-and-response song and pat with the beat.

Tina Singu

Song from Lesotho
As Sung by Kathleen Hill

Call

Response

Sotho: **Ti - na sing - u   le - lu - vu - tae   - o.   Wat - sha, wat - sha,   wat - sha,**
Pronunciation: ti   na   sing   u   lɛ   lu   vu   tae   o   wat   sha   wat   sha   wat   sha

Call   Response

Ti - na,   Ti - na   sing - u   le - lu - vu - tae   - o.
ti   na   ti   na   sing   u   lɛ   lu   vu   tae   o

1.   2.   Part 2

Wat - sha,   wat - sha,   wat - sha.   wat - sha,   la   la   la   la   la
wat   sha   wat   sha   wat   sha   wat   sha   la   la   la   la   la

"Stone Pounding" was sung years ago by road workers, mostly women, as they broke large stones into smaller pieces. Now children play a game as they sing this song.

SWITCH between clapping the rhythm of the words and patting with the beat.

STONE POUNDING

Jamaican Folk Song
Transcribed by Helen H. Roberts

Three stone a stone, then a three stone a stone, then a
three stone a stone say tam-boo-lay and no quar-rel. You no
hear-e what me yer-ry? You no hear-e what me yer-ry? You no
hear-e what me hear, say tam-boo-lay and no quar-rel.

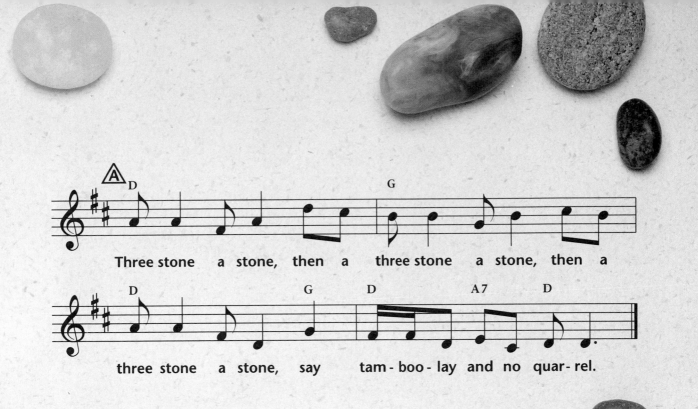

Ⓐ

D — — — G
Three stone a stone, then a three stone a stone, then a

D — G — D — A7 — D
three stone a stone, say tam-boo-lay and no quar-rel.

A NEW RHYTHM

The *short long short* pattern of sounds at the beginning of "Stone Pounding" lasts for two beats.

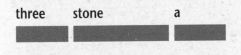

three · · stone · · · a

Find two *short long short* patterns in the following phrase. Then clap the rhythm.

When *do* is D, as in "Stone Pounding," the key signature shows two **sharps** (♯). They tell you to play F sharp (F♯) and C sharp (C♯) instead of F and C.

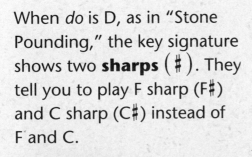

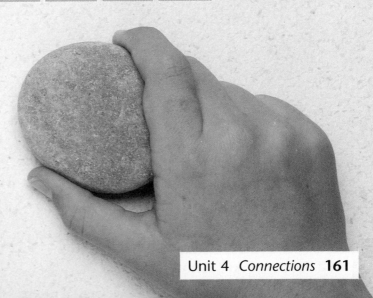

These scenes show the festive costumes and traditional instruments of Andean carnivals. A Peruvian man plays a large flute (middle right) and the Bolivian marchers (middle left) play panpipes and drums. Bolivian and Peruvian musicians (opposite page) show two types of Andean flutes called quenas.

LISTENING

Guadalquivir *Andean Dance Song*

LISTEN to "Guadalquivir" and raise your hand each time you hear the phrase with the *short long short* pattern. How many times do you hear the phrase?

"Guadalquivir" is a carnavalito. Carnavalitos blend South American Indian and Spanish musical traditions. They are usually sung and danced during festivals called carnivals.

Village carnivals may celebrate weddings, holy days, or anniversaries special to the village. People wear masks and fancy costumes, and enjoy singing, dancing, feasting, and parades.

PERFORM this step with the A section of "Guadalquivir."

right   left   right left   right   left   right   left   right left

■   ■   ■   ■   ■   ■   ■   ■   ■   ■

Calypso is lively, rhythmic music of the West Indies.

SING the A section. Trace the melodic shape in the
air and find the widest skips.

Hosanna, Me Build a House

Jamaican Calypso

A

Ho - san - na, me build a house, oh,____

Ho - san - na, me build a house, oh,____

1. I built it on the sand - y ground.____
2. I built it on the sol - id ground.____

B

Me house built on the sand - y ground.__ It will fall you see.
Me house built on the sol - id ground.__ It will stand you see.

Me house built on the sand - y ground.__ It will fall you see.
Me house built on the sol - id ground.__ It will stand you see.

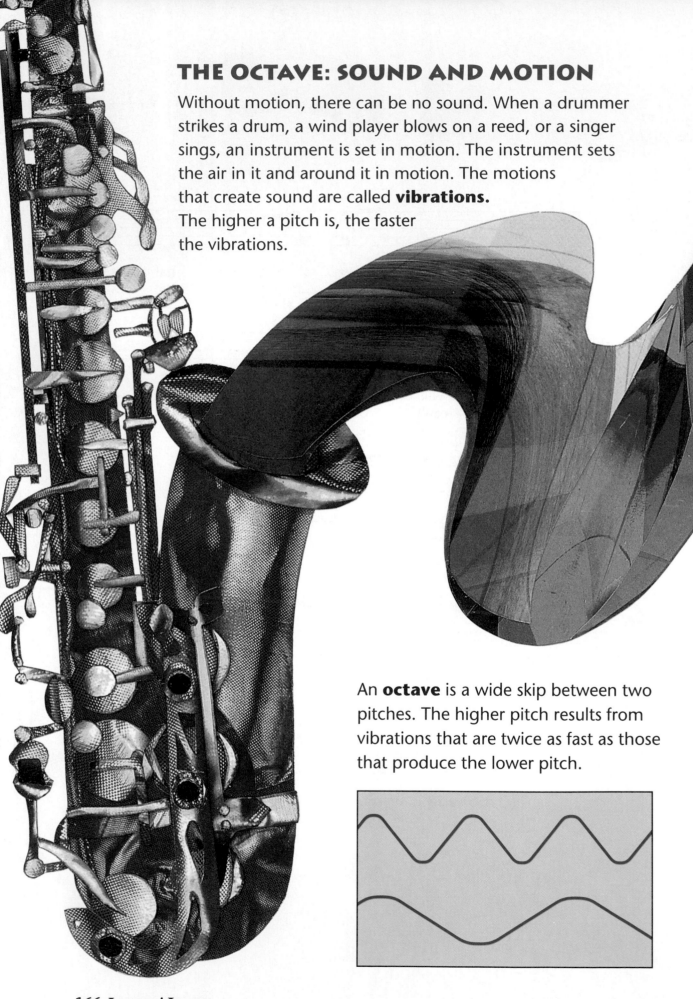

THE OCTAVE: SOUND AND MOTION

Without motion, there can be no sound. When a drummer strikes a drum, a wind player blows on a reed, or a singer sings, an instrument is set in motion. The instrument sets the air in it and around it in motion. The motions that create sound are called **vibrations.** The higher a pitch is, the faster the vibrations.

An **octave** is a wide skip between two pitches. The higher pitch results from vibrations that are twice as fast as those that produce the lower pitch.

In this folk song, nonsense words called **vocables** are used to imitate the sound of a spinning wheel.

RAISE your hand when you hear an octave.

SARASPONDA

Dutch Spinning Song

A

Sa - ra - spon - da, Sa - ra - spon - da, Sa - ra - spon - da, Ret - set - set!

Sa - ra - spon - da, Sa - ra - spon - da, Sa - ra - spon - da, Ret - set - set!

B

Ah - do - ray - oh!   Ah - do - ray - boom - day - oh!

Ah - do - ray - boom - day, Ret - set - set!   Ah - say - pa - say - oh!

CULTURAL

Spirituals were created by African Americans, who combined African rhythms with melodies they created and heard in America. Many spirituals, such as this one about David and Goliath, are based on Biblical stories.

LITTLE DAVID, PLAY ON YOUR HARP

African American Spiritual

Refrain

Lit - tle Da - vid, play on your harp, Hal - le - lu! Hal - le - lu!

Lit - tle Da - vid, play on your harp, Hal - le - lu!

End (Fine)

Verse

1. Lit - tle Da - vid was a shep - herd boy, He
2. Old David was a might - y king, and

Go back to the beginning and sing to the end (Da Capo al Fine)

slew Go - li - ath and shout - ed for joy.
all the peo - ple came to sing.

CONNECTIONS

The stone carving (left) shows a woman playing a harp. The statue comes from Ur, a city of Sumeria, Mesopotamia, about 2,000 B.C. Above are designs from buildings of other Near Eastern civilizations that existed in Biblical times.

How high and low can you sing? The larynx, or voice box, is the part of your throat that vibrates as you make sound. The muscles of the larynx can tighten or loosen to produce a wide variety of pitches and qualities.

As a boy matures, his voice changes. His larynx gradually doubles in size, and the pitch of his voice becomes about an octave lower than it was. A girl's voice changes, too. Her larynx changes in texture rather than size, so the quality of her voice changes more than the pitch does.

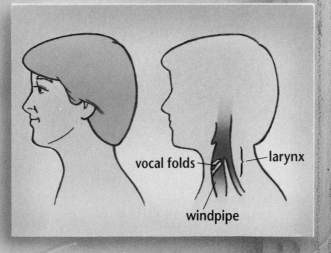

MEET JOSEPH SHABALALA

Have you ever dreamed of taking your own special music to friends, neighbors, and beyond to the far corners of the earth? This is what Joseph Shabalala, founder of Ladysmith Black Mambazo, did. Starting with his own relatives, he developed a group that shares the musical traditions of the Zulu with people all over the world.

LISTEN to Joseph Shabalala talk about his career as a composer and leader of a musical group.

CONNECTING CULTURES

Many of the songs you sang in this unit were created by people of African origin. Some of the people live there now. Others have ancestors who came from Africa.

THINK IT THROUGH

Compare the rhythms, melodies, and ideas expressed in the songs you sang. Find similarities and differences.

Drums play an important part in the music of Africa, including Zaire (top). In Haiti, people of African descent carry on the tradition of drumming (left), and in the United States, Chick Webb, an African American drummer, put together the first standard trap set (right).

COME TO

Join the festive dancing! You've danced to the A section of "Guadalquivir." Here's the formation for the B section.

DANCE to "Guadalquivir."

CARNIVAL!

CONNECTING SOUND AND SYMBOL

The *short long short* pattern can be heard in both "Guadalquivir" and "Stone Pounding."

PAT and clap these two patterns from "Stone Pounding." How are they alike? How are they different?

Pat:

hear - e   what me

Clap:

three stone   a

Hear-e what me can be written this way.

Three stone a can be written two ways. A **tie** connects the two eighth notes that sound as one quarter note.

or

FIND this rhythm pattern in the music for "Stone Pounding" on page 160.

CARRY ON THE CARNIVAL RHYTHM

The ♪♩ ♪ rhythm can be found in the music of many parts of the world. In Egypt, you might hear this pattern played on a clay or metal hand drum called a dumbek.

PERFORM the pattern below as if you were playing a dumbek. Use one palm on *dum* and the fingertips of the other hand on *tak*. Say the words as you drum.

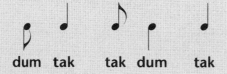

dum tak   tak dum   tak

LISTENING

Ayazein *Egyptian Folk Song*

LISTEN for the dumbek pattern in "Ayazein." Try to play along as you listen again!

Dumbeks are widely used in Middle Eastern countries, Turkey, and Greece. A floral pattern has been hammered into this metal dumbek from Turkey.

The dumbek is often played with other instruments. In this scene from Egypt, it is played with two rababas.

More About Octaves

Which part of "Sarasponda" is this? Sing
it with the "spinning words."

An octave is two pitches separated by a wide skip, with the
higher pitch vibrating twice as fast as the lower. The two
pitches have the same name. If C is the letter name of the
lower pitch, what is the letter name of the higher pitch?

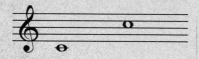

If *do* is the pitch syllable name of the lower pitch, what
name is used for the pitch one octave higher?

CREATE a melodic ostinato using low and high *do*.
Use the resonator bells C and C' and this rhythm pattern. Perform the ostinato with the A section
of "Sarasponda."

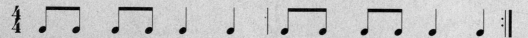

Keep the ped - al mov - ing.   Keep the wheel a - turn - ing.

176

ANNA CODDE

Maerten van Heemskerck's portrait shows
a woman with her spinning wheel. The glowing
light and calm domestic scene are typical of Dutch
paintings from the 1500s. Imagine the turning
posts, spools, and wheel making rhythmic
sounds such as *ret set set* as they
spin fleece into wool.

LISTENING

Hoedown (excerpt) from *Rodeo*
by Aaron Copland

"Hoedown" borrows musical ideas from square dances and rodeos.

SING this motive with pitch syllables. Stamp on low *do* and clap on high *do.*

LISTENING MAP   Listen to "Hoedown" and follow the map.

KEY
a
b

A

START   a a b b a a b b b b a a   bridge
22 beats

B

16 beats

SPOTLIGHT ON AARON COPLAND

Aaron Copland (1900–1990) was born in Brooklyn, N.Y. His first contact with music came from listening to his older sister practice the piano. By age 8, he was composing songs. As an adult, he became one of the first American composers to have his work known all over the world.

Copland's use of jazz and American folk tunes gave his music a sound all its own. Besides composing for concerts, the ballet, opera, radio, theater, and movies, he was a pianist and conductor. He also lectured and wrote books to help people understand and appreciate modern music.

Voices in Harmony

When you sing or play pitches to accompany a melody, you produce harmony. By playing three or more pitches at the same time, you produce a **chord.** When the chord pitches change, the harmony of the song changes.

The harmony of "Hoe Ana Te Vaka" has changing chords.

RAISE your hand each time you hear a chord change. Which instrument is playing the chords?

In the South Pacific, the canoe has long been an important form of transportation. "Hoe Ana Te Vaka" describes paddling a canoe and sighting the islands of Tahiti and Mo'orea.

Hoe Ana Te Vaka
PADDLE THE CANOE

Tahitian Folk Song
Collected and Transcribed
by Kathy B. Sorensen

NAME THAT CHORD!

Each chord has a letter name based on a pitch called the **chord root.** Usually when the pitches of a chord are arranged close to each other on the staff, the lowest pitch is the chord root and gives the chord its name.

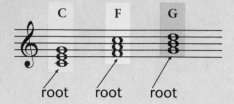

root   root   root

FIND the chord names above the music.

Me   house built_ on_ the sand-y ground._   It will fall you   see.

Me house built_ on_ the sand-y ground._   It will fall you   see.

HOSANNA!
WE BUILD A CHORD!

The colors show the harmonic pattern for the B section of "Hosanna, Me Build a House."

PLAY the harmonic pattern for "Hosanna, Me Build a House" with these three chords.

C E G F A C G B D

Rap and

Nathaniel Talking is a book of poetry by Eloise Greenfield. In the book, Nathaniel B. Free is a nine-year-old boy, and this is his rap.

Nathaniel's RAP

It's Nathaniel talking
and Nathaniel's me
I'm talking about
My philosophy
About the things I do
And the people I see
All told in the words
Of Nathaniel B. Free
That's me
And I can rap
I can rap
I can rap, rap, rap
Till your earflaps flap
I can talk that talk
Till you go for a walk
I can run it on down
Till you get out of town
I can rap
I can rap
Rested, dressed and feeling fine
I've got something on my mind

Rhythm

Friends and kin and neighborhood
Listen now and listen good
Nathaniel's talking
Nathaniel B. Free
Talking about
My philosophy
Been thinking all day
I got a lot to say
Gotta run it on down
Nathaniel's way
Okay!
I gotta rap
Gotta rap
Gotta rap, rap, rap
Till your earflaps flap
Gotta talk that talk
Till you go for a walk
Gotta run it on down
Till you get out of town
Gotta rap
Gotta rap
Rested, dressed and feeling fine
I've got something on my mind
Friends and kin and neighborhood
Listen now and listen good
I'm gonna rap, hey!
Gonna rap, hey!
I'm gonna rap!

—Eloise Greenfield

What can you tell about Nathaniel from
this poem?

**DESCRIBE how the poem could sound
when it is performed aloud as a rap.**

I Missed the Bus *by Jermaine Dupri*

In 1992 the rap duo Kris Kross recorded "I Missed the Bus."
They were 13 years old. Their special style is wearing every-
thing—hat, shirt, and jeans—backwards. But their music,
with its fresh rhythms and appealing rhymes, is what made
them successful. They've had a triple-platinum album,
Totally Krossed Out, from which "I Missed the Bus" is taken.

Rap sprang up in African American communities during
the 1970s. Rappers put together fast, catchy phrases over
rhythm tracks. Some rap is pure entertainment. Other
rappers' words turn to serious themes such as politics,
poverty, and racism.

LISTEN to "I Missed the Bus" and describe
what you hear.

Chris Smith
and Chris Kelly
of Kris Kross

In some music, stressed or **accented** sounds come between the beats instead of on the beat. Rhythm patterns with sounds between the beats are called **syncopated.**

Syncopation can be found in many kinds of music. The *short long short* pattern in "Stone Pounding" is an example of syncopation. The rhythms of rap are also very syncopated.

CREATE your own syncopated rap version of "Nathaniel's Rap."

THINK IT THROUGH

How would "Nathaniel's Rap" sound if every syllable were unaccented and on the beat? Try saying it that way. How does it compare with the recording?

MAKE YOUR OWN MELODY

Steel drums are tuned instruments made from oil drums and steel barrels. One drum can play up to thirty pitches, so a steel drum band can play both melody and harmony.

Steel drums accompany parades during Carnival. Steel drum bands, also called pan orchestras, are popular throughout the Caribbean and in other places with large numbers of West Indian people.

LISTEN to "Hosanna, Me Build a House" with steel drums playing the melody. When do the musicians make up new melodies in place of the melody of the song?

Steel drum band playing during Carnival in St. George's, Grenada. Opposite page: musicians playing steel drums on St. Lucia, a Caribbean island.

ADD SOME HIGHLIGHTS

Another way to change "Hosanna, Me Build a House" is to highlight parts of the melody by playing them on instruments. Find the pitches needed to play the tinted motives.

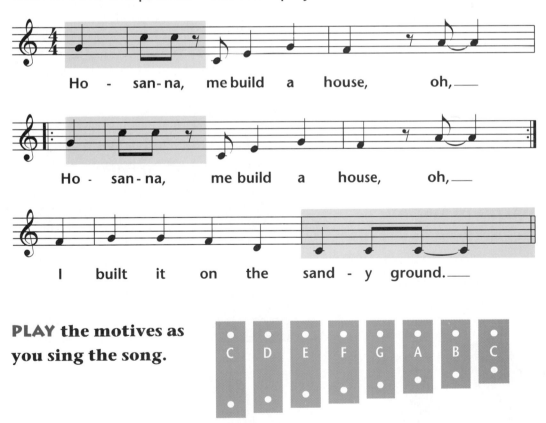

Ho - san-na, me build a house, oh, ____

Ho - san-na, me build a house, oh, ____

I built it on the sand - y ground. ____

PLAY the motives as you sing the song.

What is the skip between the lowest and highest pitches called?

THE JAZZ CONNECTION

The syncopated rhythms and melodies of **jazz** grew from the spirituals, work songs, and blues of African Americans. The roots of jazz go back to rhythms from western Africa, which African Americans mixed with harmony from classical and folk music they learned in America. Jazz appeals to people of all cultures and many play this music.

Many jazz musicians are known for their ability to **improvise,** or find new ways to play melodies and rhythm patterns each time they perform.

meet MARIAN McPARTLAND

Marian McPartland is a pianist and a songwriter who also improvises on other compositions, interpreting them her own way. She hosts a radio show, "Piano Jazz," on which she talks to and performs with other jazz pianists.

LISTEN to Marian McPartland as she discusses and demonstrates jazz improvisation.

Things Ain't What They Used to Be

by Mercer Ellington

LISTEN to Marian McPartland improvise on this jazz melody.

IMPROVISE melodies on these pitches during the verses of "Little David, Play on Your Harp."

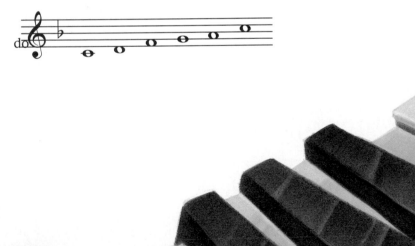

MAKING CONNECTIONS

When you meet someone new, you may first notice how that person is different from you. When you find something that is the same between you, such as an activity that you both enjoy, you have made a connection. You are on your way to being friends.

People everywhere enjoy playing together. "Stone Pounding" is a singing game from Jamaica.

Singing while you work can make the job easier. "Sarasponda" is a work song from Holland, and "Tina Singu" is one from Lesotho.

What other singing games do you know? What other work songs do you know?

CHECK IT OUT

1. How many times do you hear the *short long short* rhythm (♪ ♩ ♪) ?

   a. two times   **b.** three times   **c.** four times

2. Which rhythm do you hear?

   a.

   b.

   c.

   d.

3. Which pitches do you hear?

   a.    **c.**

   C   C

   b. 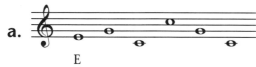   **d.**

   C   C

4. Which pitches do you hear?

   a.    **c.**

   E   E

   b.    **d.**

   E   E

CREATE

Syncopation in C

CREATE a melody using the pitches C D E G C'. Use this rhythm pattern.

Write your melody on a staff. Where does it move by steps? by skips? Mark the steps with 1 and the skips with 2.

C is *do*. Sing your pattern with pitch syllable names.

PLAY your melody as an introduction to "Sarasponda."

Write

Explore your connections to the musical experiences of your family or neighbors.

Interview an older person to find out about his or her musical experiences. Ask about the person's favorite songs from school, or the musicians and groups that he or she enjoyed. Write a newspaper article about what you learn.

MORE SONGS TO SING

SOURWOOD MOUNTAIN

Appalachian Folk Song

1. Chick - en crow - in' on Sour - wood Moun - tain,
2. My true love's a blue - eyed dai - sy,

Hey de - ing dang did - dle al - ly day.
{ So man - y pret - ty girls
  If I don't get her

I can't count them,
I'll go cra - zy,
} Hey de - ing dang did - dle al - ly day.

My true love she lives in Letch - er,
My true love lives in the hol - low,
} Hey de - ing dang

did - dle al - ly day.
{ She won't come and I won't fetch her,
  She won't come and I won't fol - low,

Hey de - ing dang did - dle al - ly day.

A Tragic Story

Music by Benjamin Britten
Words by William M. Thackeray

Start slowly *p* 1. There liv'd a sage in days of yore, And
p 2. He mus'd up-on this cu-rious case, And
More movement *mf* 3. Says he, "The mys-ter-y I've found, I'll
Getting faster *f* 4. Then 'round and 'round, and out and in, All
Faster & louder 5. And right and left, and 'round a-bout, And

he a hand-some pig-tail wore, But won-der'd much and
swore he'd change the pig-tail's place, And have it hang-ing
turn me 'round," He turn'd him 'round, He turn'd him 'round, he
day the puz-zled sage did spin; In vain it mat-ter'd
up and down, and in and out, he turn'd, But still the

sor-row'd more, Be-cause it hung be-hind him.
at his face, Not dan-gling there be-hind him.
turn'd him 'round, But still it hung be-hind him.
not a pin, The pig-tail hung be-hind him.
pig-tail stout hung stead-i-ly be-hind him.

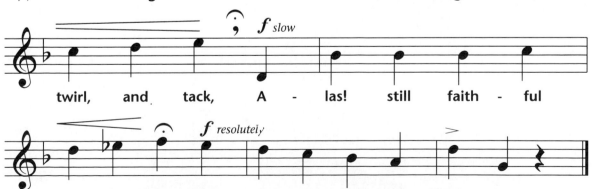

ff

Very fast 6. And though his ef-forts nev-er slack, And though he twist, and

f slow

twirl, and tack, A-las! still faith-ful

f resolutely

to his back, The pig-tail hangs be-hind him.

ENCORE
improvise!

Jazz musicians have always enjoyed the freedom of improvising. This allows them to change a piece of music as they play. Performing in this way did not start with jazz musicians. Performers have always improvised. Classical musicians such as Bach, Mozart, and Beethoven were masters of improvising at the keyboard.

SPOTLIGHT ON
CHARLIE PARKER

Charlie Parker, one of the all-time great saxophone players, was famous for his improvisations. Born in Kansas City in 1920, he began playing the alto saxophone when he was thirteen years old. During the 1940s, Parker's way of playing changed the style of jazz. His free style earned Parker the nickname "Bird."

The Charlie Parker combo in 1947, with Miles Davis playing trumpet.

Now's the Time (Versions 1 and 2)
by Charlie Parker

Listen to a twelve-bar blues piece composed by Charlie Parker. You will hear two versions. The first version was made for Bird, *a movie about Charlie Parker. Using an old recording, engineers erased the drum, bass, and piano parts. Only the saxophone parts played by Charlie Parker were kept. New musicians were hired to play the other parts. The second version is the original recording of "Now's the Time."*

DESCRIBE the differences you hear between the two recordings.

The syncopated feeling that can be heard in "Now's the Time" is also found in this song.

HAMBONE

African American Hand Jive Game

1. Ham - bone, Ham - bone, have you heard?—
2. If that mock - in' - bird don't sing,—
3. If that dia - mond ring turns brass,—
4. If that look - ing glass gets broke,—
5. Ham - bone, Ham - bone, where you been?—

Pop - pa's gon - na buy me a mock - in' - bird.—
Pop - pa's gon - na buy me a dia - mond ring.—
Pop - pa's gon - na buy me a look - ing glass.—
Pop - pa's gon - na buy me a bil - ly goat.—
"Round— the— world and— back a - gain."—

6. Hambone, Hambone, where's your wife?
   "She's in the kitchen eatin' rice."

Other artists also improvise in the way they use materials. Irene Bankhead, a quiltmaker, sews together beautiful pieces of cloth to make colorful designs. Bankhead, who started quilting when she was thirteen, can often finish a quilt in three days.

String by **Irene Bankhead**

Music with

a Message

PROVERBS BY AESOP

Slow and steady wins the race.
— *The Hare and the Tortoise*

Don't count your chickens before they are hatched.
— *The Milkmaid and Her Pail*

Appearances are often deceiving.
— *The Wolf in Sheep's Clothing*

No act of kindness, however small, is wasted.
— *The Lion and the Mouse*

Pete Seeger, an American folk singer, wrote this song. Its message is about the importance of protecting whales.

The Song of the World's Last Whale

Words and Music by Peter Seeger

1. and 6. I heard the song_____ of the world's last
2. It was down off Ber-mu-da_____ Ear - ly last

whale,_____ As I rocked in the moon - light_____
spring,_____ Near an un-der - wa - ter moun - tain_____

___ and reefed the sail,_____ It - 'll hap-pen to
___ Where the hump - backs sing._____ I_____ low-ered the

you al - so with - out fail, if it hap-pens to
mi-cro-phone A quar-ter mile_____ down, Switched_____ on the re-

me_____ sang the world's last whale._____
cor-der_____ And let the tape spin round._____

3. I didn't just hear grunting, I didn't just hear squeaks,
   I didn't just hear bellows, I didn't just hear shrieks.
   It was the musical singing and the passionate wail,
   That came from the heart of the world's last whale.

4. Down in the Antarctic the harpoons wait,
   But it's upon the land they decide my fate.
   In London Town they'll be telling the tale,
   If it's life or death for the world's last whale.

5. So here's a little test to see how you feel,
   Here's a little test for this age of the automobile.
   If we can save our singers in the sea,
   Perhaps there's a chance to save you and me.

Some Good

Here is an African song with a message: "Take time in life 'cause you got far way to go." What do you think this means?

TAKE TIME IN LIFE

Liberian Folk Song

1. I was pass - ing by, My broth - er called me in,
2. I was pass - ing by, My un - cle called me in,
3. I was pass - ing by, Some peo - ple called me in,

And he said to me, You bet - ter take time in life.
And he said to me, My neph - ew, take time in life.
And they said to me, My young man, take time in life.

Peo - ple, take time in life, Peo - ple, take time in life,
Neph - ew, take time in life, Neph - ew, take time in life,
Young man, take time in life, Young man, take time in life,

Peo - ple,
Neph - ew, } take time in life 'cause you got far way to go.
Young man,

What is the meter of "Take Time in Life"? How can you tell?

CREATE a beat pattern with movement to show how many beats are in each set.

Advice

 LISTENING

 ## D'Hammerschmiedsgesellen

Bavarian Folk Dance

The name of this dance means "The Journeyman Blacksmith." A journeyman was a young man learning a trade. Blacksmiths made horseshoes and other metal objects.

Listen to "D'Hammerschmiedsgesellen" to find the meter. Which meter signature fits the music?

2
4

3
4

4
4

CREATE a movement pattern to show how many beats are in each set.

THE STORIES YOU TELL!

Calypso is the name of Jacques Cousteau's ship. Cousteau studied underwater and coastal life in the oceans around the world. John Denver wrote this song to honor Cousteau's work.

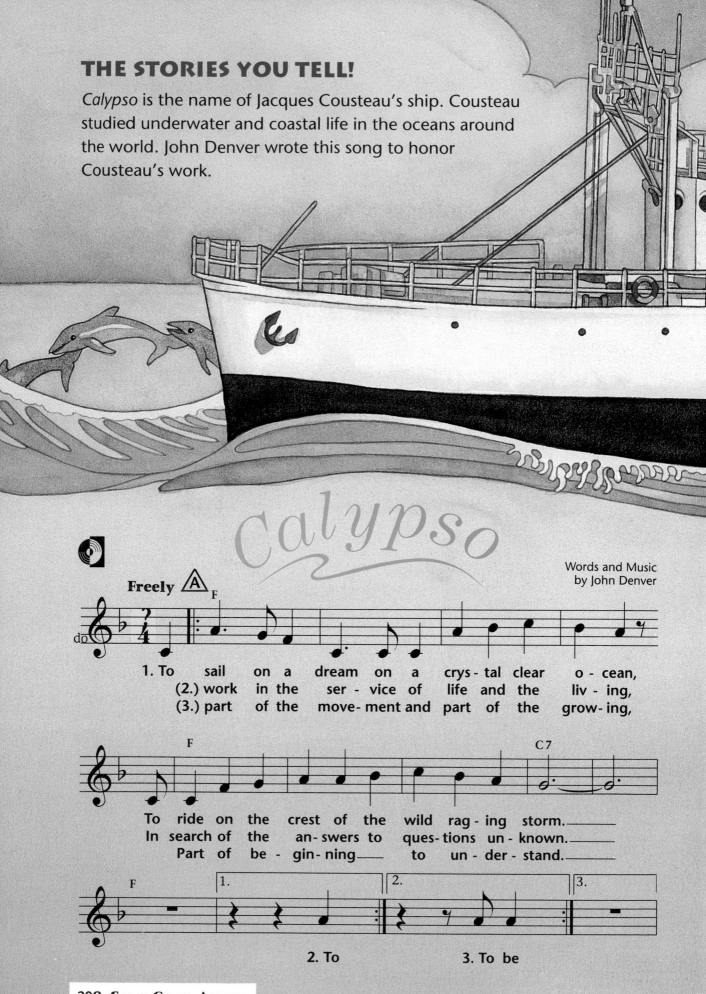

Calypso

Words and Music
by John Denver

1. To sail on a dream on a crys - tal clear o - cean,
(2.) work in the ser - vice of life and the liv - ing,
(3.) part of the move - ment and part of the grow - ing,

To ride on the crest of the wild rag - ing storm.
In search of the an - swers to ques - tions un - known.
Part of be - gin - ning to un - der - stand.

2. To

3. To be

B Dm

Aye, ____ Ca - lyp - so, the plac - es you've been to, The
Aye, ____ Ca - lyp - so, I sing to your spir - it, To

Gm   C7   1. Dm   2. Dm

things that you've shown us, the sto - ries you tell! well. Hi - dee -
those who have served you so long and so

C F   C7   1. F   2. F

ay ee oo ____ oh - dle - oh oo ____ Hi - dee - oo ____

Which meter signature goes at the beginning of
"Calypso"? 2/4 3/4 4/4

What riddles do you know? Riddles make you think about things in new ways. Find the riddles in "Tum-Balalaika."

Tum-Balalaika

Russian Yiddish
Folk Song

Verse

1. Maid - en, maid - en, can you ex - plain,
2. Fool - ish boy, I can____ ex - plain, A

What can grow with - out an - y rain?
stone can grow with - out an - y rain.

What____ can burn for man - y a year?
True love can burn for man - y a year. A

What____ can cry, and shed not a tear?
sad heart can cry, and shed not a tear.

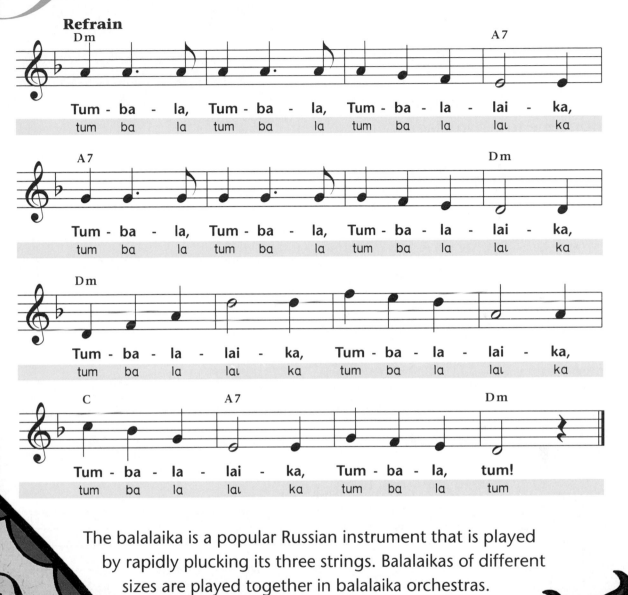

Refrain

Dm   A 7

Tum - ba - la,   Tum - ba - la,   Tum - ba - la - lai - ka,
tum   ba   la   tum   ba   la   tum   ba   la   laı   ka

A 7   Dm

Tum - ba - la,   Tum - ba - la,   Tum - ba - la - lai - ka,
tum   ba   la   tum   ba   la   tum   ba   la   laı   ka

Dm

Tum - ba - la - lai - ka,   Tum - ba - la - lai - ka,
tum   ba   la   laı   ka   tum   ba   la   laı   ka

C   A 7   Dm

Tum - ba - la - lai - ka,   Tum - ba - la,   tum!
tum   ba   la   laı   ka   tum   ba   la   tum

The balalaika is a popular Russian instrument that is played by rapidly plucking its three strings. Balalaikas of different sizes are played together in balalaika orchestras.

COUNTING IN MAORI

Children everywhere sing alphabet and counting songs. In New Zealand, Maori children count with this chant. Try counting from one to ten in Maori.

HEI TAMA TU TAMA

Sing three times counting 1 - 9

Traditional Maori Children's Counting Game

Maori: **Ka ta - hi, Hei ta - ma tu ta - ma**
Pronunciation: ka ta hi hei ta ma tu ta ma

Ka ru - a, Hei ta - ma tu ta - ma
ka ru a hei ta ma tu ta ma

Start here 4th time to count 10

Ka to - ru, Hei ta - ma tu ta - ma,
ka to ru hei ta ma tu ta ma

After 3rd time go to

Hei ta - ma tu ta - ma, Hei ta - ma tu ta - ma.
hei ta ma tu ta ma hei ta ma tu ta ma

Tahi, rua, toru are the words for "one, two, three."
Wha, rima, ono are "four, five, six."
Whitu, waru, iwa are "seven, eight, nine."
Tekau is "ten" and *tama* means "young boy."

MAJOR AND MINOR

The melodies of "Tum-Balalaika" and
"Hei Tama Tu Tama" have different sounds.
One reason is that they use different sets
of pitches. The set of pitches heard in "Tum-
Balalaika" is called **minor**. The set of pitches
in "Hei Tama Tu Tama" is called **major**.

Tempo Terms

Folk dancers dance to both slow and lively music. Sometimes the music changes speed, challenging the dancers to go slower or faster.

clap

cross

legs

DANCE to "D'Hammer-schmiedsgesellen," a folk dance from the Bavarian region of Germany.

214

right

left

both

SPEED LIMIT AHEAD!

The **tempo** is the speed of the beat of a song. Here are some Italian words used to describe the tempo of music.

adagio	slow
moderato	medium
allegro	fast
presto	very fast

Music can begin at any tempo and then change. When the music speeds up, the change is called an **accelerando**, and when it slows down, the change is called a **ritardando**. Tempo changes can take you by surprise and make the music more interesting or expressive.

LISTEN for the tempos in "D'Hammerschmiedsgesellen."

LISTENING

Presto (excerpt) from Trio for Piano, Oboe, and Bassoon
by Francis Poulenc

The bassoon *and* the oboe *are woodwind instruments in the orchestra. If the bassoon's wooden tube were straightened out, it would measure $8\frac{1}{2}$ feet long! Because it is so long, the bassoon can play very low pitches. The player blows air through a* **double reed,** *two pieces of bamboo that are tied together and connected to the bassoon. The oboe is about 22 inches long and has a smaller double reed, producing higher, sweeter sounds. These two instruments are the main members of the double-reed branch of the woodwind family.*

oboe reed

bassoon reed

LISTENING MAP *Signal when you hear the tempo change in "Presto."*

TIME FOR TI!

Listen as you sing the last phrase from "Hei Tama Tu Tama." You only sing *do* and a lower pitch. That pitch, just below *do*, is called *ti*.

The letter name for *do* in "Hei Tama Tu Tama" is F. What is the letter name for *ti*?

PLAY this phrase on an instrument.

Hei ta - ma tu ta - ma, Hei ta - ma tu ta - ma,

Hei ta - ma tu ta - ma._____

NAME the pitch syllables in this pattern.
Clue: The pattern ends on high *do* (*do*¹).

*do*¹

Raise your hand when you hear the pattern in "Aquaqua."

218

Aquaqua

Israeli Children's Game
Collected by Rita Klinger

In "Hei Tama Tu Tama," *do* is F. The key signature has a flat
(♭) on the third line. In "Aquaqua," *do* is C. How does its
key signature differ from the one in "Hei Tama Tu Tama"?

Look at the song again. A silence the length of an eighth
note is shown with an **eighth rest** (ɣ).

THE MAJOR SCALE

If you sing all the pitches from *do* to *do¹*, you will be singing a **major scale**.

The C major scale looks like this.

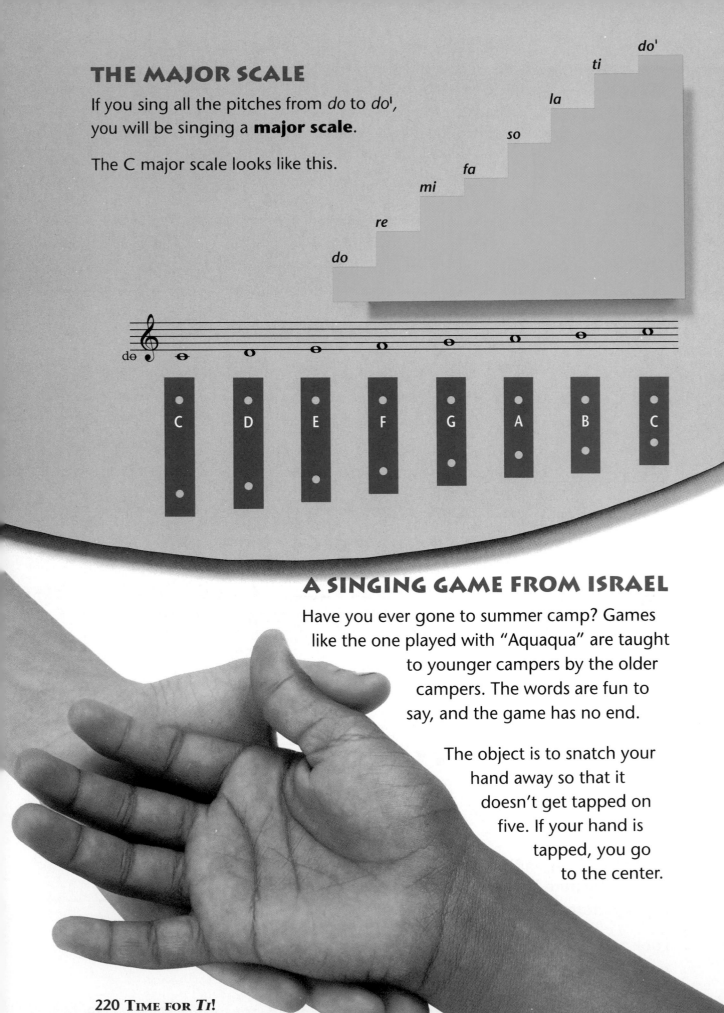

do re mi fa so la ti do¹

C D E F G A B C

A SINGING GAME FROM ISRAEL

Have you ever gone to summer camp? Games like the one played with "Aquaqua" are taught to younger campers by the older campers. The words are fun to say, and the game has no end.

The object is to snatch your hand away so that it doesn't get tapped on five. If your hand is tapped, you go to the center.

Count out and tap hands.

Continue to five.

Music That

Music can carry a personal message, and it can also pass on the knowledge and traditions of a group of people.

LISTENING

Canoe Song and Dance

As Performed by Members of the Haliwa-Saponi Nation

Throughout their history, Native Americans have used songs and dances to teach life skills, such as hunting, and to tell stories. This Eastern Woodlands social dance tells the following story.

The women of the village are paddling canoes down the river to do the washing. They see the men of the village paddling upstream. The men are tired from the hard work of hunting. At first the men pass the women, but they are so happy to see each other that the men turn around and they all paddle downstream together.

Songs such as "Canoe Song and Dance" are learned by hearing someone sing them.

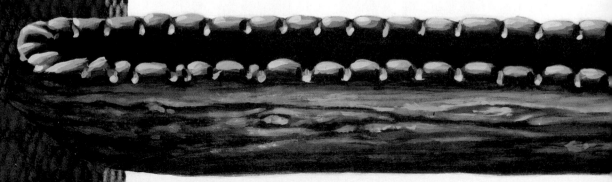

Eastern Woodlands canoe

Eastern Woodlands woven belt

Teaches Tradition

LEARN to sing "Canoe Song and Dance" by listening to these members of the Haliwa-Saponi Nation.

Canoe Dance performed by Haliwa-Saponi people of North Carolina.

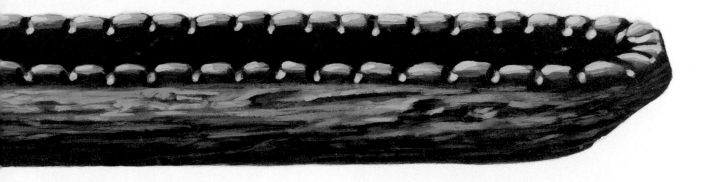

TAKE TIME FOR A NEW RHYTHM

Which line shows the rhythm you performed with the first phrase of "Take Time in Life"?

The rhythm of the first phrase could be written like this.

SING the song on page 206 and find all the ♩. ♪ patterns.

A dot following a note adds half of the note's rhythmic value. A dot after a quarter note makes it an eighth note longer.

♪ ♩ ♪ = ♩

♪ ♩ ♪ = ♩.

♩ ♪ = ♩.

A RHYTHM RIDDLE

Which pattern below shows the correct notation for the first phrase of the refrain of "Tum-Balalaika"? For the first phrase of "Calypso"?

After you've solved the riddle, sing "Tum-Balalaika" with a soloist on each verse.

THINK IT THROUGH

How long would a dotted half note sound? A dotted eighth note?

Dancing to Major and Minor

Most music is in either major or minor. Sometimes it's interesting to hear both in one piece.

SPOTLIGHT ON
Antonin Dvořák

Antonin Dvořák (1841–1904) was the son of a Czech innkeeper and butcher, who had hoped his son would stay in the business. Antonin played violin at the inn, and at 16 began to study music seriously. He learned to sing and to play violin, viola, organ, and piano. He later worked as a church organist and composer. Dvořák included Czech folk melodies in his pieces, and his tuneful, rhythmic music is still very popular.

LISTENING

Slavonic Dance Op. 46, No. 8

(excerpt)

by Antonin Dvořák

SIGNAL with your hand each time you hear a shift between minor and major.

What does the tempo marking tell you?

Allegro

A — f — 4 beats — 4 beats

B — p — 16 beats — **A** — f

C — p — 16 beats

B — $fpfpfpfp$ — 16 beats

D — p —— f — 24 beats

CODA

A — f —————— pp — 12 beats

A SPIRITUAL

The words of the song "Wade in the Water" refer to a Biblical story about the Pool of Bethesda, a pond in Jerusalem. Sometimes the water's surface ripples and moves, and this was called "troubling the waters."

People believed that the pool was brushed by the wing of an angel, and that the first person to step into the water after it moved would be healed of diseases and ailments. Many who were in poor health gathered there to wait for the water to be "troubled."

DOWN BY THE RIVERSIDE

The musicians in this 1966 wood carving by Daniel Pressley are singing and playing traditional instruments, the guitar and the harmonica. The texture and depth of the carving add to the sense of energy and feeling in their music.

LISTEN to the song. Does it sound major or minor?

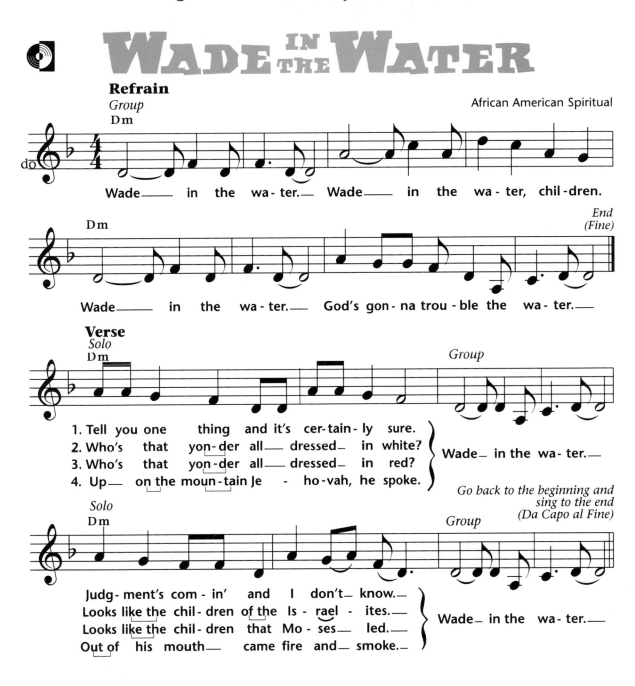

WADE IN THE WATER

Refrain

Group

Dm

African American Spiritual

Wade—— in the wa-ter.—— Wade—— in the wa-ter, chil-dren.

Dm

End (Fine)

Wade—— in the wa-ter.—— God's gon-na trou-ble the wa-ter.——

Verse

Solo

Dm

Group

1. Tell you one   thing   and it's cer-tain-ly sure.
2. Who's   that   yon-der all—— dressed—— in white?
3. Who's   that   yon-der all—— dressed—— in red?
4. Up—— on the moun-tain Je - ho-vah, he spoke.

Wade— in the wa-ter.——

Go back to the beginning and sing to the end (Da Capo al Fine)

Solo

Dm

Group

Judg-ment's com-in'   and   I   don't— know.——
Looks like the chil-dren of the Is - rael - ites.——
Looks like the chil-dren that Mo - ses— led.——
Out of   his mouth——   came fire and— smoke.——

Wade— in the   wa-ter.——

D·O·T·T·E·D
Rhythms Return

Name a song you know for each picture.

CLAP the rhythm and match it to a phrase from one of the songs.

Singing is an important part of German culture, and songs such as this canon are traditional favorites.

Find the rhythm that is always sung with the word *Musica*.

TAP or play this rhythm each time you sing it.

Music Alone Shall Live

Himmel und Erde

German Round
Words Adapted by MMH

German: Him - mel und Er - de müss - en ver - gehn;
Pronunciation: hɪ məl ʊnt ɛʁ də mö sən fɛʁ gen
English: All things will per - ish be - neath___ the sky;

a - ber die Mu - si - ca, a - ber die Mu - si - ca,
ɑ bəʁ di mu zi kɑ ɑ bəʁ di mu zi kɑ
Mu - sic a - lone shall live, Mu - sic a - lone shall live,

a - ber die Mu - si - ca blei - bet be - stehn.
ɑ bəʁ di mu zi kɑ blaɪ bət bə shten
Mu - sic a - lone shall live, nev - er to die.

Galliard *by Tielman Susato*

The galliard, an athletic and energetic dance, was one of the most popular dances in European courts during the 1500s. It was the only court dance for which the men removed their hats—which otherwise would have fallen off!

CLAP the rhythm of the A section of "Galliard." Which part is the same as the rhythm of the words *aber die Musica?*

LISTEN to all of "Galliard" to hear how many times this rhythm is played in the melody:

Boy Playing Flute by Judith Leyster. Statens Konstmuseer, Stockholm, Sweden

BOY PLAYING FLUTE

Judith Leyster painted this around 1630. The boy is playing a kind of flute which was played either to the right or to the left. On the wall are a Baroque violin and bow and a recorder.

WOODWINDS OF THE RENAISSANCE

In "Galliard" you hear several Renaissance woodwind instruments. Each section of the music is repeated. The first time through each section, the music is played on recorders.

When each section is repeated, you hear shawms and krummhorns. These are double-reed instruments that were early forms of the bassoon and oboe.

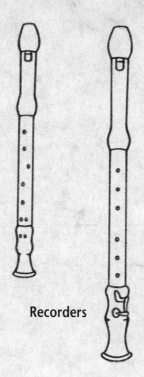

Recorders

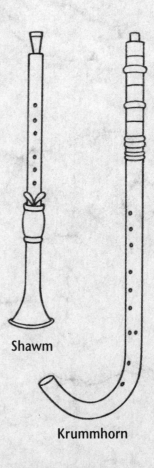

Shawm

Krummhorn

A MAJOR

"Hei Tama Tu Tama" sounds major. What is its tonal center?

When a song has *do* as its tonal center, it is in major. "Hei Tama Tu Tama" is in F major. The pitches in this song come from the F major scale.

PLAY and sing a major scale, beginning on F.

do re mi fa so la ti do¹

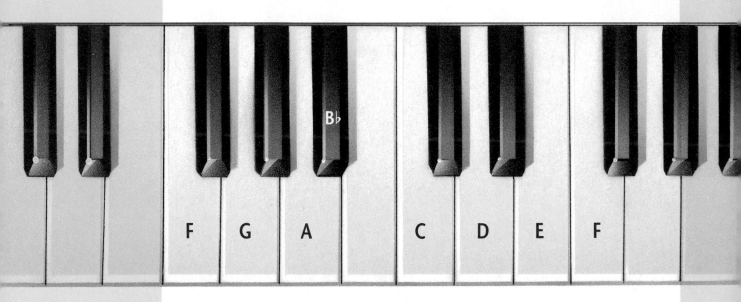

When F is *do*, there is a flat on the B line of the staff. This flat tells you to use B flat (B♭) instead of B in this song. Notice the black key (B♭) that is used in the F major scale.

EVENT

ADD MINOR HARMONY

When a song has *la* as its tonal center, it is in minor. "Wade in the Water" is in D minor. The pitches you sing come from the D **minor scale**.

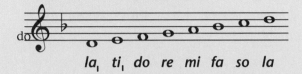

la, ti, do re mi fa so la

A scale in D minor has the same key signature as one in F major. The scale in F major begins and ends on *do*. The scale in D minor begins and ends on *la*.

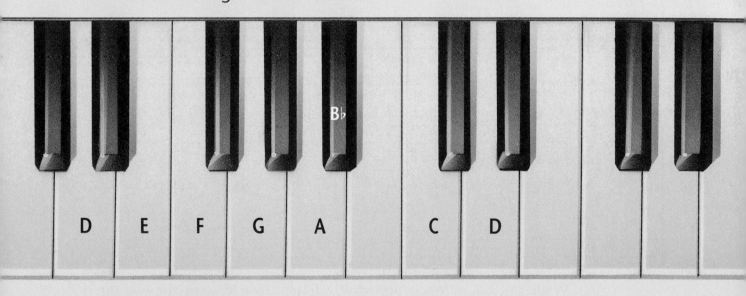

SING this harmony part with the refrain of "Wade in the Water."

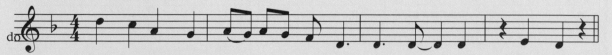

Wade on chil-dren, wade _ in the wa- ter. Wade, chil - dren,   Wade on.

PLAY a minor scale beginning on D. Remember to play a B♭.

WADE IN THE WATER

African American Spiritual

Intro.

All

Wade on chil-dren, wade in the wa-ter. Wade, chil - dren, Wade on.

Refrain

Part 1

Wade in the wa - ter. Wade in the

Part 2

Wade on chil - dren, wade in the wa - ter. Wade, chil - dren,

wa - ter, chil-dren. Wade in the wa - ter.

Wade on. Wade on chil - dren, wade in the wa-ter.

God's gon - na trou - ble the wa - ter.

Wade, chil - dren, Wade on.

Verse

Solo
Dm
Group   C   Dm

1. Tell you one   thing   and it's cer-tain-ly sure.
2. Who's_ that   yon-der all_ dressed   in white?
3. Who's_ that   yon-der all_ dressed   in red?
4. Up   on the moun-tain Je - ho-vah, he spoke.

} Wade_ in the wa-ter._

*Go back to the beginning
and sing to the end
(Da Capo al Fine)*

Solo
Dm
Group   C   Dm

Judg-ment's com-in' and   I don't_ know._
Looks like the child-ren of the Is-rael-ites._
Looks like the child-ren that Mo-ses_ led._
Out of   his   mouth_ came fire and_smoke._

} Wade_ in the wa-ter._

*Note: Cue notes may be sung or replaced with improvisation.

IMPROVISE and sing your own melodies with these
pitches. They are the pitches of the harmony part.

Use resonator bells or a keyboard to help you.

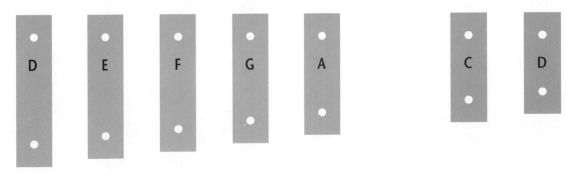

D   E   F   G   A   C   D

SONGS THAT TEACH

Think of something you learned today and how you learned it. Share that information with your neighbor.

SING the song that goes with each picture. What can each song teach you?

Hei Tama Tu Tama

Tum-Balalaika

Which songs are in minor? Major?
Which songs are in $\frac{3}{4}$? $\frac{4}{4}$?

MAKE up your own question about one
of the songs to ask your neighbor.

Take Time in Life

CHECK IT OUT

1. Which example is in ¾ ?

   a. Example 1   **b.** Example 2

2. Which example is in ⅜ ?

   a. Example 1   **b.** Example 2

3. Which rhythm do you hear?

4. Which rhythm do you hear?

CREATE

Playing with Threes

CREATE an accompaniment of four measures for "Tum-Balalaika." Use these rhythm patterns.

EXPERIMENT with different combinations of the rhythm patterns. Play them on tambourines or other percussion instruments.

Which combination of rhythms do you like with the song? Why?

Write

Which message from the songs in this unit meant the most to you?

Write several sentences explaining the message and what it means to you.

Waltzing with Bears

Words and Music by Dale Marxen

Refrain

He goes wa - wa - wa - wa - wa, waltz-ing with bears,

Rag - gy bears, bag - gy bears, shag - gy bears, too. There's

noth-ing on earth Un - cle Wal - ter won't do,_____ So

he can go waltz-ing, wa - wa-wa-waltz-ing, So he can go

waltz - ing, waltz - ing with bears._____

Verse

1. I went to his room in the mid-dle of the night, I
2. We bought Un - cle Wal - ter a___ new___ coat to wear, But

tip - toed in - side and turned on the light, But
when he comes home it's all cov - ered with hair, And

242

to my dis - may   he was no - where in   sight!_____
late - ly I've no - ticed there are sev - 'ral new   tears,_____

Go to the beginning (Da Capo)

— My un - cle Wal - ter goes waltz - ing at night.
— My un - cle Wal - ter goes waltz - ing with bears.

Coda

— Well, it all feels like fly - ing, there— is no de -

Go to the beginning and sing to the end (Da Capo al Fine)

ny - ing, And— now my pa - ja - mas are cov - ered with hair!

3. We told Uncle Walter that he should be good.
   And do all the things we say that he should,
   But I know he'd rather be off in the wood,
   We're afraid we will lose him, we'll lose him for good.
   Refrain

4. We said, "Uncle Walter, oh, please won't you stay,"
   And managed to keep him at home for a day,
   But the bears all barged in and they took him away,
   For the pandas demand at least one waltz a day!
   Refrain

5. Last night when the moon rose we crept down the stairs,
   He took me to dance where the bears have their lairs,
   We danced in a bear hug with nary a care, *(to Coda)*

Las mañanitas
The Morning Song

Mexican Folk Song
English Version by MMH

Spanish: **És** - tas son las ma - ña - ni - tas
Pronunciation: es tas son las ma nya ni tas
English: **Now** we sing *las ma - ña - ni - tas,*

que can - ta - ba el Rey Da - vid,
ke kan ta βael ɾei ða βið
as King Da - vid long a - go

a las mu - cha - chas bo - ni - tas
a las mu cha chaz βo ni tas
sang a song to greet the morn - ing,

se las can - ta - mos a - sí:
se las kan ta mos a si
to greet the sun - light's first glow.

Des - pier - ta, mi bien, des - pier - ta,
des pyeɾ ta mi βyen des pyeɾ ta
A - wak - en, dear one, a - wak - en

mi - ra que ya a - ma - ne - ció,
mi ɾa ke ya ma ne syo
and wel - come the ros - y dawn.

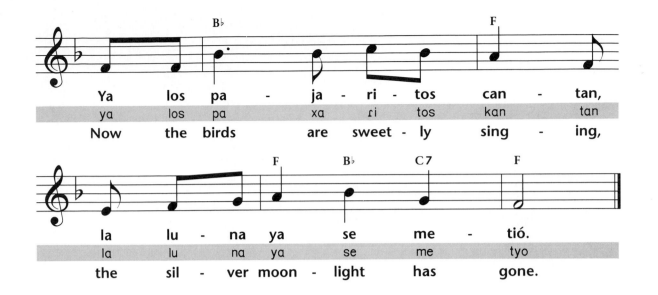

Ya los pa - ja - ri - tos can - tan,
ya los pa xa ri tos kan tan
Now the birds are sweet - ly sing - ing,

la lu - na ya se me - tió.
la lu na ya se me tyo
the sil - ver moon - light has gone.

Push the Business On

English Singing Game

We'll hire a horse and grab a rig; And all the world will dance a jig;

And we will do what - ev - er we can to push the busi- ness on. ___

To push the busi- ness on. ___ To push the busi- ness on. ___

And we will do what - ev - er we can to push the busi- ness on. ___

Singing Reeds

Have you ever held two blades of grass together with your thumbs, and blown between them? You might have heard the same sound early musicians heard thousands of years ago when they tried this.

A double-reed instrument is a wind instrument with two blades, or reeds, that vibrate together when air passes between them. These reeds may be made of cane, metal, or even plastic.

The two double-reed instruments that are the most familiar to us today are the oboe, a higher-pitched in-strument, and the bassoon, a larger, lower-pitched instrument.

Sounds of the Oboe

LISTEN to the sound of an oboe. How would you describe this sound?

Some form of the oboe has been popular since 3000 B.C. The oboe comes from the shawm, a simple pipe with a double reed. Shawms were played in India, China, Egypt, and Greece before they were brought to western Europe.

Playing the ancient oboe, or aulos, was one of the main athletic events in the original Olympic Games in Greece. The aulos was so difficult to blow that these players became real heroes. Often the sound of the aulos accompanied Roman gladiators as they fought in the arena, or soldiers as they marched into battle.

A Grecian cup, painted about 460 B.C. in the province of Attica, shows a young man playing an aulos.

The Nagasvaram shawm of India comes from an ancient Persian shawm. It has a loud tone which makes it a popular instrument in outdoor ceremonies.

Sounds of the Bassoon

One early name for the bassoon was dulcian. *Dulcian is from the Latin word* dulcis, *which means "soft" or "sweet." In the 1500s, the dulcian developed into the early bassoon.*

LISTEN to the bassoon. **Why do you think it is related to the dulcian?**

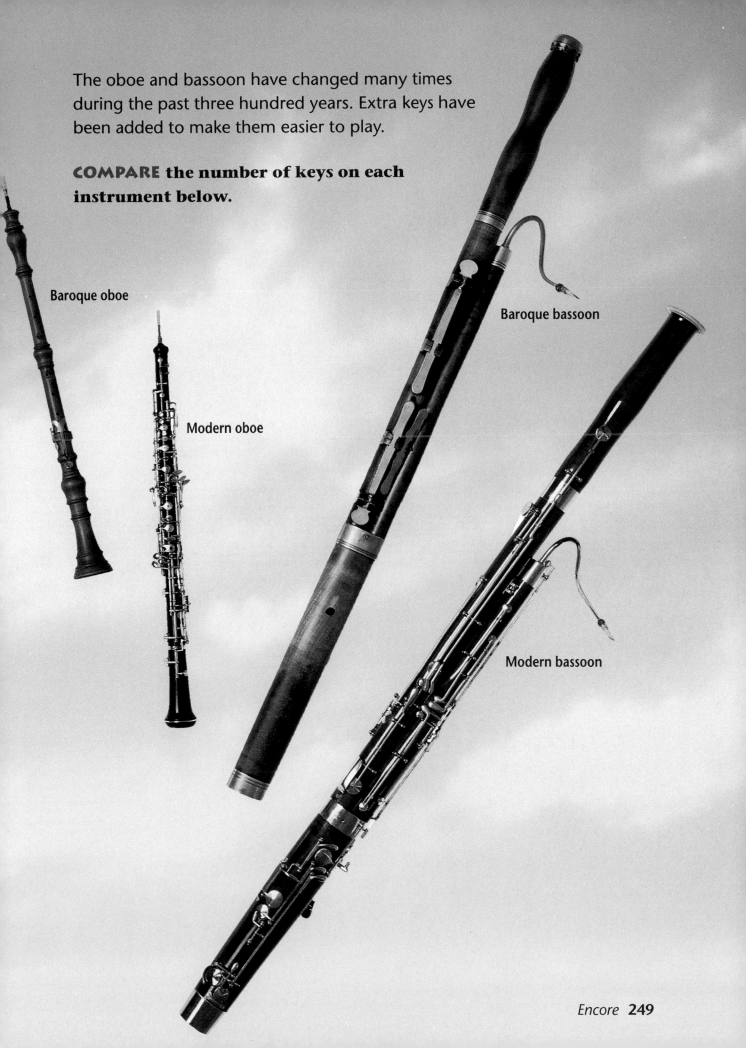

The oboe and bassoon have changed many times during the past three hundred years. Extra keys have been added to make them easier to play.

COMPARE the number of keys on each instrument below.

Baroque oboe

Modern oboe

Baroque bassoon

Modern bassoon

A WORLD

ROCKS

Big rocks into pebbles
Pebbles into sand.
I really hold a million million rocks here in my hand.

—*Florence Parry Heide*

OF CHANGE

Comes Once in a Lifetime

Music by Jule Styne
Words by Betty Comden and Adolph Green

Ev - 'ry day _____ just go _____ a - long,
Take each day _____ and gath - er the

Dawn till sun - down, _____
rose - buds in it, _____

Here's the run - down, _____ Ev - 'ry
Fill each min - ute, _____ Ev - 'ry

1. day that comes, comes once _____ in a life - time.

2. day that comes, comes once _____ in a life - time.

Think of now, _____ To - mor - row is

wait - ing in the wings. _____

MAKE A CHANGE

Who or what is changing in this song?
How will this change happen?

I Can Be

Words and Music by
Anthony Q. Richardson

Introduction

This is the day,___ I will make a change,___ all I have to do___

Sing bracketed section twice

Part 1 **Make a change.**___

Part 2 **It's up to me.**___

I can be what-

ev - er I want to be. All I do is try a lit - tle

hard - er. I can do what - ev - er I want to do.

Repeat 1st time only

All I do is try a lit - tle hard - er.

254

SING the first page with the dynamics as marked.

How do you think the change in dynamics brings out the meaning of the words?

CHOOSE dynamics that help to express the feelings in this song.

THIS PRETTY PLANET

Words and Music by
John Forster and Tom Chapin

This pret - ty plan - et spin - ning through space.— You're a gar - den. You're a har - bor. You're a ho - ly place.— Gold - en

sun go - ing down.— Gen - tle blue gi - ant, spin us a - round.— All through the night. Safe 'til the morn - ing light.—

Korobushka *Russian Folk Song*

LISTENING

In Russia, a korobushka is a trunk in which a peddler carries all sorts of items for sale.

LISTEN for musical changes in "Korobushka." Move to the music.

CHANGING AC

Read the lyrics. How would you change the accompaniment with each verse?

THE CAT CAME BACK

American
Folk Song
Arranged by
Mary Goetze

Verse **Freely**

1. Old Farm - er John - son had trou - bles all his own. He
2. Farm - er John - son's neigh - bor swore he'd chase him out of sight. He

had a lit - tle cat that would - n't leave his home. He
donned his fast - est shoes and he ran with all his might. The

tried and he tried to give that cat a - way! He
cat was quick, he ran a - way and John - son's neigh - bor fell.

Refrain

gave it to a man go - ing far, far a - way.— But the
Peo - ple came from miles a - way be - cause they heard him yell.— But the

Part 1

cat came back— the ver - y next day.— The

Part 2

cat came back!— We thought he was a gon - er. The

258

COMPANIMENT

cat came back!— We thought he was a gon-er, but the

cat came back!— We thought he was a gon-er. The

cat came back,— He just would-n't stay a-way.—

cat came back,— He would-n't stay a-way.——

Interlude *(Sing after 1st, 2nd, and 4th Refrain)*

Part 1

Part 2

Du- du- du-doop! Me-ow!— Du- wa,— du-du-du-doop! Me-ow!—

Go to Coda after 4th Refrain **Coda**

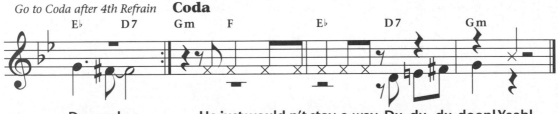

Du- wa!— He just would-n't stay a-way. Du-du- du-doop! Yeah!

3. He gave it to a man
   going up in a balloon.
   Told him to give it
   to the man up in the moon.
   The balloon came down
   about ninety miles away.
   What happened to the man?
   I really couldn't say. *Refrain*

4. A great tornado came
   just the other day.
   The wind began to blow,
   the trees began to sway.
   Thunder struck, lightning flashed,
   darkness took the day.
   The people were so frightened,
   they knelt right down to pray. *Refrain*

A MUSICAL TALL TALE

"Old Joe Clark" is based on an old fiddle tune.
What does the song tell you about Old Joe?

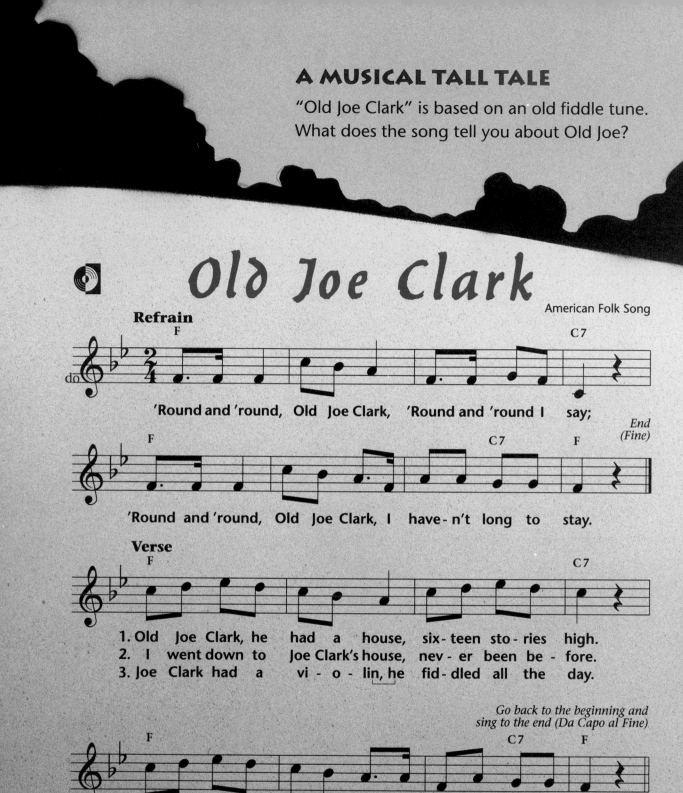

Old Joe Clark

American Folk Song

Refrain

'Round and 'round, Old Joe Clark, 'Round and 'round I say;

End (Fine)

'Round and 'round, Old Joe Clark, I have-n't long to stay.

Verse

1. Old Joe Clark, he had a house, six-teen sto-ries high.
2. I went down to Joe Clark's house, nev-er been be-fore.
3. Joe Clark had a vi-o-lin, he fid-dled all the day.

Go back to the beginning and sing to the end (Da Capo al Fine)

Ev'-ry sto-ry in that house was full of chick-en pie.
He slept on the feath-er bed and I slept on the floor.
An-y-bod-y start to dance and Joe would start to play.

Many people have enjoyed making up verses
about Old Joe.

WRITE your own verse for this tall tale.

CREATE A RHYTHMIC ACCOMPANIMENT

Choose a word or idea from each verse. Create a four-beat rhythmic ostinato to accompany that verse. Here are some examples for the first verse.

Chick, chick, chick-en chick-en

How high?——— Oh my!

Bring me some pie.

PLAY an ostinato with each verse using different combinations of sounds.

CHANGING COLORS

Each instrument pictured here
has its own special sound, or tone color.
As you listen to "The Court of King Carraticus,"
each instrument's sound will cue you to move differently. The pictures show you the motions.

PLAY the sound cue game!

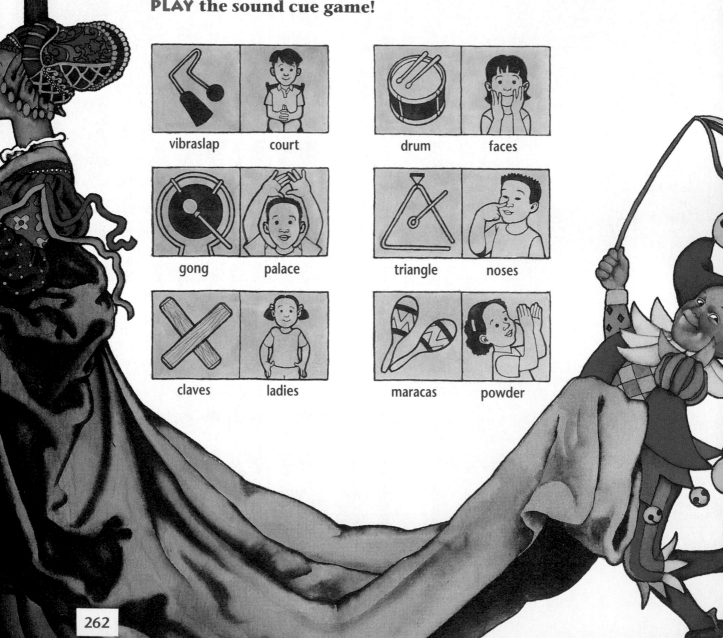

vibraslap   court

drum   faces

gong   palace

triangle   noses

claves   ladies

maracas   powder

PERFORM the motion that goes
with each tone color as you hear it.

The Court of King Carraticus

American
Nonsense Song

verses accumulate

1. Oh, the court of King Car-ra-ti-cus is just pass-ing by;
2. Oh, the pal-ace of the court of King Car-ra-ti-cus

Oh, the court of King Car-ra-ti-cus is just pass-ing by;
Oh, the pal-ace of the court of King Car-ra-ti-cus

Oh, the court of King Car-ra-ti-cus is just pass-ing by;
Oh, the pal-ace of the court of King Car-ra-ti-cus

Oh, the court of King Car-ra-ti-cus is just pass-ing by.
Oh, the pal-ace of the court of King Car-ra-ti-cus

Add one phrase on each repetition of the song.

3. ladies of the palace of the court of King Carraticus are just passing by.

4. faces of the...

5. noses of the...

6. powder on the...

7. If you want to take a photo of the...

(spoken at end)
It's too late! They just passed by!

From FIRESIDE BOOK OF FUN & GAME SONGS by Marie Winn and Alan Miller. © 1974. Reprinted by permission of the publisher, Simon & Schuster, Inc., New York.

A RAINBOW OF PERCUSSION INSTRUMENTS

This song teases Michie Banjo for his fancy clothes. Listen for the tone colors in the accompaniment of this song.

Michie Banjo

Creole Bamboula
English Words by
Margaret Marks

Refrain

Look at Mich - ie Ban - jo,   Fan - cy Mich - ie Ban - jo,
mi shi

Strut - tin'   down   the   street.

Verse

1. Cha - peau   cocked on   one   side,   Mich - ie Ban - jo,
   sha po
2. Dia - mond   pin in his   tie,   Mich - ie Ban - jo,

High   but - ton shoes   that   squeak.
Bright   yel - low gloves   so   neat.

Walk - in' stick a - swing - in'   wide, Mich - ie Ban - jo,
Trou - sers pleat - ed   way   up   high, Mich - ie Ban - jo,

Go back to the beginning and sing to the end
(Da Capo al Fine)

Ev' - ry - thing's   all   com - plete.
Ev' - ry - thing's   all   com - plete.

End (Fine)

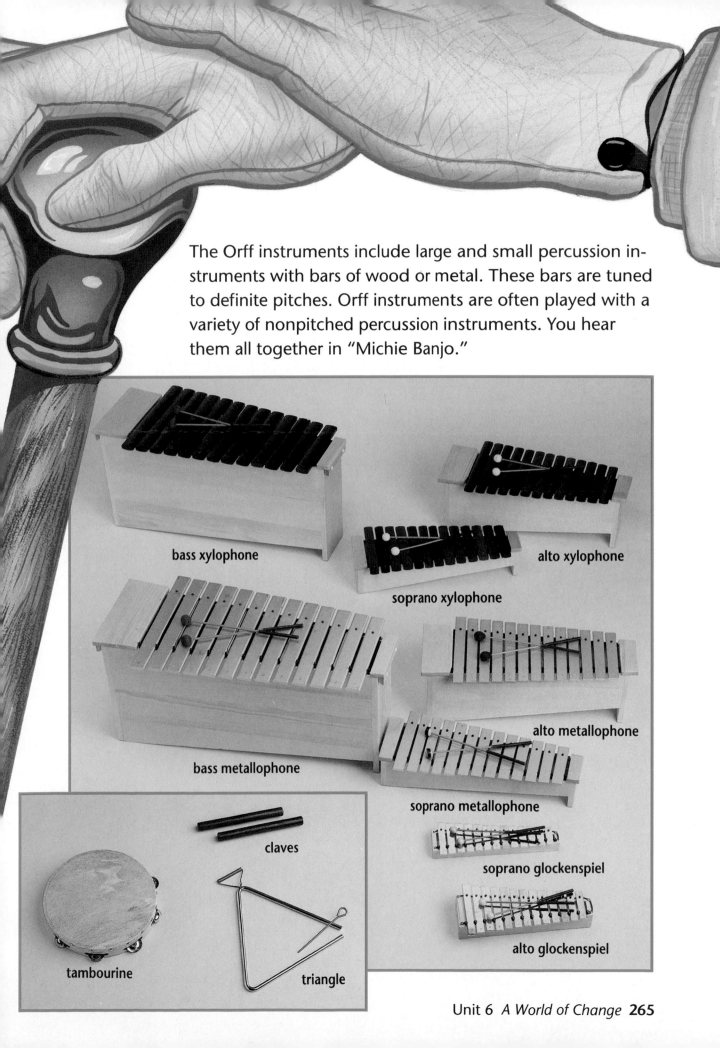

The Orff instruments include large and small percussion instruments with bars of wood or metal. These bars are tuned to definite pitches. Orff instruments are often played with a variety of nonpitched percussion instruments. You hear them all together in "Michie Banjo."

bass xylophone

soprano xylophone

alto xylophone

bass metallophone

alto metallophone

soprano metallophone

soprano glockenspiel

alto glockenspiel

claves

tambourine

triangle

A MINOR CHANGE

meet Anthony Richardson

The composer of "I Can Be," Anthony Richardson, wrote this song for his music students at an elementary school in Memphis, Tennessee.

LISTEN as Anthony Richardson talks about why he wrote this song. Then sing "I Can Be" on page 254. Sing in three parts as shown in the score.

A sharp (♯), a flat (♭), or a **natural** (♮) sign that appears next to a pitch and is not in the key signature is called an **accidental.** The accidental changes how the pitch should be sung.

G♭ sounds a little lower than G.

G♯ sounds a little higher than G.

G♮ reminds you to sing G.

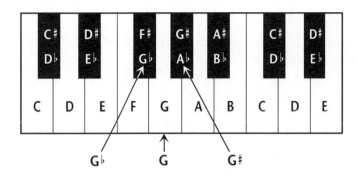

MAJOR OR MINOR?

Listen to a major scale beginning on E, then to a minor scale beginning on E.

SING each scale with the correct pitch syllables.

do   re   mi   fa   so   la   ti   do'
E major scale

la₁   ti₁   do   re   mi   fa   so   la
E minor scale

Look at "Korobushka" as you listen to it. Does its melody use the pitches of a major scale or a minor scale? How do you know?

SIMPLY BEAUTIFUL

The Shakers, a religious group, live a strict and simple life. They organize their time, tools, and homes carefully, wasting nothing.

SING "Simple Gifts," a well-known Shaker song.

This chair and lamp stand show the simple, graceful design typical of the Shakers, who make everything they use.

SIMPLE GIFTS

Shaker Song

DOUBLE the Fun

FIND the connection between the two patterns on each line.

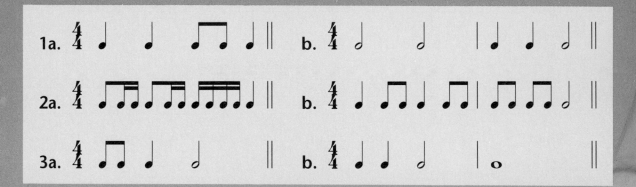

A **whole note** (𝅝) shows a sound that lasts for four beats in 𝄴.

When you change a rhythm by making it twice as long, you **augment** it. To augment means to make larger. For example, when you augment a sound one beat long, it becomes a sound two beats long. In 𝄴, each quarter note will become a half note.

If you augment a rhythm in 𝄴, what would a half note become?

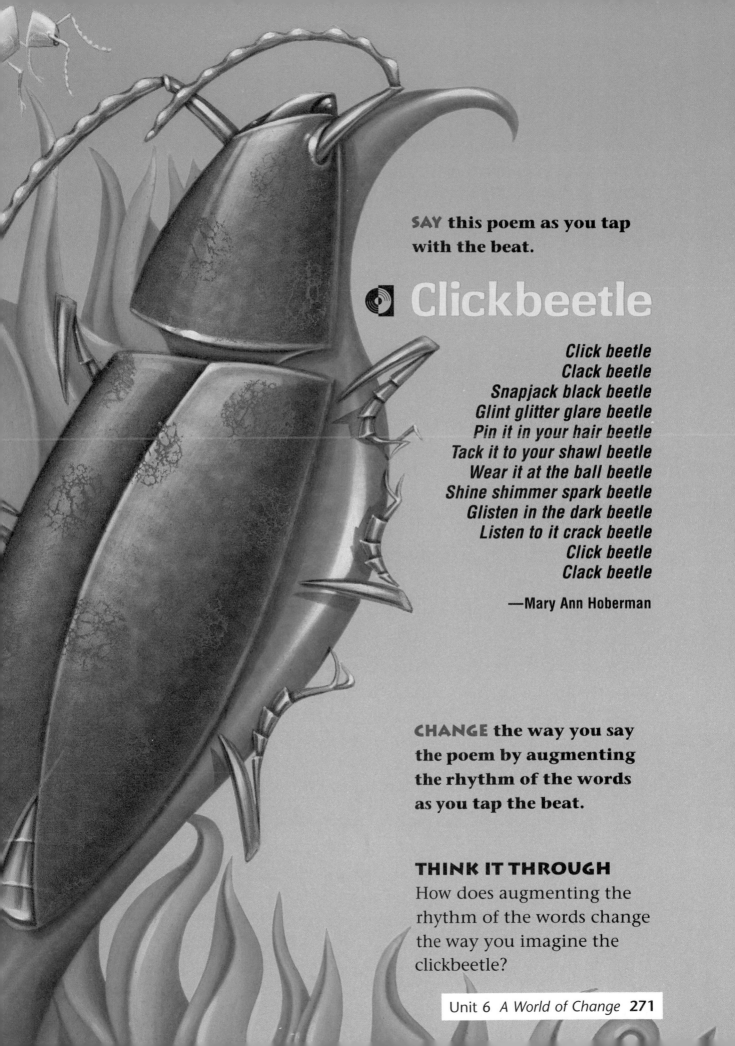

SAY this poem as you tap with the beat.

Clickbeetle

Click beetle
Clack beetle
Snapjack black beetle
Glint glitter glare beetle
Pin it in your hair beetle
Tack it to your shawl beetle
Wear it at the ball beetle
Shine shimmer spark beetle
Glisten in the dark beetle
Listen to it crack beetle
Click beetle
Clack beetle

—Mary Ann Hoberman

CHANGE the way you say the poem by augmenting the rhythm of the words as you tap the beat.

THINK IT THROUGH

How does augmenting the rhythm of the words change the way you imagine the clickbeetle?

Appalachian Spring (excerpt)
by Aaron Copland

The ballet Appalachian Spring *is about a pioneer couple's wedding day. Copland's music for the ballet includes the melody of "Simple Gifts." The melody is repeated and changed in a variety of ways. You will hear its rhythm augmented and also hear the melody played as a canon.*

OFF FRANKLIN OR NOLENSVILLE PIKE, NASHVILLE

Mayna Treanor Avent's painting shows the sunny rural beauty that may have inspired *Appalachian Spring.*

PAT with the beat and sing this phrase of "Simple Gifts."

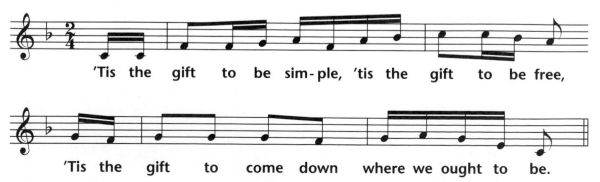

'Tis the gift to be sim-ple, 'tis the gift to be free,

'Tis the gift to come down where we ought to be.

PAT with the beat and sing the same phrase, this time augmenting the rhythm.

'Tis the gift to be sim-ple, 'tis the gift to be free,

'Tis the gift to come down where we ought to be.

Listen for the augmentation of "Simple Gifts" in *Appalachian Spring.*

THE CLARINET

The **clarinet** is a woodwind instrument that comes in a variety of sizes. A musician blows on a single **reed,** a piece of cane attached to the mouthpiece, to make the air inside the instrument vibrate and produce sound. Listen as the clarinet begins the music from *Appalachian Spring.*

clarinet

single reed

CHANGING

Sing "This Pretty Planet." As you sing, pat with the beats that feel strongest and clap with the other beats. How are the beats grouped?

MOVE **to "This Pretty Planet" in $\frac{4}{}$.**

1. Walk clockwise, then counterclockwise.

2. Face the center of the circle and raise your arms, then lower your arms.

METER

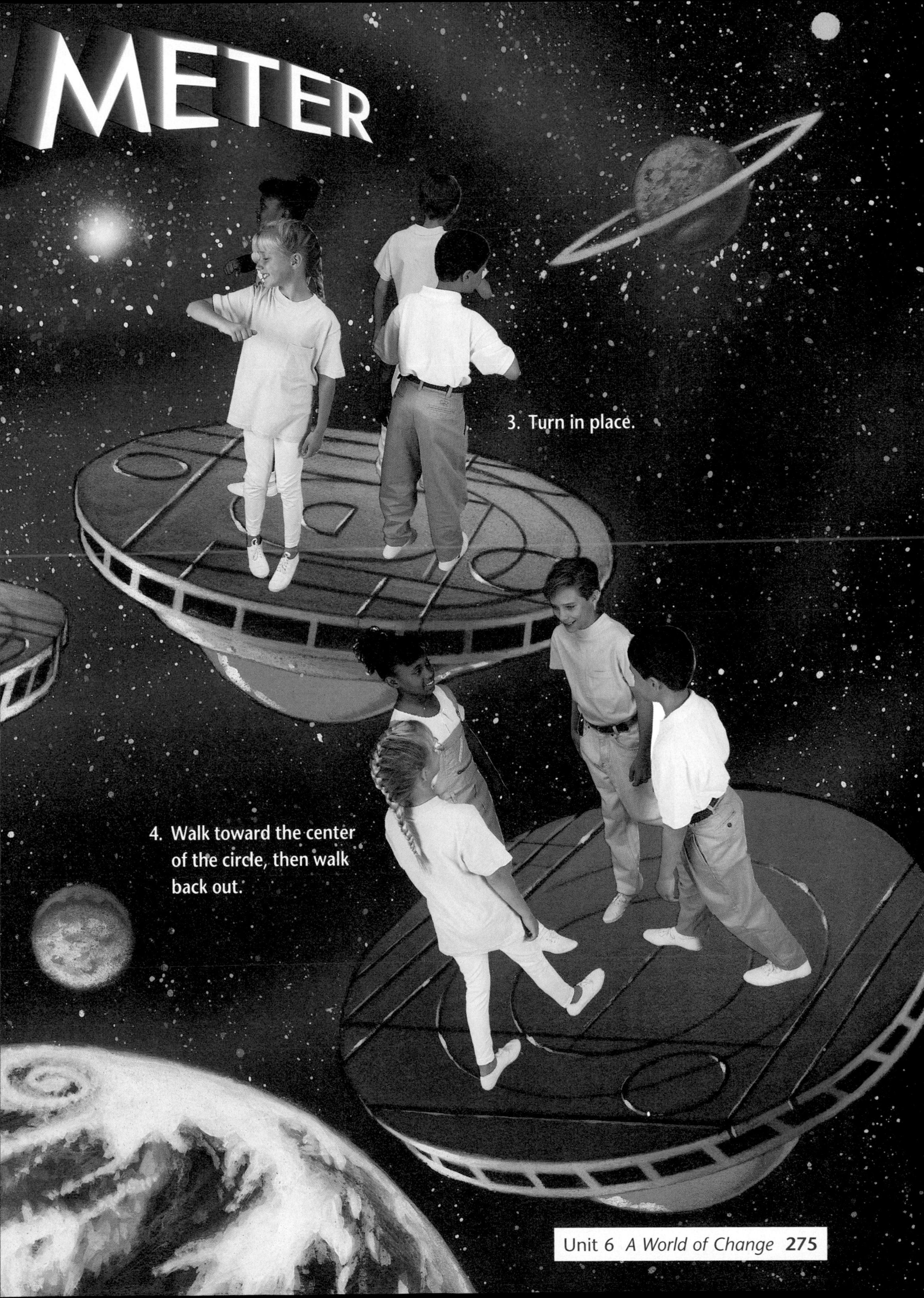

3. Turn in place.

4. Walk toward the center
of the circle, then walk
back out.

NEW PLANET

Changing the meter of a song gives a new feeling to the music. Here is "This Pretty Planet" in $\frac{6}{8}$. Compare it with the same song in $\frac{4}{4}$ on page 257.

SING the song with two different meters.

This Pretty Planet

Words and Music by
John Forster and Tom Chapin
Adapted by MMH

This pret - ty plan - et spin - ning through space. You're a

gar - den. You're a har - bor. You're a ho - ly place.

Gold - en sun go -ing down. Gen-tle blue gi - ant, spin us a- round.

All through the night. Safe 'til the morn - ing light.

THINK IT THROUGH

What happens to the sets of beats when the meter changes? Which meter do you prefer, and why?

Some songs stay in the same meter; others change meter.

PAT with the beats that feel strongest as you listen to "The Court of King Carraticus." What happens?

UNTITLED
Keith Haring's artwork expresses his wish for people to join together to enjoy and take care of the planet Earth.

PLAIN and FANCY

Compare each pair of objects. How are they different?

One of each pair is simple and the other is ornate, or decorated. Music can be ornate also. A song can be decorated by adding pitches to the melody. This is called **ornamentation.**

COMPARE the pictures in the frames below.

This shows the original melody of "Music Alone Shall Live."

Him - mel und Er - de müss- en ver - gehn;

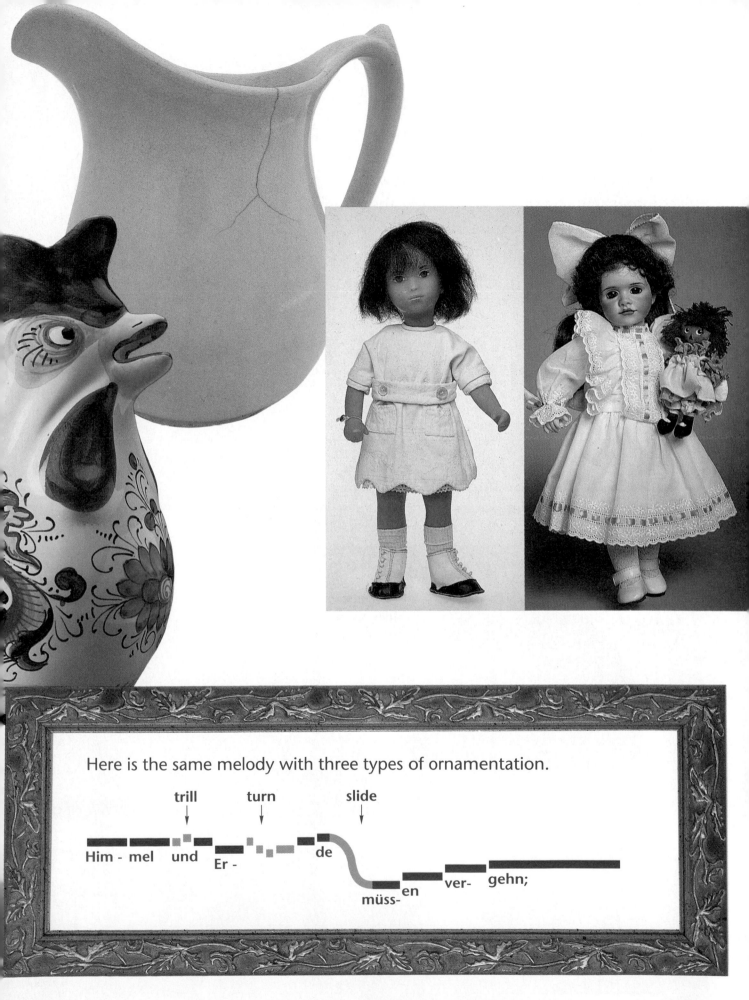

Here is the same melody with three types of ornamentation.

trill   turn   slide

Him - mel   und   Er -   de   müss-   en   ver-   gehn;

ORNAMENTS FROM AROUND THE WORLD

Vocal ornamentation is practiced by singers from all over the world. In some styles of music, the composer suggests how to ornament the melody. In others, the performers are creative in adding pitches to the song.

LISTENING

Vocal Ornamentation Montage

Listen to how these singers use ornamentation.

African American–
turns, slides

Indian–
trills, slides

Hopi—slide

Palestinian—trills, turns

FANCY THAT!

Here's the beginning of the refrain of "Old Joe Clark."

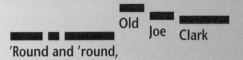
'Round and 'round, Old Joe Clark

How would "Old Joe Clark" sound with ornamentation? Try these versions.

1. slide

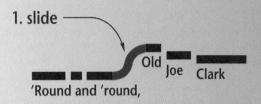
'Round and 'round, Old Joe Clark

2. trill

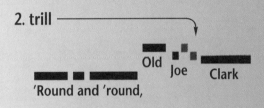
'Round and 'round, Old Joe Clark

3. turn

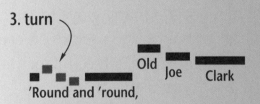
'Round and 'round, Old Joe Clark

CHOOSE the way you'd like to ornament "Old Joe Clark." Then sing the song and use your ornamentation at the beginning of the refrain.

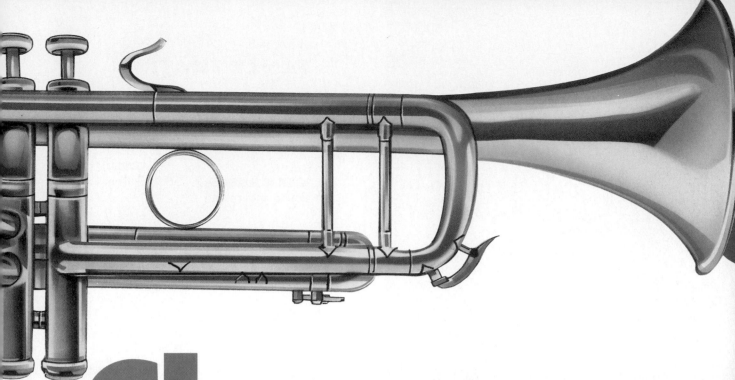

Change= Variation

One of the many ways to change or vary a piece of music is to change the melody. A composer writes music based on a melody. Different treatments of that melody follow. The form of the music is called **theme and variations.** The original melody is the theme, and each changed version of the melody is called a variation. The theme sounds different in each variation, but you can still recognize it.

Look at these seven ways to vary a melody. Name the songs that were varied in these ways.

- dynamics
- meter
- tempo
- pitch
- tone color
- accompaniment
- rhythm

LISTENING

Variations on an American Theme

by Linda Worsley

LISTENING MAP   *The theme, "The Battle Hymn of the Republic," is presented first, followed by the variations. Listen for all the ways the theme is varied.*

INTRODUCTION
AND THEME
All

VARIATION 1
LIVELY
Woodwinds

VARIATION 2
LYRICAL
Woodwinds

VARIATION 5
PLAYFUL
**Unpitched
Percussion**

VARIATION 4
SINGING
Brass

VARIATION 3
MARCHING
Brass

VARIATION 6
MARCHING
**Pitched
Percussion**

VARIATION 7
LYRICAL
**Arco
Strings**

VARIATION 8
LIVELY
**Pizzicato
Strings**

THEME
A SECTION
STATELY
All

THEME
B SECTION
STATELY
All

CODA
All

283

VARIATIONS ON "MUSIC ALONE SHALL LIVE"

Now it's your turn to be the composer!

CREATE a set of variations using "Music Alone Shall Live" as your theme. Divide into groups and choose one of these ideas to change the theme.

Rhythm and Meter

Change the meter from $\frac{3}{4}$ to $\frac{4}{4}$. For example, change the rhythm of the words *aber die Musica.*

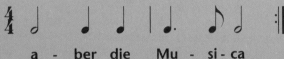

a - ber die Mu - si - ca

Tone Color

Change the vocal tone color by whispering or speaking. Or play the song on percussion instruments.

Accompaniment

Decide whether to perform the song as a two- or three-part canon. Decide when each part will start.

Dynamics

Use any or all of these markings to change dynamics.

$f,\ p,\ mf,\ mp,$ ⎯⟨⎯, ⎯⟩⎯

Tempo

Decide which tempos and tempo changes to use.

adagio, moderato, allegro, presto, accelerando, ritardando

Pitch

You can slide, trill, or turn to ornament the melody.

PERFORM your variation as part of a class performance of "Variations on 'Music Alone Shall Live.'"

ALL KINDS OF CHANGES

Describe the musical changes you see. What other ways can you make changes?

Make some changes as you sing "Simple Gifts," "The Cat Came Back," and "I Can Be."

CHECK IT OUT

1. Listen to two examples. Is the second rhythm an augmentation of the first?

   a. Yes   **b.** No

2. Listen to two examples. Is the second rhythm an augmentation of the first?

   a. Yes   **b.** No

3. Which phrase is in minor?

   a. Phrase 1   **b.** Phrase 2   **c.** Phrase 3   **d.** Phrase 4

4. Listen to two examples. How do the dynamics and tempo change in the second example?

   a. faster and louder   **c.** slower and louder

   b. faster and softer   **d.** slower and softer

5. Listen to two examples. How does the accompaniment change in the second example?

   a. A rhythmic ostinato is added.

   b. A vocal melodic line is added.

   c. The melody is sung as a canon.

   d. There is no change.

CREATE

Melody in Minor

CREATE a melody for part of the poem "Clickbeetle."

Every time you and your partner have the word "beetle," play the pitch A. Choose the rest of your pitches from the minor scale that starts on A.

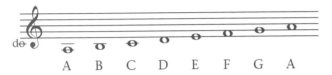

A B C D E F G A

Write the pitch letter names you choose on a sheet of paper. Play your part in a performance of the whole poem.

Write

What do you like most about music class? What would you like most to change? What would you like to learn more about?

Write a letter to your teacher explaining your favorite and least favorite music class, and what musical activities you look forward to in the future.

Garden Song

Words and Music by David Mallett

1. Inch by inch, row by row,___ Gon-na make this
2. Pull-in' weeds and pick-in' stones,___ We are made of
3. Plant your rows straight and long,___ Temp-er them with

gar-den grow,___ All it takes is a
dreams and bones,___ Feel the need to___
prayer and song,___ Moth-er Earth will___

rake and a hoe and a piece of fer-tile ground.___
grow my___ own 'cause the time is close at hand.___
make you___ strong, if you give her love and care.___

Inch by inch, row by row,___ Some-one bless the
Grain for grain, sun and rain,___ Find my way in
Old crow watch-ing hun-gri-ly___ From his perch in

seeds I sow, Some-one warm them from be-low__ 'til the
na-ture's chain, Tune my bod-y and my brain_ to the
yon-der tree. In my gar-den I'm as free__ as that

rain comes tum-bl-ing down.
mu-sic from___ the land.
feath-ered thief___ up there.

290

DONNA, DONNA

Music by Sholom Secunda
Words by Aaron Zeitlin

Verse

mp

1. On a wag - on bound for mar - ket,
2. "Stop com - plain - ing," said the farm - er,
3. Calves are eas - i - ly bound and slaugh - tered,

there's a calf with a mourn - ful eye, High a - bove— him
"who told you a— calf to be, Why don't you— have
nev - er know - ing the rea - son why, But who - ev - er

there's a swal - low wing - ing swift - ly— through the sky.
wings to fly— with, like the swal - low so proud and free?"
treas - ures free - dom, like the swal - low has learned to fly.

Refrain *f*

How the winds are laugh - ing, they laugh with all their might,

Laugh and laugh the whole day through, and half the sum - mer's night.

mf Don - na, don - na, don - na, don - na,

f Don - na, don - na, don - na,— don.

mf Don - na, don - na, don - na, don - na,

Don - na, don - na, don - na, don.

ENCORE
FOR THE RECORD

The Granger Collection

When Thomas Edison shouted "Mary had a little lamb" into the mouthpiece of his invention, in 1877, he recorded the first sounds on the first phonograph.

Edison's first "record" was a small metal cylinder. The recorded sound was very weak. After many improvements, people could listen to their favorite music on discs played on the gramophone.

By 1925, phonograph records were developed. Early records were large and easily broken. Each side held about six minutes of sound. By the late 1940s, long-playing records that held about thirty minutes of sound on each side began to replace the older records.

...or let 'em spin

The phonograph at left is a very early model. Radio/record players such as the one above were used for long-playing records.

By the 1950s, the sound quality of records was improved. Through stereophonic sound, two separate tracks of sound, one on the left and one on the right, give the impression of a live performance. When the two tracks are combined, the sound seems to surround the listener.

Left to right: records called 45s, a record player insert for playing 45s, jukebox, cassette tape, portable tape player, CDs.

At one time, music stores were filled with rows of record albums. But today, the racks are filled with tapes and CDs. Cassette tapes became popular when small tape recorders were developed. A tape player can be easily carried to the beach or park.

The CD, or compact disc, is much smaller than the record. The sound is very clear. There are no slight hissing noises which records sometimes pick up.

A CD player uses laser technology. When a laser beam passes over one side of the disc, it crosses many pits, which contain the information that will become the music you hear. Now, you can enjoy eighty minutes of music on one CD.

New types of CDs and tapes are still being developed. The CDs and tapes of the future will be even smaller and lighter than those popular today.

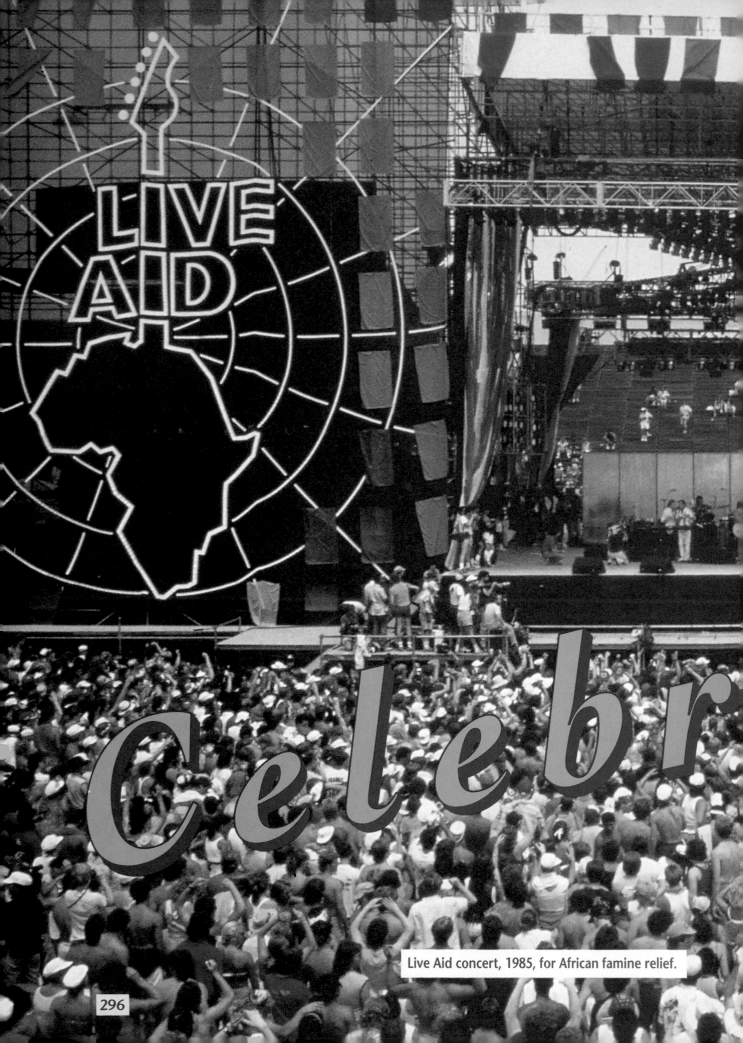

Live Aid concert, 1985, for African famine relief.

Celebr

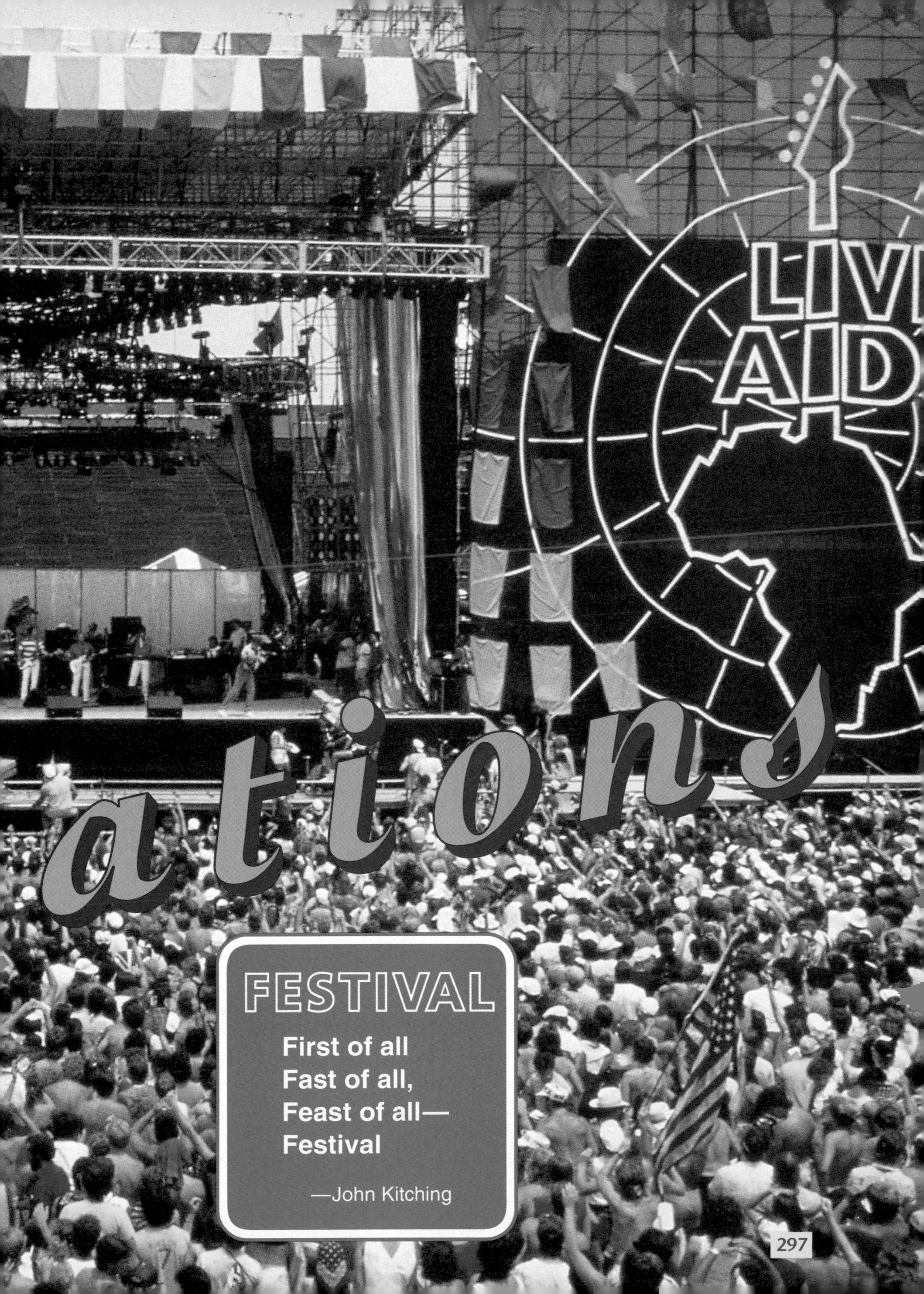

ations

LIVE AID

FESTIVAL

First of all
Fast of all,
Feast of all—
Festival

—John Kitching

Cheer for the U.S.A.

People play and sing the national anthem of their country on official occasions, at athletic events, and to honor the country's leader.

"The Star-Spangled Banner" is the national anthem of the United States. The words of the song recall an important event in the history of the country.

THE STAR-SPANGLED BANNER

Music Attributed to J. S. Smith
Words by Francis Scott Key

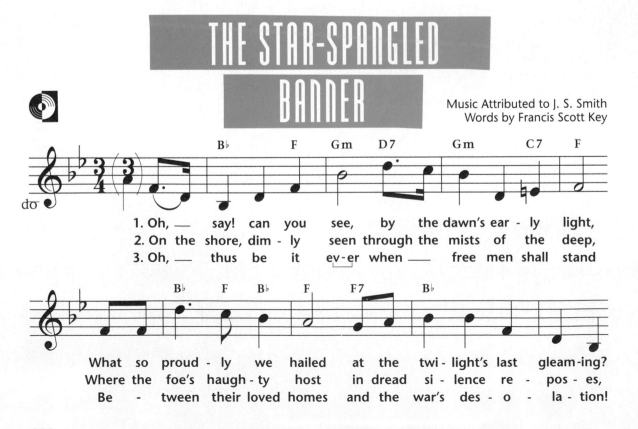

1. Oh, — say! can you see, by the dawn's ear - ly light,
2. On the shore, dim - ly seen through the mists of the deep,
3. Oh, — thus be it ev - er when — free men shall stand

What so proud - ly we hailed at the twi - light's last gleam-ing?
Where the foe's haugh - ty host in dread si - lence re - pos - es,
Be - tween their loved homes and the war's des - o - la - tion!

Whose broad stripes and bright stars, through the per - il - ous fight,
What is that which the breeze, o'er the tow - er - ing steep,
Blest with vic - t'ry and peace, may the heav'n res - cued land

O'er the ram - parts we watched were so gal - lant - ly stream-ing?
As it fit - ful - ly blows, half con - ceals, half dis - clos - es?
Praise the Pow'r that hath made and pre - served us a na - tion.

And the rock - ets' red glare, the bombs burst - ing in air,
Now it catch - es the gleam of the morn - ing's first beam,
Then —— con - quer we must, for our cause it is just,

Gave proof through the night that our flag was still there.
In full glo - ry re - flect-ed now —— shines on the stream;
And this be our mot-to, "In —— God is our trust."

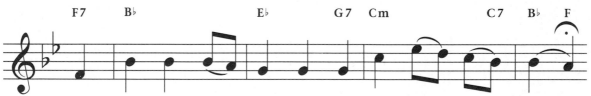

Oh, say, does that —— Star - Span - gled Ban - ner —— yet —— wave ——
'Tis the Star - Span - gled —— Ban - ner, oh, long may—— it—— wave ——
And the Star - Span-gled —— Ban - ner in tri - umph — shall —— wave ——

O'er the land —— of the free and the home of the brave?
O'er the land —— of the free and the home of the brave!
O'er the land —— of the free and the home of the brave!

Katharine Lee Bates traveled across the United States about a hundred years ago. Her trip inspired the poem that became "America, the Beautiful." The words capture not only the beauty of the American landscape, but also the pride Bates felt for her country.

America, the Beautiful

Music by Samuel Ward
Words by Katharine Lee Bates

1. O beau-ti-ful for spa-cious skies, For am-ber waves of grain.
2. O beau-ti-ful for pil-grim feet, Whose stern im-pas-sioned stress
3. O beau-ti-ful for he-roes proved In lib-er-at-ing strife,
4. O beau-ti-ful for pa-triot dream That sees be-yond the years,

For pur-ple moun-tain maj-es-ties a-bove the fruit-ed plain.
A thor-ough-fare for free-dom beat a-cross the wil-der-ness.
Who more than self their coun-try loved, and mer-cy more than life.
Thine al-a-bas-ter cit-ies gleam Un-dim'd by hu-man tears.

A-mer-i-ca! A-mer-i-ca! God shed His grace on thee,
A-mer-i-ca! A-mer-i-ca! God mend thine ev'-ry flaw,
A-mer-i-ca! A-mer-i-ca! May God thy gold re-fine,
A-mer-i-ca! A-mer-i-ca! God shed His grace on thee,

And crown thy good with broth-er-hood, From sea to shin-ing sea.
Con-firm thy soul in self-con-trol, Thy lib-er-ty in law.
Till all suc-cess be no-ble-ness, And ev'-ry gain di-vine.
And crown thy good with broth-er-hood, From sea to shin-ing sea.

Although people across the world have different languages and cultures, we can all share a desire for peace, as expressed in this song.

Sing a Song of Peace

Words and Music by Jill Gallina

mf

Sing a song of peace through the world,

'til ev-'ry land is sing-ing.

Sound the bells of peace through the world,

cresc.

with ev-'ry na-tion ring-ing.

cresc.

Land by land 'cross moun-tain and plain, Hand in hand one

long, lov-ing chain; Un-til peace and

free-dom___ reign from sea___ to___ shin-ing sea.

The words to "America" were first recited at a children's Fourth of July picnic in Boston in the 1800s. Later, Reverend Smith, the man who wrote the words, chose a hymnlike tune from a collection of German melodies to set the words to music.

AMERICA

Music by
Henry Carey
Words by
Samuel F. Smith

1. My coun-try, 'tis of thee, Sweet land of
2. My na-tive coun-try thee, Land of the
3. Let mu-sic swell the breeze, And ring from
4. Our fa-thers' God, to Thee, Au-thor of

lib - er - ty, Of thee I sing.
no - ble free, Thy name I love.
all the trees Sweet Free-dom's song;
lib - er - ty, To Thee we sing.

Land where my fa-thers died, Land of the Pil-grim's pride,
I love thy rocks and rills, Thy woods and tem-pled hills;
Let mor-tal tongues a-wake, Let all that breathe par-take,
Long may our land be bright With Free-dom's ho-ly light;

From ev' - ry__ moun-tain-side Let__ free-dom ring.
My heart__ with__ rap-ture thrills Like__ that a - bove.
Let rocks__ their__ si - lence break, The__ sound pro - long.
Pro - tect__ us__ by Thy might, Great__ God, our King!

LISTENING

Variations on "America" (excerpts)

by Charles Ives

Musical variations are different versions of the same tune. Ives wrote these variations as a teenager. The music is humorous and somewhat outrageous. One section of the music is in two different keys at the same time—one key in the right hand and another in the left.

LISTENING MAP   *You will hear the basic theme, followed by variations. Listen for the dramatic changes and playful surprises.*

FRIGHT NIGHT

The fun of fright and "things that go bump in the night" makes Halloween a playful holiday.

THE BOOGIE WOOGIE GHOST

Words and Music by
Nadine M. Peglar

1. There was a ghost on Hal-low-een, He real-ly made the ghost-ie scene,
2. He'd go out spook-ing late at night, And giv-ing ev'-ry-one a fright,

He was the Boo-gie-Woo-gie Ghost, He was the ghost-ie with the most,
He knew some wit-ches, two or three, And they would all go on a spree,

And when the kid-dies came a-round, He'd give out with a ghost-ly sound,
And when the morn-ing came a-round, He'd give one last mys-te-rious sound,

He'd go,—— "Boo-oo-oo-oo-ooo."   ooo."

Whisper a spooky vocal ostinato to help express the chilling message of this song.

The Ghost of JOHN

Words and Music
by Martha Grubb

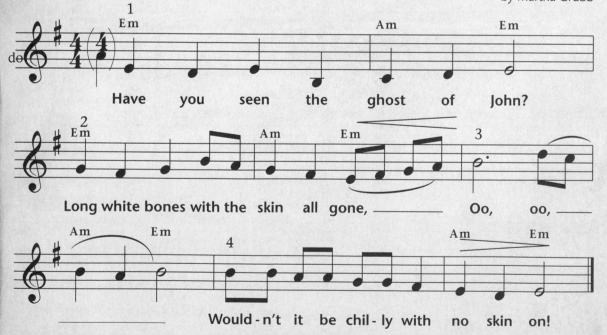

Have you seen the ghost of John?

Long white bones with the skin all gone, Oo, oo,

Would-n't it be chil-ly with no skin on!

Theme in YELLOW

I spot the hills
With yellow balls in autumn.
I light the prairie cornfields
Orange and tawny gold clusters
And I am called pumpkins.
On the last of October
When dusk is fallen
Children join hands
And circle round me
Singing ghost songs
And love to the harvest moon;
I am a jack-o'-lantern
With terrible teeth
And the children know
I am fooling.

—*Carl Sandburg*

LISTENING

Scary Music Montage

A suspense film or television program uses scary music to heighten the effect of what is happening on the screen. The frightening effect of music, however, is not only used in television and film. For a long time, composers have used minor keys, crescendos, and surprises to build tension and startle their listeners. As you listen to the "Scary Music Montage," you will hear music that makes you feel uneasy. Determine why the music might have an unsettling effect.

The rhythm of this song may get your skeleton moving!

DRY BONES

African American Spiritual

A **Freely**

E - ze - kiel cried, "Them dry bones!" E - ze - kiel cried, "Them dry bones!"

E - ze - kiel cried, "Them dry bones, Now hear the Word of the Lord!" E -

gradually getting faster

Lord!" The foot bone con - nect - ed to the leg bone,

The leg bone con - nect - ed to the knee bone,

The knee bone con - nect - ed to the hip - bone,

The hip - bone con - nect - ed to the back - bone,

The back - bone con - nect - ed to the shoul - der bone,

The shoul - der bone con - nect - ed to the neck bone,

The neck bone con - nect - ed to the jaw - bone,

The jaw - bone con - nect - ed to the head bone,

Now hear the Word of the Lord.

Them bones, them bones gon - na walk a - round, Them

bones, them bones gon - na walk a - round, Them bones, them bones gon - na

walk a - round, Now hear the word of the Lord.

Every day of the year, crops are gathered somewhere in the world. Whenever and wherever the harvest comes, it is a time for celebration and thanksgiving.

For Health and Strength

Old English Round

For health and strength and dai - ly food

We praise Thy name, Oh, Lord.

During the 1800s, there were many Shaker villages in the eastern part of the United States. Kathy Jakobsen's painting, shown below, depicts the simple life-style of Shaker communities. This Shaker song welcomes visitors.

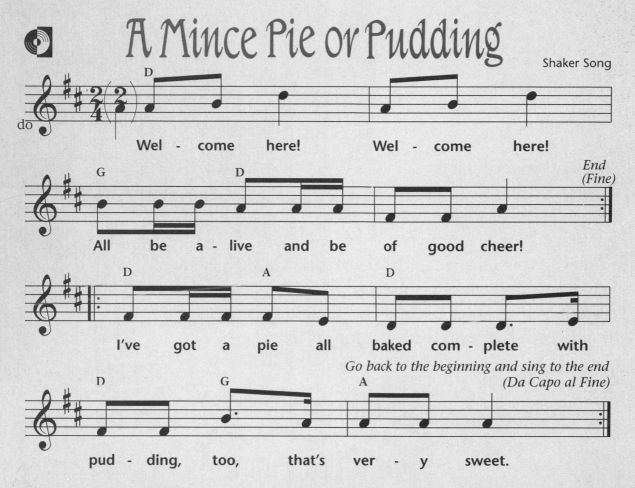

A Mince Pie or Pudding

Shaker Song

Wel - come here! Wel - come here!

All be a - live and be of good cheer!

I've got a pie all baked com - plete with

Go back to the beginning and sing to the end
(Da Capo al Fine)

pud - ding, too, that's ver - y sweet.

North Union, Shaker Village, Kathy Jakobsen, 1984

Winter Carnival

Winters are very cold in Canada. Each year, however, Canadians of all ages gather to "discover the warmth of winter" at the Quebec Carnival. Parades, fireworks, snow sculpture competitions, sporting events, and concerts are all part of the winter celebration. The festivities are led by Bonhomme Carnaval, a smiling snowman.

Bonhomme! Bonhomme!

Canadian Folk Song
English Version by MMH

French: Bon - homme, Bon - homme, sais - tu jou - er? Bon - homme, Bon -
Pronunciation: bɔ nɔm bɔ nɔm sɛ tü ʒu e bɔ nɔm bɔ
English: 1.-3. Bon - homme, Bon - homme, can you play this? Bon - homme, Bon -

homme, sais - tu jou - er? Sais - tu jou - er de ce vi - o - lon -
nɔm sɛ tü ʒu e sɛ tü ʒu e də sə vi ɔ lɔ̃
homme, can you play this? Can you play this on the vi - o -
Can you play this on the ti - ny
Can you play this on the big____ bass

312

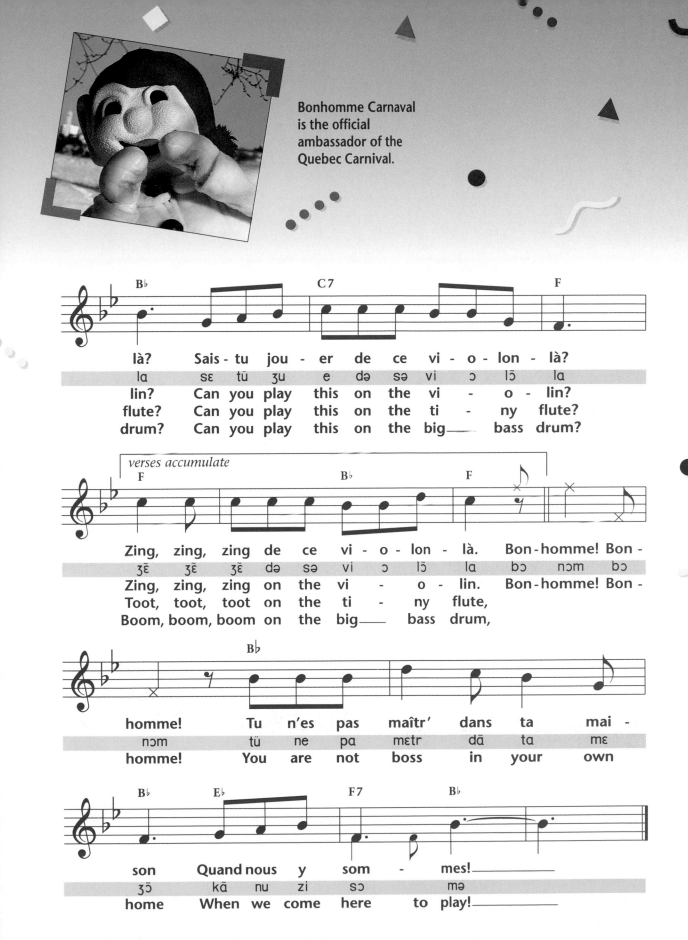

Bonhomme Carnaval is the official ambassador of the Quebec Carnival.

là? Sais - tu jou - er de ce vi - o - lon - là?
la sɛ tü ʒu e də sə vi ɔ lɔ̃ la
lin? Can you play this on the vi - o - lin?
flute? Can you play this on the ti - ny flute?
drum? Can you play this on the big___ bass drum?

verses accumulate

Zing, zing, zing de ce vi - o - lon - là. Bon-homme! Bon -
ʒɛ̃ ʒɛ̃ ʒɛ̃ də sə vi ɔ lɔ̃ la bɔ nɔm bɔ
Zing, zing, zing on the vi - o - lin. Bon-homme! Bon -
Toot, toot, toot on the ti - ny flute,
Boom, boom, boom on the big___ bass drum,

homme! Tu n'es pas maîtr' dans ta mai -
nɔm tü ne pa mɛtr dɑ̃ ta mɛ
homme! You are not boss in your own

son Quand nous y som - mes!___
ʒɔ̃ kɑ̃ nu zi sɔ mə
home When we come here to play!___

4. Can you play this on the great big horn?
   Ta-ta-ra on the great big horn, . . .

Add a partner song to "Jingle Bells" to create harmony.

WINTER FANTASY

Words and Music
by Jill Gallina

mf

do — Snow - flakes fall - ing all o - ver town,

mf

do — Dash - ing through the snow in a one - horse o - pen sleigh,

Slip - ping, slid - ing ev' - ry - bod - y rush - in' 'round.

O'er the fields we go, laugh - ing all the way.

There's an i - cy chill in the air,

Bells on bob - tails ring, mak - ing spir - its bright. What

Tell - ing us that win - ter's real - ly here. Oh!

fun it is to laugh and sing a sleigh - ing song to - night. Oh!

I'm so glad that win-ter is here.

Jin-gle bells, jin-gle bells, jin-gle all the way.

Grab your sled and let out a hap-py cheer Be-cause it's

Oh, what fun it is to ride in a one-horse o-pen sleigh.

snow-ing, blow-ing, all through the day.

Jin-gle bells, jin-gle bells, jin-gle all the way.

Win-ter winds will sure-ly blow all your cares a-way. Hey!

Oh, what fun it is to ride in a one-horse o-pen sleigh! Hey!

The Miracle of Lights

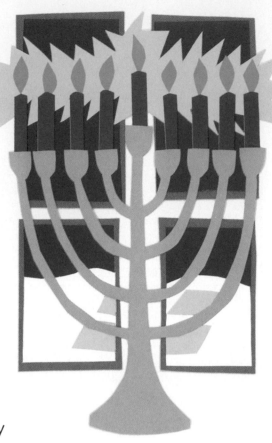

Lighting candles for Hanukkah honors a special event in Jewish history. Long ago, the people of Jerusalem wanted to relight their holy lamp, but there was only enough oil for one day. Miraculously, the small amount of oil lasted for eight days.

IN THE WINDOW

Hebrew Folk Song
Arranged by Mary Goetze

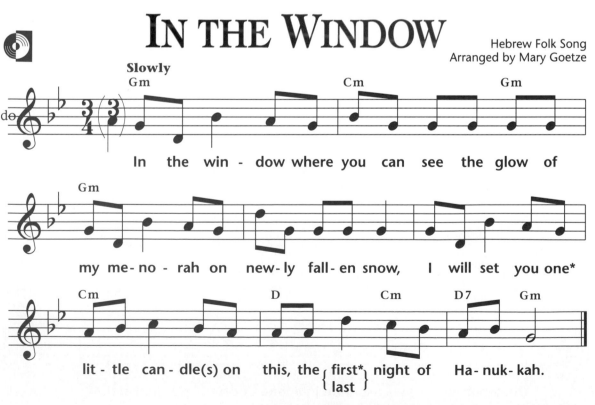

Slowly

In the win - dow where you can see the glow of my me - no - rah on new - ly fall - en snow, I will set you one* lit - tle can - dle(s) on this, the { first* } night of Ha - nuk - kah. { last }

*On each of the nights of Hanukkah, sing the correct number.
On the eighth verse, sing the word "last."

Add this part to some of the verses.

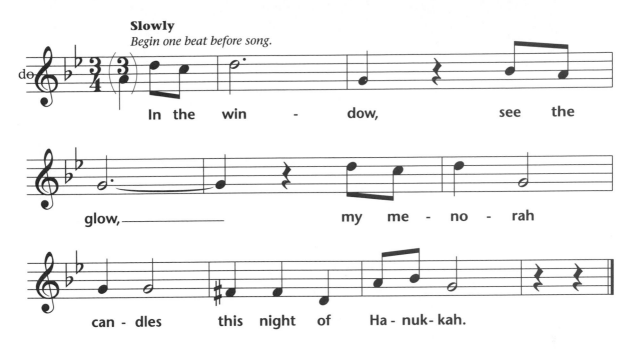

In the win - dow, see the glow,_____ my me - no - rah can - dles this night of Ha - nuk - kah.

Add this part to some other verses. Try singing all three parts together.

In the win- dow where you can see the glow, my me - no - rah on the fal - len snow. I will set____ my lit - tle can- dles on this____ night of Ha - nuk - kah.

MEXICAN CHRISTMAS SEASON

In Mexico and the southwestern United States, *Las Posadas* is a highlight of the Christmas season. The celebration begins on December 16 and lasts nine nights until Christmas Eve. Songs tell the story of Mary and Joseph's trip to Bethlehem.

There are two parts to "Para pedir posada." The first part of the song is a question, the second an answer. As the song begins, Joseph asks for shelter. The answer is that there is no room.

Para pedir posada

Mexican Folk Song
English Version by MMH

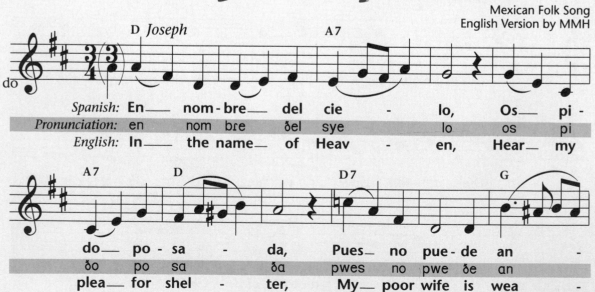

Spanish: En nom-bre del cie - lo, Os pi-
Pronunciation: en nom bɾe ðel sye lo os pi
English: In the name of Heav - en, Hear my

do po-sa - da, Pues no pue-de an -
ðo po sa ða pwes no pwe ðe an
plea for shel - ter, My poor wife is wea -

318

Each evening of *Las Posadas*, groups of friends walk from home to home, stopping to sing. Mary and Joseph are tired and need a place to rest. The word posada actually means "inn or shelter." The people at home answer, but the travelers are not allowed to come in.

At last, after being turned away again and again,
Mary and Joseph are welcomed.

Entren santos peregrinos

Enter, Holy Pilgrims

Mexican Folk Song
English Version by MMH

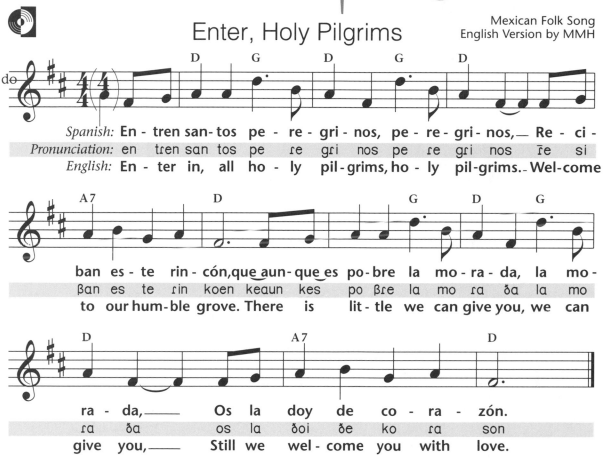

Spanish: En - tren san - tos pe - re - gri - nos, pe - re - gri - nos,— Re - ci -
Pronunciation: en tɾen san tos pe ɾe gɾi nos pe ɾe gɾi nos ɾe si
English: En - ter in, all ho - ly pil - grims, ho - ly pil - grims.— Wel - come

ban es - te rin - cón, que aun - que es po - bre la mo - ra - da, la mo -
βan es te ɾin koen keaun kes po βɾe la mo ɾa ða la mo
to our hum - ble grove. There is lit - tle we can give you, we can

ra - da,—— Os la doy de co - ra - zón.
ɾa ða os la ðoi ðe ko ɾa son
give you,—— Still we wel - come you with love.

When the posadas procession ends, the owner of the home opens the door, and everyone comes in for a festive party that includes breaking a piñata.

Dale, dale, dale!

Mexican
Folk Song
English Version
by MMH

Verse

Spanish: En las no - ches de po - sa - das,
Pronunciation: en las no ches ðe po sa ðas
English: On the nights of Las Po - sa - das,

la pi - ña - ta es lo me - jor,
la pi nya taes lo me xoɾ
chil - dren laugh and try with all their might,

Y los ni - ños más a - le - gres
i los ni nyos mas a le gɾes
To win the bright pi - ña - ta's trea -

le pe - gan con gran fer - vor.
le pe gang kong gran feɾ βoɾ
sure they swing and swing all night.

Refrain

Da - le, da - le, da - le, no pier - das el ti - no,
ða le ða le ða le no pyeɾ ðas el ti no
Da - le, da - le, da - le, do not lose el ti - no,

Mi - de la dis - tan - cia, que hay en el ca - mi - no.
mi ðe la ðis tan sya keai en el ka mi no
Turn a - round and find it on—— *el ca - mi - no.*

Que si no le das de un pa - lo - te pi - no,
ke si no le ðas ðeun pa lo te pi no
For if you should miss it with *pa - lo - te pi - no,*

Por - que tie - nes ca - ra, de pu - ro pe - pi - no.——
poɾ ke tye nes ka ɾa ðe pu ɾo pe pi no
You will feel as fool - ish as *pu - ro pe - pi - no.*——

This song is from the program *Rudolph, the Red-Nosed Reindeer*.

A Holly Jolly Christmas

Words and Music
by Johnny Marks

Have a hol - ly jol - ly Christ-mas, it's the best time of the year.

I don't know if there'll be snow but have a cup of cheer.

Have a hol - ly jol - ly Christ -mas, and when you walk down the street

Say hel - lo to friends you know and ev' - ry - one you meet.

Oh, ho, the mis - tle - toe hung where you can see.

Some - bod - y waits for you, kiss her once for me.

Have a hol - ly jol - ly Christ - mas, and in case you did - n't hear,

Oh, by gol - ly, have a hol - ly jol - ly Christ - mas this year. Have a

Christ - mas ___ this year. ___

This German carol reminds us that decorating an evergreen tree is a favorite Christmas tradition. Sometimes we create our own traditions for celebrating a holiday, as expressed in the song on the next page. What are your unique holiday traditions?

O Tannenbaum!
O Christmas Tree!

German Carol
English Version by MMH

German: O Tan - nen - baum, O Tan - nen - baum, wie
Pronunciation: o ta nən baʊm o ta nən baʊm vi
English: O Tan - nen - baum, O Tan - nen - baum, your

treu sind dei - ne Blät - ter! Du grünst nicht nur zur
trɔɪ zɪnt daɪ nə blɛ tər du grünst nɪçt nur tsur
leaves are ev - er faith - ful! Not on - ly green when

Som - mers - zeit, Nein, auch im Win - ter,
zɔ mər tsaɪt naɪn aʊx ɪm vɪn tər
sum - mer glows, But in the win - ter

wenn es schneit. O Tan - nen - baum, O
vɛn ɛs shnaɪt o ta nən baʊm o
when it snows, O Tan - nen - baum, O

Tan - nen - baum, wie treu sind dei - ne Blät - ter!
ta nən baʊm vi trɔɪ zɪnt daɪ nə blɛ tər
Tan - nen - baum, your leaves are ev - er faith - ful!

Somewhere in My Memory

Music by John Williams
Words by Leslie Bricusse

Can - dles in the win - dow, shad - ows paint - ing the ceil - ing, gaz - ing at the fire glow, feel - ing that "gin - ger - bread" feel - ing. Pre - cious mo - ments, spe - cial peo - ple, hap - py fac - es I can see. Some - where in my mem - 'ry, Christ - mas joys all a - round me, liv - ing in my mem - 'ry, all of the mu - sic, all of the mag - ic, all of the fam - 'ly home here with me.

In Italy, during the nine days before Christmas, people celebrate with fairs, fireworks, and bonfires. The Christmas Eve celebration honors the birth of Jesus with prayers and carols. This Italian carol is a lullaby for the baby.

Dormi, dormi

Sleep, Sleep

Italian Carol
English Text
by George K. Evans

According to the Christmas story, three wise men, or kings, brought gifts to the newborn child on January 6. In Latin American countries, this day is known as Three Kings Day. It is the day that children receive gifts.

We Three Kings

Words and Music
by John Henry Hopkins

Verse

We three kings of O - ri - ent are,
Bear - ing gifts we trav - erse a - far,

Field and foun - tain, moor and moun - tain,

Fol - low - ing yon - der star.

Refrain

O_____ Star of won - der, star of night,
Star with roy - al beau - ty bright,

West - ward lead - ing, still pro - ceed - ing,

Guide us to thy per - fect light.

There are twelve days between Christmas and Epiphany,
the day when the three kings arrived with their gifts.

The Twelve Days of Christmas

English Carol

1. On the first day of Christ-mas my true love sent to me: A par-tridge— in a pear tree.
2. On the sec-ond day of Christ-mas my true love sent to me: Two tur-tle doves, and a par-tridge— in a pear tree.
3. On the third day of Christ-mas my true love sent to me: Three French—hens, two tur-tle doves, and a par-tridge— in a pear tree.
4. On the fourth day of Christ-mas my true love sent to me:

Four col-ly birds, two tur-tle doves, and a par-tridge— in a pear
three French— hens,

tree. 5. On the fifth day of Christ-mas my true love sent to me:

Five gold-en rings, four— col-ly birds, three French hens,

End
(Fine)

two— tur-tle doves, and a par-tridge— in a pear tree.

6.-12. On the sixth day of Christ-mas my true love sent to me:
(seventh, etc.)

Go back to the sign and sing to the end
(Del Segno al Fine)

6. Six geese a - lay - ing,

7. Seven swans a-swimming,   11. Eleven ladies dancing,

8. Eight maids a-milking,   12. Twelve lords a-leaping,

9. Nine drummers drumming,

10. Ten pipers piping,

ASIAN NEW

For Asians and Asian Americans, celebrating the new year may last for several weeks. The exact date of the holiday depends upon each country's traditions.

In Vietnam and China, the Kitchen God goes to the heavens and reports on the family at the end of the old year. After cleaning and decorating the house, families send the Kitchen God off with firecrackers, food, and gifts in hopes of a good report.

In Vietnam, the new year celebration is called Tet. During the first days of the new year everyone tries to be happy. To be angry could bring bad luck.

Buying mume blossoms is part of preparing for Tet.

YEAR CELEBRATIONS

In Laos, the new year usually begins in April. In preparation, houses and temples are washed. Splashing and throwing water becomes a festive part of the celebration. People are joyful because they believe that the happier you are, the happier the year to come will be.

Suk san wan pi mai
New Year's Song

Laotian Song
Collected and Transcribed by
Kathy B. Sorensen
English Version by MMH

Preparation for the Chinese New Year begins at least a month in advance. In addition to cleaning the house, families paint their front doors red–the color red means happiness. When the new year actually arrives, the celebration lasts for fifteen days.

Chinese Lion Dance *Chinese Folk Music*

On the third to fifth days of the Chinese New Year, the Chinese Lion dances through the crowds in the streets. Martial-arts students perform the lion dance. Listen to the rhythm of the Chinese drum and cymbal.

The lion asleep.

Lion Dance Drum Pattern

Lion Dance Cymbal Pattern

The lion awakening.

The Chinese Lion, danced by students of the Wan Chi Ming Hung Gar Institute in New York City.

The lion bowing.

Dr. King's DREAM

The powerful speeches of Dr. Martin Luther King, Jr., inspired many people to work for equal rights. His words still give people hope and encouragement.

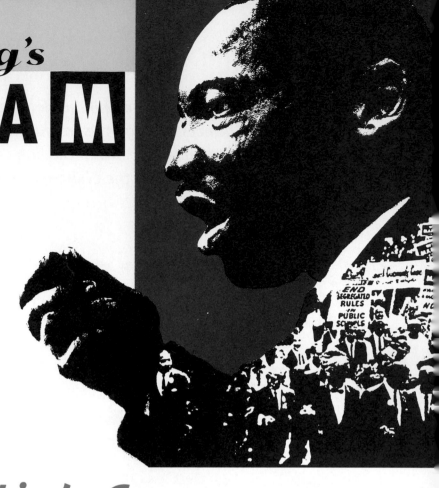

Martin's Cry

Words and Music by Vernon Clark

1. There was a man— named Mar - tin Lu - ther King, who said,
2. King took a stand— for civ - il rights a - cross the land,
3. King led a march— to Wash - ing - ton and said a - gain,

"Let free - dom— ring!—
Let free - dom— ring!—
"Let free - dom— ring!"

I have a dream— that one day this na - tion will
No mat - ter where— his foot - steps led him, he would
He gave his life— so one day all peo - ple could

rise   and   sing;_____   that
rise   and   sing;_____   "Yes,
rise   and   sing;_____   "Yes,

all   men   are   cre - a - ted   e - qual:

black,   white,   red,   or   yel - low   or   brown._____

I   have   a   dream,_____   I   have   a   dream,_____

Let   free - dom_____   ring!"

"Let   free - dom ring!_____   Let   free - dom ring!_____

from   the   Al - le - ghe - nies to   the   red   clay   in   Geor - gia,_____

Go back to 𝄋 *and Sing to the end*
(Del Segno al Fine)

Let   free - dom   ring!"_____   "Yes,

In 1983, the birthday of Martin Luther King, Jr., became a national holiday. It is a day to celebrate his dream of equality for all people. People sing songs like this African American spiritual to honor Dr. King's belief in peace and freedom.

DOWN BY THE RIVERSIDE

African American Spiritual

1. Gon-na lay down my sword and shield,
2. Gon-na lay down my bur - den,
3. Gon-na try on my star - ry crown, } Down by the riv-er - side,
4. Gon-na meet my dear old fath - er,
5. Gon-na meet my dear old moth - er,

Down by the riv-er - side, Down by the riv-er - side,

Gon - na lay down my sword and shield,
Gon - na lay down my bur - den,
Gon - na try on my star - ry crown, } Down by the riv-er - side,
Gon - na meet my dear old fath - er,
Gon - na meet my dear old moth - er,

Gon - na stud - y war no more.

Refrain

I ain't gon-na stud - y war no more,

Ain't gon - na stud - y war no more,

1.
Ain't gon - na stud - y war no more,

2.
stud - y war no more.

The Civil Rights Memorial in Montgomery, Alabama, was designed by Maya Lin. Ms. Lin also designed the Vietnam Memorial in Washington, D.C.

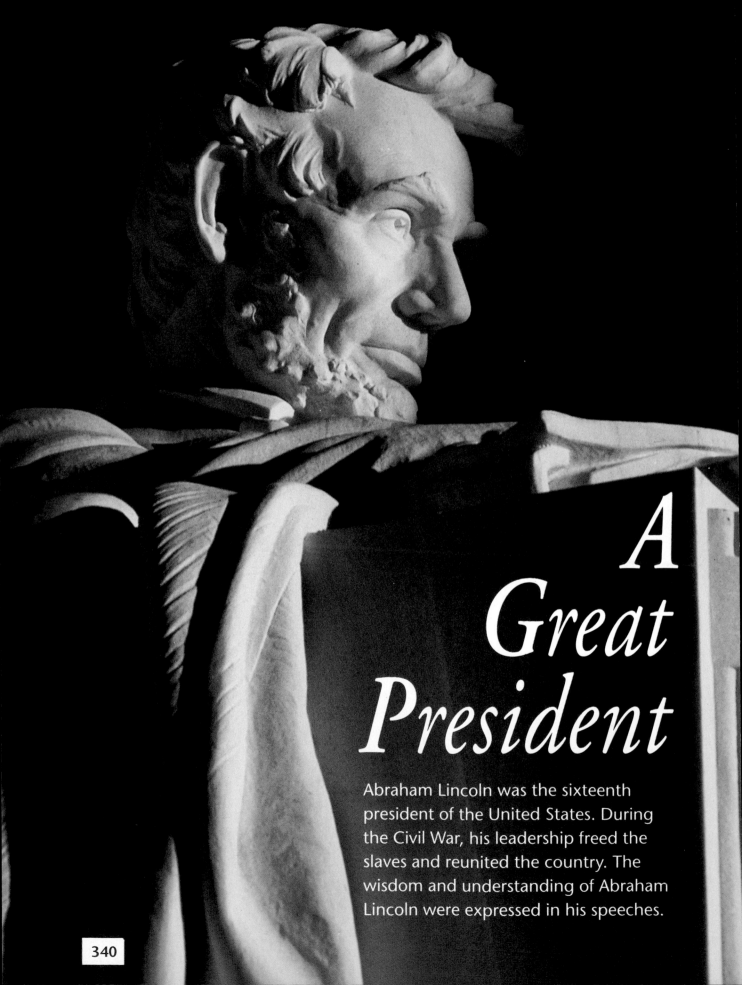

A Great President

Abraham Lincoln was the sixteenth president of the United States. During the Civil War, his leadership freed the slaves and reunited the country. The wisdom and understanding of Abraham Lincoln were expressed in his speeches.

LISTENING

Lincoln Portrait

(excerpts) *by Aaron Copland*

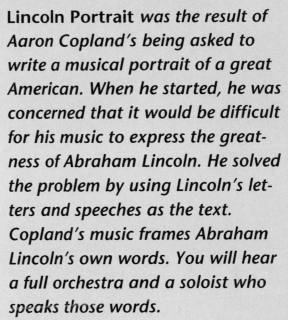

Lincoln Portrait *was the result of Aaron Copland's being asked to write a musical portrait of a great American. When he started, he was concerned that it would be difficult for his music to express the greatness of Abraham Lincoln. He solved the problem by using Lincoln's letters and speeches as the text. Copland's music frames Abraham Lincoln's own words. You will hear a full orchestra and a soloist who speaks those words.*

To Meet
MR. LINCOLN

If I lived at the time
That Mr. Lincoln did,
And I met Mr. Lincoln
With his stovepipe lid

And his coalblack cape
And his thundercloud beard,
And worn and sad-eyed
He appeared:

"Don't worry, Mr. Lincoln,"
I'd reach up and pat his hand,
"We've got a fine President
For this land;

And the Union will be saved,
And the slaves will go free;
And you will live forever
In our nation's memory."

— Eve Merriam

Celebrations *Presidents' Day* **341**

MARCHING ON

Macnamara's Band

Music by Shamus O'Connor
Words by John J. Stamford

Verse

F

1. Oh! me name is Mac - na - mar - a, I'm the lead - er of the band,—
2. Right— now we are re - hears - in', for a ver - y swell af - fair,—
3. Oh! my name is Un - cle Yul - ius and from Swe - den I have come,—
4. Oh! I wear a bunch of sham - rocks and a un - i-form of green,—

Bb F C

Al - though we're few in num - bers we're the fin - est in the land.
The an - nual cel - e - bra - tion, all the gen - try will be there.
To play with Mac - na - mar - a's band and beat the big bass drum,
And I'm the fun - niest look - ing Swede that you have ev - er seen.

C F

We play at wakes and wed - dings and at
When Gen - 'ral Grant to Ire - land came he
And when I march a - long the street the
There's O' - Bri - ens and Ry - ans and Shee -hans and Mee -hans, they

F Bb

ev' - ry fan - cy ball,— And when we play to
took me by the hand,— Says he, "I nev - er
la - dies think I'm grand,— They shout, "There's Un - cle
come from Ire - land,— But by Yim-min - y I'm the

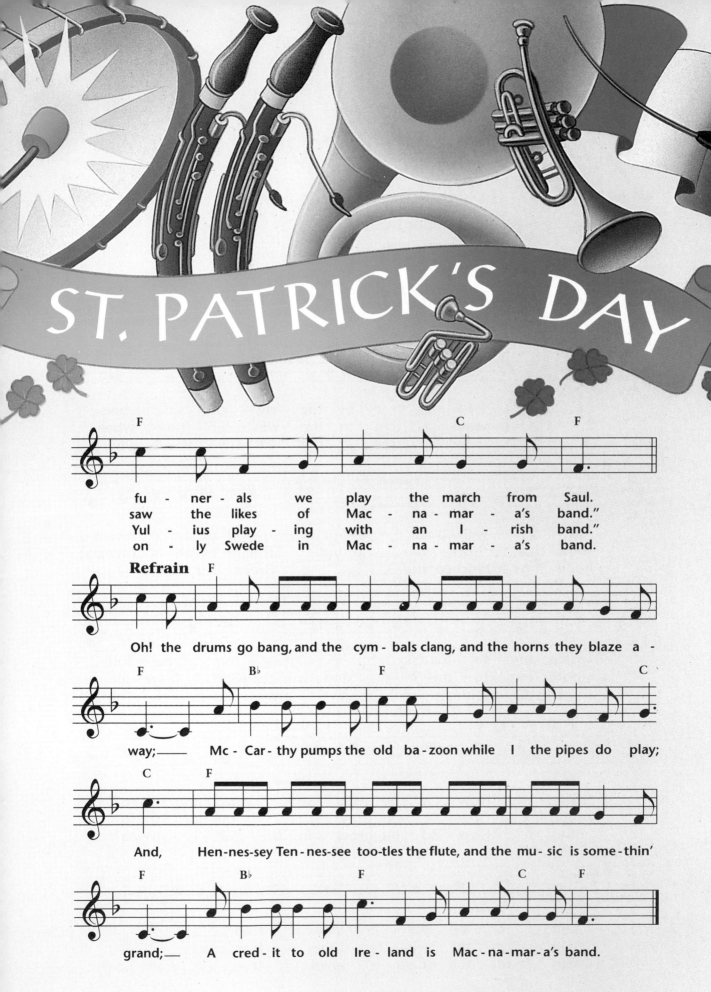

ST. PATRICK'S DAY

fu - ner - als we play the march from Saul.
saw the likes of Mac - na - mar - a's band."
Yul - ius play - ing with an I - rish band."
on - ly Swede in Mac - na - mar - a's band.

Refrain

Oh! the drums go bang, and the cym - bals clang, and the horns they blaze a -

way;____ Mc - Car - thy pumps the old ba - zoon while I the pipes do play;

And, Hen - nes - sey Ten - nes - see too - tles the flute, and the mu - sic is some - thin'

grand;____ A cred - it to old Ire - land is Mac - na - mar - a's band.

Arbor Day
Plant a Tree

Arbor Day is a holiday to honor trees.

TREE SONG

Words and Music
by Ken Medema

More Songs to Read

Feel the Beat! Conduct the Meter!

I Love the Mountains

Traditional Round

I love the moun-tains, I love the roll-ing hills,

I love the flow-ers, I love the daf-fo-dils;

I love the fire-side when all the lights are low.

Boom-dee-ah-da, Boom-dee-ah-da, Boom-dee-ah-da, Boom-dee-ah-da.

Practice with Phrases

LISTEN to find the phrases in these songs. How many different pitches does each song use? 3

GO 'ROUND THE MOUNTAIN

Illinois Play Party Song

1. Go 'round the moun-tain;⎫
2. Swing 'round your part-ner;⎭ To- di- did- dle- um, To- di- did- dle- um,

Go 'round the moun-tain;⎫
Swing 'round your part-ner;⎭ To- di- did- dle- um, To- di- did- dle- um- dum.

3. Back 'round the mountain; . . .
4. Girls through the window; . . .
5. Boys through the window; . . .
6. Find you a new love; . . .

NIGHT SONG

German Folk Song

All through the night,   the moon is sil - ver bright.

Crick - et sings his   ti - ny song,   sings it through the

whole night long.   All   through the   night.

Reading Rhythm

IDENTIFY the meter and read the rhythm in this song. These are the rhythms used:

♩ quarter note

♫ two eighth notes

♩ half note

Virginia Folk Song

Bab - y - lon's fall - in', fall - in', fall - in',

Bab - y - lon's fall - in' to rise no more.

Reading *Do Re Mi So La*

SING two songs that use only *do re mi so la.*

la

so

mi

re

do

Page's Train

North Carolina Folk Song

do

1
D

Pa - ge's train   runs   so   fast,

2
D   A7   D

Can't   see   noth-ing   but   the   win - dow   glass.

I Am a Cat

Music by Marilyn Copeland Davidson
Anonymous Poem

do

F

I   am   a   cat!   I'm   ver - y   ver - y   fat!   I

F

sit   on   a   mat   and   that   is   that!

Practice *Do Re Mi So La*

SING these two patterns with pitch syllables. Then listen to "Down the Road" to find each pattern.

SING these patterns.

1.

2.

3.

4.

5.

6.

Lady, Come Down and See

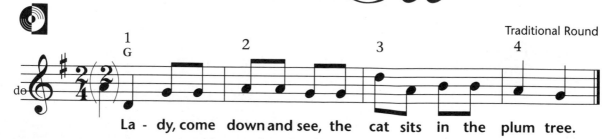

Traditional Round

La - dy, come down and see, the cat sits in the plum tree.

FIND the pitch below *do.*

Four Sounds to a Beat

FIND the beats with four sounds.

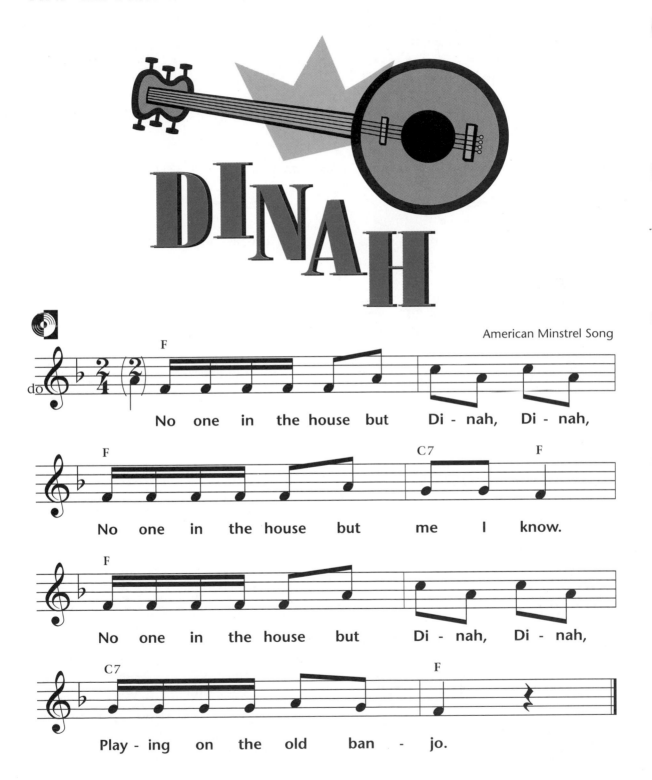

American Minstrel Song

No one in the house but Di - nah, Di - nah,

No one in the house but me I know.

No one in the house but Di - nah, Di - nah,

Play - ing on the old ban - jo.

Reading Sixteenth Notes

PAT these patterns. Use them with "Ida Red."

Refrain

Group 1:
Wish I'd get some mail! Wish I'd get some mail!

Verse

Group 2:
Mail! Please bring some Mail! Please bring some

Group 3:
Let-ters and cards! Let-ters and cards!

Ida Red

Kentucky Folk Song

Refrain

Down the road and a-cross the creek,

Can't get a let-ter but once a week.

Verse

I - da Red, I - da Blue,
I - da Red, I - da Green,
I - da Red, I - da Gold,
I - da Red, I - da Red,

I got stuck on I - da too.
pret-ti-est girl you've ev-er seen.
she is some-thin' to be-hold.
that girl's sweet-er than gin-ger-bread.

Discover a Song

SING the pitches and rhythms of these phrases to discover the name of the song.

SING these patterns.

Using What You Know

THE OLD CHISHOLM TRAIL

Cowboy Song

Verse

1. Come a - long boys, and lis - ten to my tale.

I'll tell you of my trou - bles on the old Chis - holm trail.

Refrain

Come a ti yi yip - py, yip - py ay, yip - py ay,

Come a ti yi yip - py, yip - py ay.

2. I woke one mornin' on the old Chisholm trail,
   A rope in my hand and a cow by the tail. *Refrain*

3. I started up the trail on October twenty-third,
   Started up the trail with the old cow herd. *Refrain*

4. On a ten dollar horse and a forty dollar saddle,
   I'm gonna punch those Texas cattle. *Refrain*

5. It's bacon and beans 'most ev'ry day,
   I'd as soon be a-eatin' prairie hay. *Refrain*

6. It's cloudy in the west and it looks like rain,
   And I left my old slicker in the wagon again. *Refrain*

7. I'm gonna see the boss, gonna get my money,
   Goin' back home to see my honey. *Refrain*

354

Steps, Skips, and Repeats

SING this song two pitches at a time. After every two pitches, tell if you just sang a step, a skip, or a repeated pitch.

Old Tar River

American Folk Song

1. Way____ down in North Car' - lin - a, *Whistle*
2. My old dog he won't go with me,
3. Rac- coon, Pos - sum had a fray,____
4. Old dog watch, smelled all a- round,____
5. Di - nah, I am going to leave you;

On the banks of Old Tar Riv - er, *Whistle*
He'd rath-er hunt far's I can see.____
Fought all night un - til next day,____
Found Rac - coon just left the ground,____
When I'm gone don't let it grieve you,

Go from there to Al - a - bam - a, *Whistle*
He smells some-thing up the hill,____
When day broke went Poss' to the hol- low,
Then he bark right up the tree,____
First to the win - dow, then to the door,____

For to see my old Aunt Han - nah. *Whistle*
If I don't find it, he sure will.____
Rac - coon says, "I bet - ter fol- low."
Rac - coon says, "You can't catch me."____
Look - ing for to see my ban - jo.

New Meter Ahoy!

LISTEN to this song to decide if you hear equal or unequal sounds to the beat.

Heave-HO Me Laddies

Sea Chantey

Oh if I were a sail-or out a sail-ing on the sea,

I real-ly am quite cer-tain a cap-tain I would be.

Heave-ho me lad-dies. Fast-en down the sails.

This lust-y wind will take us a-sail-ing o'er the sea. sea.

Reading New Pitches

FIND a new pitch in this song.
Hint: It is below low *so*.

My Horses Ain't Hungry

Tennessee Folk Song

1. My hors-es ain't hun-gry, They won't eat your hay,
2. I know you're my Pol-ly, I'm not going to stay,
3. With all our be-long-ings, We'll ride till we come

So I'll get on my po-ny, I'm go-ing a-way.
So— come with me dar-ling, We'll feed on our way.
To— a lone-ly cab-in, We'll call it our home.

PLAY an ostinato with the song.

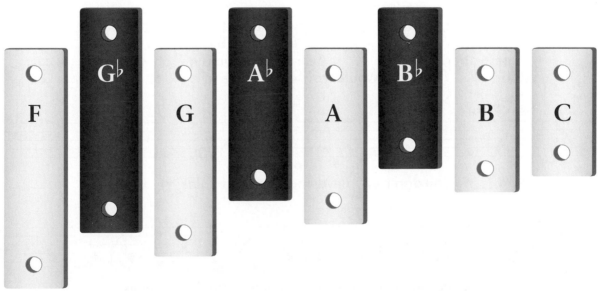

Reading in $\frac{6}{8}$ ($\frac{2}{}$.) Meter

THE DERBY RAM

English Folk Song
Ozark Version

Verse F

do

1. As I went down to Der - by town, all
2. The wool up - on this ram's___ back It
3. The horns up - on this ram's___ head They
4. The ears up - on this ram's___ head They
5. Oh ev' - ry tooth this ram___ had would

F   C 7   F

on a sum - mer's day,___ It's there I saw the
drug___ to the ground,___ I hauled it to the
reached___ to the moon,___ the butch-er went up on
reached___ to the sky,___ the ea - gle built his
hold a bush-el of corn,___ And ev' - ry foot he

B♭   C 7   F

fin - est ram, that's ev - er fed on hay.___
mar - ket, And it weighed ten thou - sand pounds.___
Feb - ru - ar-y, And nev-er got back till June.___
nest there, For I heard the young ones cry.___
stood___ on, Would cov-er an a-cre of ground.___

Refrain F   C 7

And if you don't be - lieve me,___ And think I tell a lie,___

F   B♭   C 7   F

Just you go down to Der-by, And you'll see the same as I.___

358

A 𝄴 Song from Newfoundland

Lots o' Fish in Bonavist' Harbor

Newfoundland Folk Song

Verse

1. There's lots o' fish in Bon - a - vist' Har - bor,
2. Oh, Sal - ly went to church ev' - ry Sun - day,

Lots o' fish right in a - round here.
Not for to sing nor for____ to hear.

Boys and girls are fish - in' to - geth - er,
But to see the fel - ler from For - tune

For - ty - five from Car - bon - ear.
What was down here fish - in' last year.

Refrain

Oh, catch - a - hold this one, catch - a - hold that one,
Dance a - round this one, dance a - round that one,

1.
Swing a - round this one, swing a - round she;

2.
Did - dle dum dee dum, did - dle dum dee.

Find the *Short Long Short* Pattern

LISTEN for the *short long short* pattern.

Old Dan Tucker

American Folk Song
Folk version of Dan Emmett's minstrel song

Verse

1. Old Dan Tuck-er's a fine old man.
2. Old Dan Tuck-er be - gan in ear-ly life, To

Washed his face in a fry - ing pan,
play the ban - jo_____ and the fife. He'd

Combed his head with a wag - on wheel And
play the head boys and_____ gals to sleep, And

died with a tooth - ache in his heel.
then in - to his bunk he'd creep.

Refrain

Get out the way, Old Dan Tuck - er, You're too late to

get your sup - per. Sup - per's o - ver and din - ner's cook - in' And

Old Dan Tuck - er's just stand - in' look - in'.

360

Octave Skips

My Dame Hath a Lame, Tame Crane

Traditional English Round

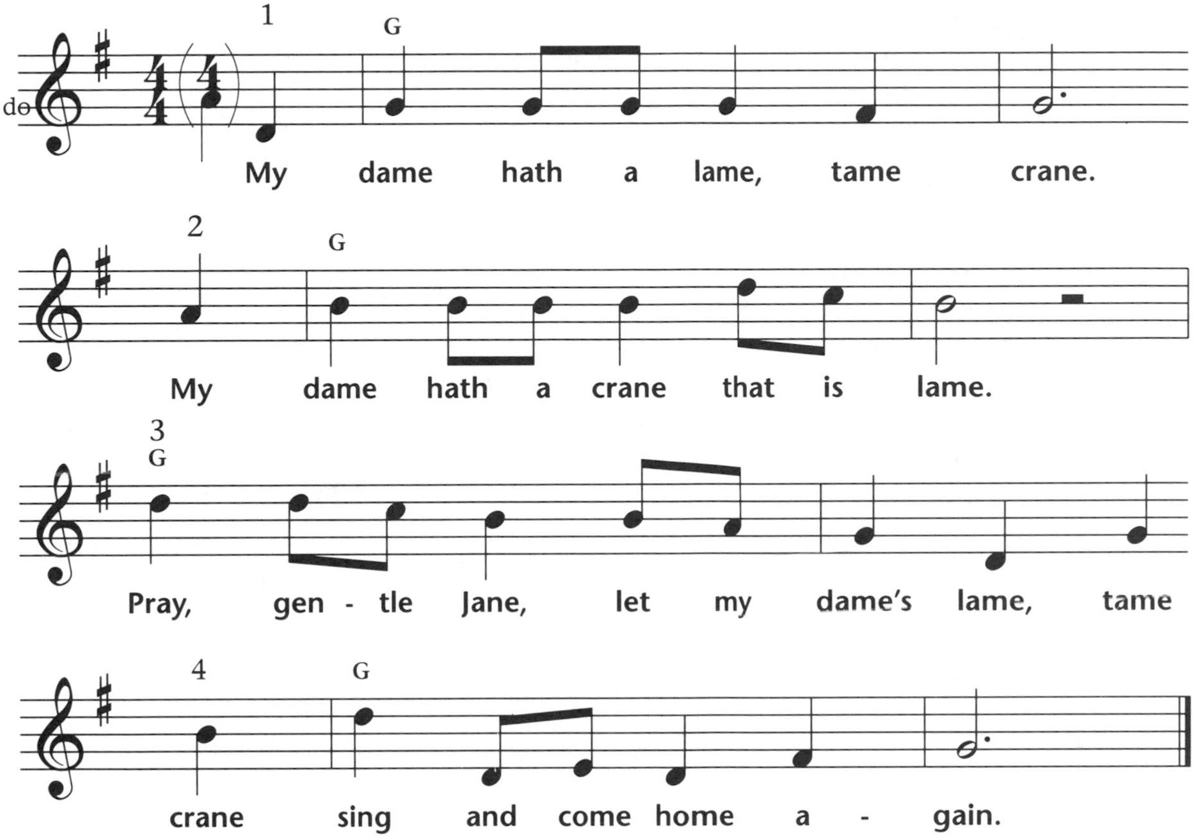

1 G

My dame hath a lame, tame crane.

2 G

My dame hath a crane that is lame.

3 G

Pray, gen - tle Jane, let my dame's lame, tame

4 G

crane sing and come home a - gain.

To Stop the Train

English Round

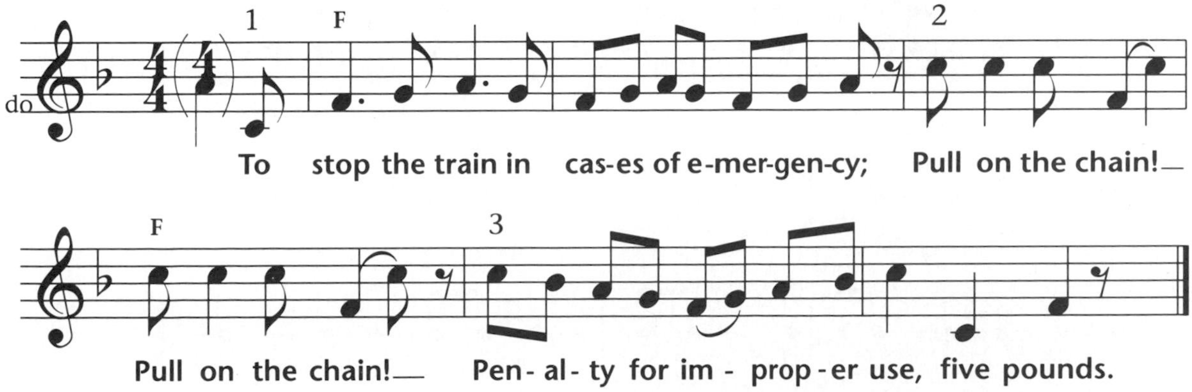

1 F   2

To stop the train in cas-es of e-mer-gen-cy; Pull on the chain!—

F   3

Pull on the chain!— Pen - al - ty for im - prop - er use, five pounds.

Using What You Know

FIND the measures with the *short long short* pattern. Then identify and read the pitches.

Before Dinner

Zairian Folk Song

Call ... *Response*

First we go to hoe our gar-den, } Ya, ya, ya, ya.
Next we car-ry jugs of wa-ter,

Call ... *Response*

Then we pound the yel-low corn, } Ya, ya, ya, ya.
Then we stir our pots of mush,

Call ... *Response*

Now we eat, come gath-er 'round the camp-fire, Ya, ya, ya, ya.

ADD these instrument parts to the song.

Arranged by Carol King

Agogo Bells

Shakers

Drum

362

Hearing and Using Octaves

RAISE your hand when you hear these pitches.

FIND the octave skip in the song below. Sing the song with pitch syllables. Then, accompany it with an octave pattern.

Shaker Song

Hop up and jump up and whirl 'round, whirl 'round,

Gath - er love, here it is all 'round, all 'round,

Here is love flow - ing 'round, catch it as you whirl round,

Reach up and reach down, here it is all 'round.

Reviewing Meter

Oliver Cromwell

English Folk Song

1. Ol - i - ver Crom-well lay bur - ied and dead, Hee haw,
(2.) ap - ples were ripe____ and read - y to fall, Hee haw,
(3.) sad - dle and bri - dle, they lie on the shelf, Hee haw,

bur - ied and dead. There grew an old ap - ple tree
read - y to fall. There came an old wo - man to
lie on the shelf. If you want an - y more you can

o - ver his head, Hee haw, o - ver his head. 2. The
gath - er them all, Hee haw, gath - er them all. 3. The
sing it your - self, Hee haw, sing it your - self.

Who's Got a Fishpole?

American Song

1. Who's got a fish - pole? We do. Who's got a fish - pole? We do.
2. Who's got a line?____ We do. Who's got a line?____ We do.
3. Who's got a hook?__ We do. Who's got a hook?____ We do.

Who's got a fish - pole? We do. Fish - pole needs a line.
Who's got a line?____ We do. Line____ needs a hook.
Who's got a hook?____ We do. Hook____ needs a worm.

364

Major or Minor?

Southern Folk Song
Arranged by Mary Goetze

Verse

1. The Boll Wee - vil am a lit - tle black bug from
2. The first time I saw Boll Wee - vil,____ He was
3. The Boll Wee - vil to the farm - er said, "You'd
4. The mer - chant took____ half the cot - ton.____ The

Mex - i - co they say. Come all the way to Tex - as just to
sit - tin' on the square. The next time I saw Boll Wee - vil, He had
bet - ter leave me a - lone. I done eat all your cot - ton, Now I'm
Boll Wee - vil took the rest. He on - ly left the farm - er Just a

Refrain

find a place to stay.
his whole fam' - ly there.   } Just a look - in' for a home.
start - in' on your corn."
sin - gle rag - ged vest.

Just a look - in' for a home.

Just a look - in' for a home.

Just a look - in' for a home.

Tunes with *Ti*

FIND *do* in each song. Where is *ti*?   ti

ALLELUIA, AMEN

Traditional Round

Al - le - lu - ia, al - le - lu - ia,

A - men, a - men.

San lun tsa
Three-Wheeled Taxi

Taiwanese Folk Song
Collected and Transcribed by Kathy B. Sorensen
English Version by MMH

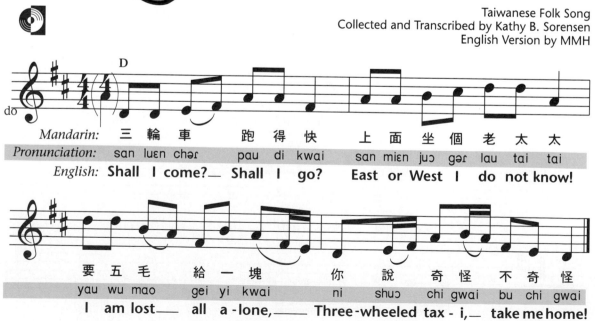

Mandarin: 三 輪 車 跑 得 快 上 面 坐 個 老 太 太
Pronunciation: san luɛn chər pau di kwai san miɛn juɔ gər lau tai tai
English: Shall I come?— Shall I go? East or West I do not know!

要 五 毛 給 一 塊 你 說 奇 怪 不 奇 怪
yau wu mao gei yi kwai ni shuɔ chi gwai bu chi gwai
I am lost — all a - lone,— Three-wheeled tax - i,— take me home!

Reading Rhythms

JOHN KANAKA

American Sea Chantey

Verse

1. I heard, I heard the Old Man say,
2. We'll work to - mor - rer, but no work to - day,
3. We're bound a - way for 'Fris - co Bay,
4. A Yan - kee ship wid a Yan - kee crew,
5. Oh, haul a - way, oh, haul a - way!

John Ka - na - ka, na - ka, Tu - lai - ay!

To - day, to - day is a hol - i - day,
We'll work to - mor - rer, but no work to - day,
We're bound a - way at the break of day,
Oh, we're the buck - os fer to push 'er through.
Oh, haul a - way, an' make your pay.

John Ka - na - ka, na - ka, Tu - lai - ay.

Refrain

Tu - lai - ay, Oh! tu - lai - ay,

John Ka - na - ka, na - ka, Tu - lai - ay.

Tools for Expression

AH, POOR BIRD

Old English Melody

1. Ah, poor bird, take your flight, Far a-bove the sor-rows of this sad night.
2. Ah, poor bird, as you fly, Can you see the dawn of to-mor-row's sky?

From GROWING WITH MUSIC, Book 3 TE, by Wilson et al. © 1970
Prentice-Hall, Inc., Englewood Cliffs, NJ. Arrangement adapted.

Chickalileeo

Southern Folk Song

1.–4. La la la chick - a - li - lee - o,
La la la chick - a - li - lee - o.

(1.) I'm goin' to mar - ry who I please,
(2.) I'm goin' to mar-ry lit - tle John - ny Green
(3.) He's gone___ off to the war a - way,
(4.) Yon - der he comes I do be - lieve,

La la la chick - a - li - lee - o.

Bet you I will if you mar - ry me,
He's the prett-'est boy I've___ ev - er seen,
He'll come___ back some___ pret-ty fair day,
I hope___ he will___ mar - ry me,

La la la chick - a - li - lee - o.

Adding Parts, Changing Texture

ADD an accompaniment to change the texture of this song.

Artsa Alinu
Our Land

Israeli Dance Song
English Version by MMH

Hebrew: אַר - צָה עָ - לִי - נוּ, אַר - צָה עָ - לִי - נוּ,
Pronunciation: aɾ tsa a li nu aɾ tsa a li nu
English: Ar - tsa a - li - nu, Ar - tsa a - li - nu.

End (Fine)

Hebrew: צָה אַר עָ - לִי - נוּ.
aɾ tsa a li nu
Ar - tsa a - li - nu.

Hebrew: כְּ - בָר חָ - רַשׁ - נוּ וְ גַם זָ - רַ - עְ - נוּ,
kəvaɾ xa ɾash nu ve gam za ɾa nu
To our land, we come to our land.

*Go back to the beginning
and sing to the end
(Da Capo al Fine)*

Hebrew: אֲ - בָל עוֹד לֹא קָ - צַ - רְ - נוּ.
a val od lo ka tsaɾ nu
Here we have plowed and plant - ed.

Singing in Minor

Korobushka

Russian Folk Song
Russian Words by Nikolay Kekrasov
English Version by MMH

A

Russian: Ой, пол - на, пол - на ко - ро - буш - ка,
Pronunciation: ɔi pɔl na pɔl na kɔ ɾɔ bush kə
English: "See what I have here in my ko - ro - bush - ka!"

Есть и сит - цы и пар - ча.
yɛst i si tsɪ i paɾ cha
We can hear the ped - dler's cry.

B

По - жа - лей мо - я за - зно - буш - ка
pɔ ʒa lye ma ya za zno bush kə
"I am on - ly a rag - ged ped - dler, but
Lace and sat - in and col - ored rib - bon, and

Мо - ло - дец - ко - го пле - ча.
ma la dyɛts ka vɔ plyɛ cha
I have treas - ures you can buy:
shin - y beads to catch your eye!"

Exploring Augmentation

~ O musique ~

French Folk Song
English Version by MMH

French: O mu-si-que no-tre_a-mie, Sour-ce pure et frai-che.
Pronunciation: o mü zi kə nɔ tɾa mi suɾ sə pü ɾe fɾɛ ʃшə

Alouette

French Canadian Folk Song

Refrain

French: A - lou-et - te, gen - tille a - lou-et - te,
Pronunciation: a lw ɛ tə ʒã ti ya lw ɛ tə

A - lou-et - te, je te plu - me-rai.
a lw ɛ tə ʒə tə plü mə ɾe

Verse *Leader* *Group*

1. Je te plu - me-rai la tête, Je te plu - me-rai la tête,
   ʒə tə plü mə ɾe la tɛt ʒə tə plü mə ɾe la tɛt
2. Je te plu - me-rai le bec, Je te plu - me-rai le bec,
   ʒə tə plü mə ɾe lə bɛk ʒə tə plü mə ɾe lə bɛk

Leader *Group*

Go back to the beginning and sing to the end
(Da Capo al Fine)

No repeat first time

1. Et la tête, et la tête. A - lou-ette, a - lou - ette. Oh!
   e la tɛt e la tɛt a lw ɛt a lw ɛt o
2. Et le bec, et le bec.
   e lə bɛk e lə bɛk
   Et la tête, et la tête.
   e la tɛt e la tɛt

3. Le nez   lə ne   5. Les pattes   le pat
4. Le dos   lə do   6. Le cou   lə ku

Choral Anthology

The words of this song link the image of the moon with the image of the sea. The long smooth melody also suggests moonlight, while the gentle rhythms might suggest the sea.

What are some words from the song that describe the moon and the sky? The wind and the sea?

LIST two words to describe how you want to sing this song.

The Path to the Moon

Music by Eric H. Thiman
Words by Madeline C. Thomas

1. I long to sail the path to the moon On a
2. So will I sail on a star - ry night On the

deep_____ blue night, when the wind is cool:
path to the moon_____ a sea - bird's flight;

A glist - 'ning path, that runs out to sea,
Skim - ming the waves where the fish - es play,

The words to this song were written by the author of "Winnie-the-Pooh." As you look at the song, find places where you think the composer is describing the wind.

Wind on the Hill

Music by Victoria Ebel-Sabo
Words by A. A. Milne

No one can tell me, _____ no - bod - y

knows _____ Where the wind comes from, _____ where the wind

goes, _____ goes, _____ where the wind goes.

It's fly - ing from some - where fast as it can. _____ I could - n't keep

up with it, _____ not if I ran. _____ No one can

LOOK at the song and decide its form.

Does the rhythm of this song use mostly short or long sounds? Consider the rhythm when deciding what singing style to use.

Hasidic Round
Arranged by Henry Leck

Like the word *lah*, the syllables traditionally sung in "Haida" are without specific meaning.

Allundé, Alluia

African Lullaby/Prayer
As sung and arranged by
Margaret Campbelle-Holman

Refrain *Gently Rocking*

do

Al- lun- dé, al - lun- dé._____ Al- lun- dé, al-
a lʊn de a lʊn de a lʊn de a

Echo — Use after verse 2

do

Al- lun- dé, al - lun- dé._____
a lʊn de a lʊn de

lu- ia. Al- lun- dé, al - lun- dé._____
lu ya a lʊn de a lʊn de

Al- lun- dé, al - lu- ia._____ Al- lun- dé, al-
a lʊn de a lu ya a lʊn de a

3rd time go to Coda ⊕

Al- lun- dé, al - lu- ia._____
a lʊn de a lu ya

3rd time go to Coda ⊕

lun- dé._____ Al- lun- dé, al - lu- ia._____
lʊn de a lʊn de a lu ya

And Where Is Home?

Words and Music by Margaret Campbelle-Holman

Unison

Lai lai lai   lai   lai lai lai lai lai   Lai lai lai lai

1., 2., 3., 4. to Verses   *5.* last time only   Fine

lai lai lai   Lai lai   lai _____   lai. _____

Verse

1. I was walk-ing, I was dream-ing, Saw a man up-
2. I was laugh-ing, I was sing-ing, Sang a song I
3. I was danc-ing, I was fly-ing, Turned and saw a
4. We are walk-ers, we are dream-ers. We sing songs that

on the stair. He was lost and asked me simp-ly,
did not know. Joy reached out and wrapped a-round me,
friend's de-spair; Pulled her up and sent her soar-ing,
say a prayer. We are danc-ers, we are soar-ing,

Refrain

"Lead me to my home."
Brought me to my home.
Streng-thened by her home.
Guide us to our home.

And where is

378

LOOK at both parts of "Don't Let the Music Stop."

One part uses mostly long notes and the other uses mostly short notes. Use your voice to emphasize the difference between them. Learn to sing the parts separately and then combined.

Words and Music
by Eugene Butler

Don't let the mu-sic stop,___ let's

I hear___ A - mer - i - ca

keep it firm and strong; Don't let the

sing - ing, I hear her sing-ing, Var - ied

mu - sic stop,___ let's sing the whole day long.

car - ols I hear.___

SING the first part of the song in a legato style and the second part in a staccato style. Is this easy or difficult? Identify why the composer wrote each part in a different style.

YOU'RE
INVITED

Choral

CONCERT

LISTENING

CHORAL CONCERT

Clément Janequin   Le chant des oyseaux
      (about 1485-1560)   (excerpt)

George Frideric Handel   Hallelujah Chorus
      (1685-1759)   (excerpt) from *Messiah*

Traditional/Arranged by
Ralph Vaughan Williams   Turtle Dove
      (1872-1958)   (excerpt)

P R O G R A M   N O T E S

Le chant des oyseaux
Clément Janequin

Clément Janequin wrote many songs that
imitate sounds of everyday life, including
Paris street noises, bird songs, battles, and
hunting expeditions. Can you tell what is
imitated in this song?

I magine that you're seated at a choral concert. You may have been greeted by an usher as you came in. The usher can help you find your seat and give you a program to read before the concert starts.

Choral singers combine their voices to achieve a special blended sound. Singers with the highest voices stand near each other because they sing the same part. The same is true for those with the middle and lowest voices. All watch the conductor, who helps them sing expressively together.

In the "Hallelujah Chorus," listen for times when the whole chorus sings together and when groups of singers sing different parts.

The soloist in "Turtle Dove" steps forward from the group as he begins. Does the rest of the chorus respond after the solo or sing along softly during the solo?

Listening

Some of the music listed below is very old, and some is new. Listen to these pieces. Which type of music would you like to learn more about?

Hallelujah Chorus
from *Messiah*

GEORGE FRIDERIC HANDEL
1741

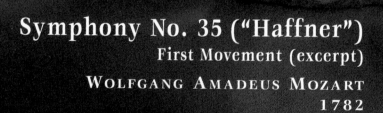

Symphony No. 35 ("Haffner")
First Movement (excerpt)

WOLFGANG AMADEUS MOZART
1782

Erlkönig

FRANZ SCHUBERT
1815

Discoveries

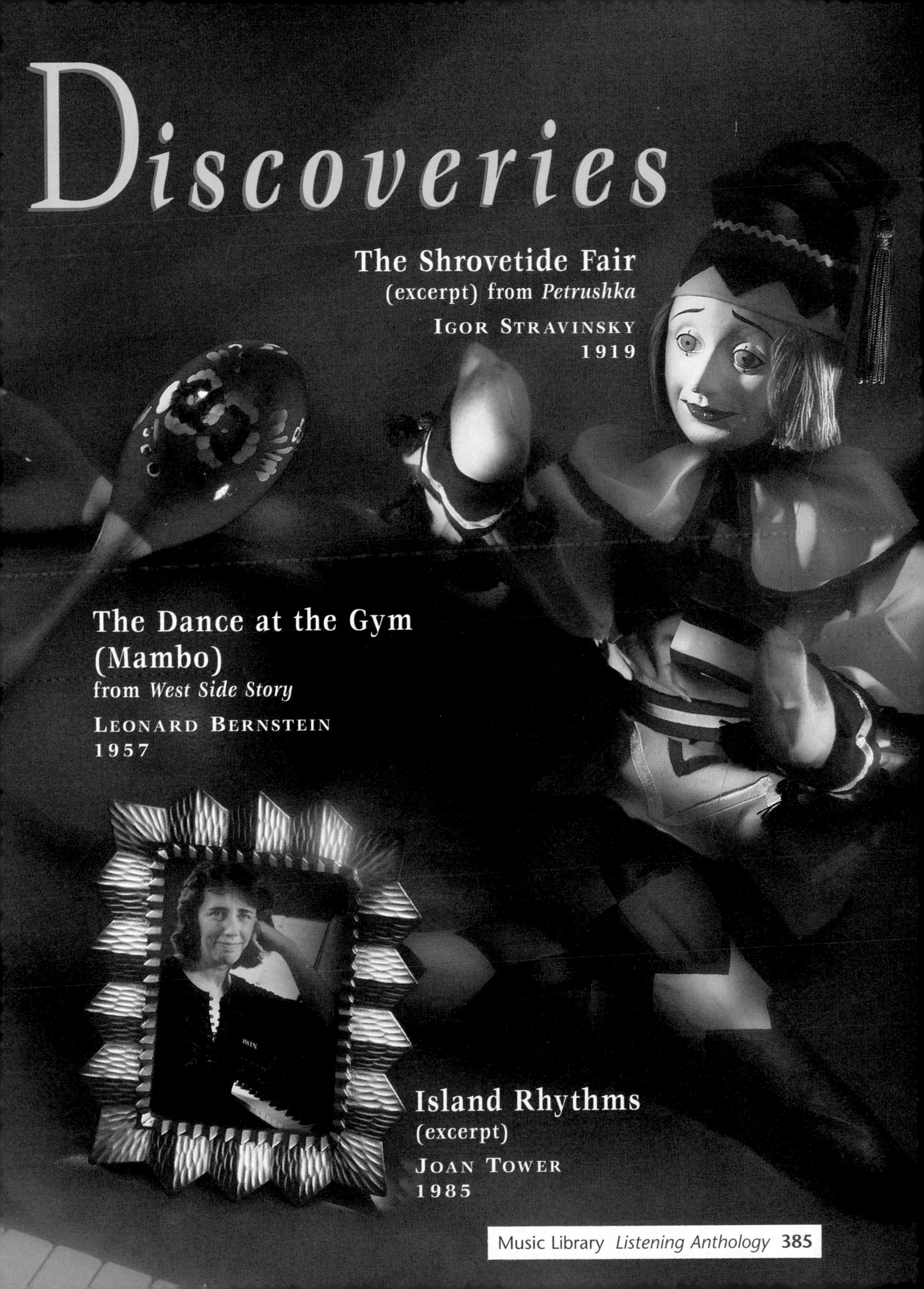

The Shrovetide Fair
(excerpt) from *Petrushka*

IGOR STRAVINSKY
1919

The Dance at the Gym
(Mambo)
from *West Side Story*

LEONARD BERNSTEIN
1957

Island Rhythms
(excerpt)

JOAN TOWER
1985

The Golden Goose

An original musical by Linda Worsley
based on a story by the Brothers Grimm

HAPPINESS

Words and Music by Linda Worsley

I *Chorus:* **Hap - pi - ness, And ad - ven - ture, What a great sen - sa - tion!**
II *Ned:* **Hap - pi - ness, And ad - ven - ture, What a great sen - sa - tion!**
III *Ned:* **Hap - pi - ness, And con - tent - ment! What a fine sen - sa - tion!**

If you try, you will find it, use your i - mag - i - na - tion.
If I try, I see cas - tles, in my i - mag - i - na - tion.
There's a farm I'll___ live in, not just i - mag - i - na - tion.

Hap - pi - ness, and ex - cite - ment, That's what
Tess: **Doom and gloom, and de - pres - sion, That's all**
Ned: **Hap - pi - ness, and en - chant - ment! I know**
Princess: **Gloom and doom, and de - pres - sion! That's all**

you will see here! Hap - pi - ness, all a - round you,
I can see there! *Ned:* **Hap - pi - ness, all a - round us,**
we can make it! Come with me, We can find it,
I could see here! *Ned:* **Hap - pi - ness, all a - round us,**

C Bm G F♯ Bm   F♯m

Feel it and it will be here! When you are will - ing,
Feel it and it will be there! May - be a ship is
Reach out a hand and take it! *Tess:* May - be our house will
Feel it and it will be here! *Chorus: as in I, to end*

F   Em   G   F♯m

when you be - lieve it, you'll make it through,
wait - ing to take us far, far a - way!
burn to the ground! Or may - be we'll freeze,

Em/A D   Bm   F♯m

And when you do, You will dis - cov - er
Tess: May - be I'll stay! *Ned:* Or there's a treas - ure
Ned: Or if you please, You'll be a he - ro

F   C   Em

you can a - chieve it, Make up your mind,
just for the ask - ing! May - be I'll find...
may - be the king will Ask you to tea!

Em *Repeat in II only* A7 D   Em/D

then you will find, Hap - pi - ness! And ad - ven - ture,
Tess: May - be you're blind! *Ned:* Hap - pi - ness, and ex - cite - ment,
Tess: That I've got - ta see!

D   Em/D   C

Reach out, help each oth - er, Some - where,
I just looked a - round me, Sud - den - ly,

F   C   Bm G F♯

some - one needs you, Strang - er, or friend or broth - er.
in a mo - ment, hap - pi - ness came and found me.

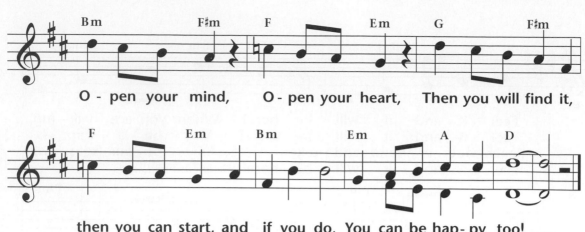

real - ly have to mean it. *Ned:* **A** prom - ise is a
real - ly have to mean it?

prom - ise is a prom - ise. **You**
(A prom - ise is a prom - ise.)

have to keep your word, it means a lot! (It means a

2nd time - all

lot!) *Both:* **So, don't ev - er make a prom - ise you can't**

prom - ise is a prom - ise, **and** no mat - ter when, no

mat - ter how, no mat - ter who you make a prom - ise, **the**

prom - ise must be kept no mat - ter what! *Chorus:* **A**

what! *Soloists:* **No mat - ter what?** *All:* **No mat - ter what!**

Ned finds the golden goose, who says, "Take me to the king!" On the way they meet a milkmaid. She wants a feather, but when she touches the goose she becomes stuck. Tess runs up to pull the maid away and can't let go. Both of them must now go with Ned to the king.

In another part of the forest, a farmer is singing of the joys of farming and his new harvest of carrots.

THINGS THAT GROW

First time Farmer; on repeat, Chorus, with Farmer on echo phrases.

Words and Music by Linda Worsley

Things that grow, (Things that grow,) In the gar - den, (In the gar - den,) Things that grow, (Things that grow,) In the sun. (In the sun.) Plant the seeds, when it's breez - y, pull the weeds, nice and ea - sy, hope for

rain and the job will be done! In the

fall, (In the fall,) dig the car-rots, (dig the

car-rots,) Crisp and sweet, (Crisp and sweet,) ev-'ry

one! (ev-'ry one!) Bless the sun and the

rain and bless the earth be-low for the

things that grow!

things that grow! _____

A peddler approaches with a tray of goods. The farmer admires a silver ring on the tray and the peddler eyes the bright orange carrots.

BARTER SONG

Words and Music by
Linda Worsley

Farmer C / Peddler / Farmer / Peddler

I'll trade you three car-rots. (ten car-rots,) four car-rots, (nine
trade you five car-rots, (eight car-rots,) six car-rots, (Well,)

C / Farmer / Both / Dm7 / G / Peddler Am / Farmer

2nd time to Coda

car-rots,) five car-rots for one shin-y ring! (the ring is of sil-ver!) Or
Both: How a-bout sev-en for one shin-y ring?

Am / Peddler / Farmer / Both

brass! (With a dia-mond!) Or glass! but it's real-ly a

Am / C7 / F / G / C / Em

beau-ti-ful thing! Bar-ter, bar-ter and trade!

F / G / C / Em / Am / Am/G♯

That's how bar-gains are made! Each side,

C/G / Am/F♯ / G7 / G7

D.S. al Coda
Farmer

giv-ing a lit-tle, un-til we can see, that we can a-gree. I'll

392 THE GOLDEN GOOSE

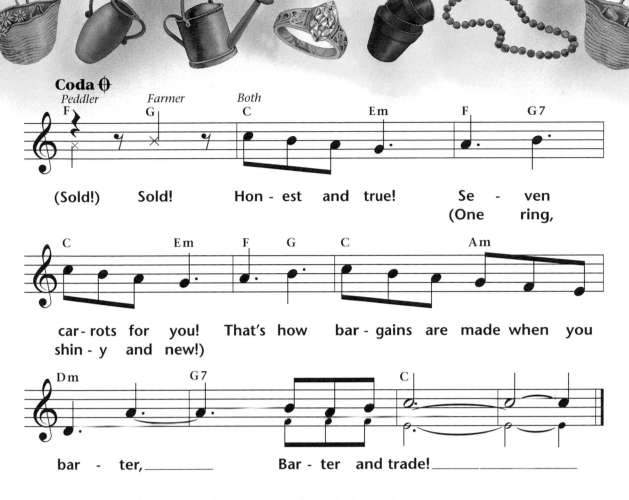

Coda ⊕

Peddler · Farmer · Both

(Sold!) Sold! Hon - est and true! Se - ven
(One ring,

car - rots for you! That's how bar - gains are made when you
shin - y and new!)

bar - ter,_____ Bar - ter and trade!_____

The farmer and the peddler see Ned and the others, try to help, and become stuck.

Meanwhile, at the palace, the king is losing hope that anything will cheer his daughter. She is sad because she wants to be an ordinary person instead of a princess.

BIRD IN THE WATER

Words and Music by
Linda Worsley

Slowly

King · F/C · B♭/C · Princess · F/C

It's im - pos - si - ble! I just

In tempo
5

B♭/C

have to be - lieve that it's pos - si - ble!

chiev - a - ble! King in the kit - chen, Cook on a
ter - ri - ble. Girl of the pa - lace, Child of the

throne! It could - n't hap - pen and you've al - ways
king! You are a prin - cess, a won - der - ful

known it's im - pos - si - ble! Just
thing, *Princess:* **But** it's pos - si - ble! If
Guard, Lady: **Im - pos - si - ble!**

lis - ten to me! Can't you see? You
I could be free! Can't you see? You

are what you are and that's what you were
are what you are and that's what you were

1. meant to be! But may - be... I could

2. meant to be!_____ But may - be... Im - pos - si - ble!

The princess bursts into laughter at the sight of Ned
and the others. The king rewards Ned with a farm.

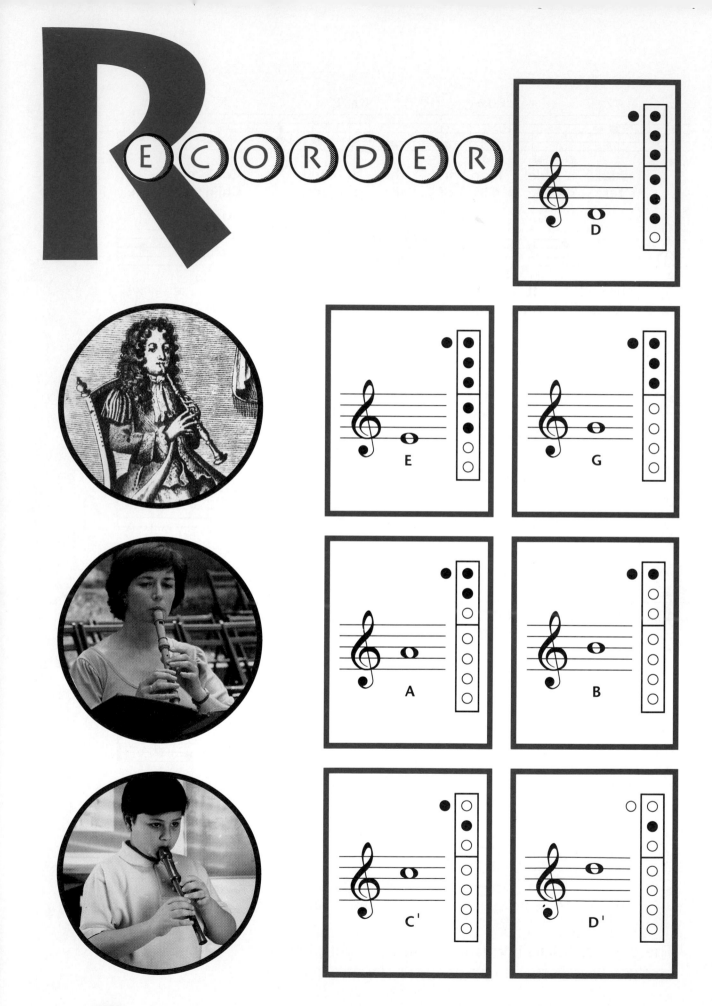

RECORDER

GLOSSARY

A

accelerando to get faster gradually, **215**

accent stress on a note or chord, **187**

accidental a flat (♭), sharp (♯), or natural sign (♮) that appears before a note and shows how the pitch should be changed, **267**

adagio slow, **215**

allegro fast, **215**

augment to change a rhythm by making it last twice as long, **270**

B

bar line (|) a line that divides notes into sets, showing the measures, **26**

bassoon a double-reed woodwind instrument that can play very low pitches, **216**

beat the pulse felt in music, **13**

C

call-and-response describes a song form in which each phrase sung by a solo leader is followed by a phrase sung by the group, **17**

canon song form with two or more voices performing the same melody but starting at different times, so that they overlap like a round, **21**

chord three or more pitches sounded together, **180**

chord root pitch on which a chord is built and that gives the chord its letter name, **182**

clarinet a woodwind instrument that uses a single reed, **273**

coda an ending section to a piece of music, **25**

crescendo (◁) to get louder gradually, **136**

cumulative describes a song form in which more words are added each time a verse is sung, **22**

D

decrescendo (▷) to get softer gradually, **136**

dotted quarter note (♩.) a note equal to one quarter note plus one eighth note, **128**

double reed two pieces of bamboo tied together, through which air is blown to produce the sound in some woodwind instruments, **216**

dynamics loudness and softness of music, **118**

E

eighth note (♪) two eighth notes (♫) equal one quarter note, **24**

eighth rest (𝄾) the symbol for a silence the length of an eighth note, **219**

F

flat (♭) a symbol in the key signature or in front of a note that means the pitch should be sung or played a half step lower, **133**

form the order of phrases or sections in music, **32**

forte (*f*) loud, **136**

H

half note (♩) a symbol for a sound the length of two quarter notes, **24**

harmony two or more pitches sung or played at the same time, **133**

heavier register a quality of speaking or singing that usually gives louder, fuller, and lower sound, **20**

I

improvise to make up music while playing it, **190**

interlude a short musical connection between sections or verses of a musical piece, **87**

J

jazz a style of music, often using improvisation and syncopation, that grew from the spirituals, work songs, and blues created by African Americans, **190**

K

key signature the sharps or flats at the beginning of each staff, **133**

L

ledger line a line added above or below the staff, **29**

lighter register a quality of speaking or singing that gives quieter, generally higher sound, **20**

M

major the sound of music that has do for its tonal center and uses the pitches of a major scale, **213**

major scale a specific set of eight pitches from *do* to *do¹*, **220**

measure the set of notes and rests between two bar lines, **26**

melody the tune; a series of pitches that moves upward, downward, or stays the same, **16**

meter signature a symbol that shows how many beats are in each measure and what kind of note equals one beat, **14**

mezzo forte (*mf*) medium loud, **136**

mezzo piano (*mp*) medium soft, **136**

minor the sound of music that has *la* for its tonal center and uses the pitches of a minor scale, **213**

minor scale a specific set of eight pitches from *la*₁ to *la*, **235**

moderato medium tempo, **215**

motive a short pattern used often in a piece of music, **85**

N

natural (♮) a symbol in front of a note that means the pitch should be played or sung as written, without a flat or sharp, **267**

O

oboe a double-reed woodwind instrument with a higher, sweeter sound than that of the bassoon, **216**

octave a skip of seven steps between two pitches; the distance between two pitches that have the same name, **166**

orchestra a large instrumental group, usually including four families of instruments: strings, woodwinds, brass, and percussion, **68**

ornamentation extra pitches or groups of pitches added to a melody to decorate it, **278**

ostinato a rhythmic or melodic pattern that repeats over and over, **40**

overture an instrumental piece that begins an opera or other large musical work; it often introduces the main musical ideas of the work, **85**

P

phrase a complete musical idea, **16**

piano (*p*) soft, **136**

pitch the highness or lowness of a sound, **16**

pitch syllable the name of a pitch, such as *do* or *mi*, **28**

presto very fast, **215**

Q

quarter note (♩) the symbol for one sound to a beat in $\frac{4}{4}$, **24**

quarter rest (𝄽) a symbol for a silence the length of a quarter note, **24**

R

reed a single piece of cane attached to the mouthpiece of some woodwind instruments, through which air is blown to produce sound, **273**

repeated notes one way a melody moves; to move by staying on the same pitch, **109**

ritardando to gradually slow down, **215**

S

sharp (♯) a symbol in the key signature or in front of a note that means the pitch should be played or sung a half step higher, **161**

sixteenth note (♪) four sixteenth notes equal one quarter note (♫♫), **72**

skip one way a melody moves; to move higher or lower by jumping over one or more pitches, **109**

spiritual a type of song created by African Americans, who combined African rhythms with melodies they created and heard in America, **168**

staff the five lines and four spaces on which musical notes are written, **29**

step one way a melody moves; to move by going to the next higher or lower pitch, **109**

syncopation happens when stressed sounds occur between the beats instead of on the beats of a rhythm pattern, **187**

T

tempo the speed of the beat, **215**

theme the main musical idea of a piece, **282**

theme and variations a musical form that has a main idea followed by changed versions of the idea, **282**

tie (⌣) a curved line that connects two notes of the same pitch and means that the sound is held for the length of both notes, **173**

tonal center the home tone or pitch around which a melody is centered, **59**

tone color the sound that is special to each instrument and voice, **22**

treble clef (𝄞) the symbol at the beginning of the staff that wraps around the G line, **78**

U

upbeat a note or notes that come before the first complete measure of music, **75**

V

variation a changed version of a theme or melody, **282**

vibration a motion that creates sound, **166**

vocables sung syllables that have no specific meaning, **167**

W

whole note (𝅝) a symbol for a sound the length of four quarter notes, **270**

ACKNOWLEDGMENTS *continued*

CPP/Belwin, Inc. for *Donna Donna* by Sholom Secunda and Aaron Zeitlin. Copyright © 1940, 1950 (Renewed 1968) MILLS MUSIC INC., c/o EMI MUSIC PUBLISHING. World Print Rights Administered by CPP/BELWIN, INC. All Rights Reserved. For *Petrushka* by Igor Stravinsky. Copyright © E.M. KALMUS ORCHESTRA SCORES. Used by Permission of CPP/Belwin, Inc., Miami, FL. All Rights Reserved. For *Singin' in the Rain* by Nacio Herb Brown & Arthur Freed. Copyright © 1929 (Renewed 1957) METRO-GOLDWYN-MAYER, INC., Rights Assigned to ROBBINS MUSIC CORP. All Rights of ROBBINS MUSIC CORP. Assigned to EMI CATALOGUE PARTNERSHIP. All Rights Controlled and Administered by EMI ROBBINS CATALOG, INC. International Copyright Secured. Made in U.S.A. Used by Permission. For *Sir Duke* by Stevie Wonder. © 1976 by JOBETE MUSIC CO., INC., and BLACKBULL MUSIC, INC., Hollywood, CA. International Copyright Secured. Made in USA. All Rights Reserved.

Dover Publications Inc. for *The California Song* from SONGS THE WHALEMEN SANG by Gale Huntington. © 1970 Dover Publications, Inc.

Follett Publishing Co. for *Voices of the World* by Stefi Samuelson, 1963 Follett Publishing Co., used by permission of Prentice-Hall.

Fox Film Music Corporation for *Somewhere in My Memory* by John Williams and Leslie Bricusse.

Ganymede Music for THE GOLDEN GOOSE. © 1999 by Linda Worsley.

Hap-Pal Music for *The Eagle* by Hap Palmer and Martha Cheney. © 1976 Hap-Pal Music.

Harcourt Brace Jovanovich, Inc. for *Hi! Ho! The Rattlin' Bog* from HI! HO! THE RATTLIN' BOG AND OTHER FOLK SONGS FOR GROUP SINGING, copyright © 1969 by John Langstaff, reprinted by permission of Harcourt Brace Jovanovich, Inc.

HarperCollins Publishers Ltd. for *Roads Go Ever Ever On* from THE HOBBIT by J.R.R. Tolkien. Published by George Allen & Unwin Ltd., an imprint of HarperCollins Publishers Ltd.

Florence Parry Heide for *Rocks* by Florence Parry Heide. Copyright Florence Parry Heide.

The Heritage Music Press for *Don't Let the Music Stop* by Eugene Butler.

Houghton Mifflin Co. for *Roads Go Ever Ever On* from THE HOBBIT by J.R.R. Tolkien. Copyright © 1966 by J.R.R. Tolkien. Reprinted by permission of Houghton Mifflin Co. All rights reserved.

Neil A. Kjos Music Co. for *La Pájara Pinta* from CANTEMOS EN ESPANOL BOOK 1, © 1948, ren. 1975 Max and Beatrice Krone. Reprinted with permission 1992.

Rita Klinger for *Aquaqua del a Omar*, Israeli children's singing game, collected in Jerusalem, Israel, by Rita Klinger, 1980.

The Last Music Co. for *This Pretty Planet* by John Forster & Tom Chapin. © 1988 Limousine Music Co. & The Last Music Co. (ASCAP).

Limousine Music Co. for *This Pretty Planet* by John Forster & Tom Chapin. © 1988 Limousine Music Co. & The Last Music Co. (ASCAP).

Gina Maccoby Literary Agency for *Clickbeetle* from BUGS by Mary Ann Hoberman. Reprinted by permission of Gina Maccoby Literary Agency. Copyright © 1976 by Mary Ann Hoberman.

Margaret K. McElderry Books for *Finding a Way* by Myra Cohn Livingston. Reprinted with permission of Margaret K. McElderry Books, an imprint of Macmillan Publishing Company, from THERE WAS A PLACE AND OTHER POEMS by Myra Cohn Livingston. Copyright © 1988 by Myra Cohn Livingston. Used also by permission of Marian Reiner for the author.

McGraw-Hill Ryerson Ltd. for *The Old Carrion Crow*, a Nova Scotian folk song from TRADITIONAL SONGS FROM NOVA SCOTIA by Helen Creighton. © McGraw-Hill Ryerson Ltd.

Dale Marxen for *Waltzing with Bears* by Dale E. Marxen. © 1986 Dale Marxen.

MMB Music, Inc. for *The Cat Came Back* from THE CAT CAME BACK by Mary Goetze. © 1984 MMB Music, Inc., Saint Louis. Used by Permission. All Rights Reserved. For *Fed My Horse* from THE CAT CAME BACK by Mary Goetze. © 1984 MMB Music, Inc., Saint Louis. Used by Permission. All Rights Reserved. For *Mongolian Night Song* from SONGS OF CHINA by Gloria Kiester and Martha Chrisman Riley. © 1988 MMB Music, Inc., Saint Louis. Used by Permission. All Rights Reserved.

Page Mortimer for the movement instructions for *Down the Road*.

Acknowledgments for Hal Leonard Showstoppers are on page HL18.

ART & PHOTO CREDITS

COVER DESIGN: Robert Brook Allen, *A Boy and His Dog*

COVER PHOTOGRAPHY: All photographs are by the McGraw-Hill School Division except as noted below.

Clarinet photograph by Jim Powell Advertising Photography for MHSD.

ILLUSTRATION

Steven Adler, 70, 84-85, 126-127; Zita Asbaghi, 192-193; Susan Ash, 128-129; Steve Atkinson, 76-77; Jim Kagan Batelman, 122-123; Karen Bell, 254-255; Doron Ben-Ami, 88-89; Bob Bennett, 292-293; (calligrapher) Steven Bennett, 46, 80, 56, 72, 122, 127, 172-173, 304, 316, 338; Ami Blackshear, 208-209, 239, 231; Karen Blessen, 298-299; Maxine Boll, 164-165; Sue Ellen Brown, 330-331; Thomas Buchs, 204-205; Shirley Chapman, 232-233; Judith Cheng, 272-273; Eva Vagreti Cockrille, 54-55; Sally Wern Comport, 104-105; Mary Collier, 300-301, 330-331, 344-345; Eulala Conner, 39, 71; Neverne Covington, 284-285; David Csicsko, 286-289; Margaret Cusack, 138-139; Dee Deloy, 14-15; Darius Detwiler, 20-21; David Diaz, 8-9; Nancy Doniger, 316-317; Janice Lee Durrand, 258-259; Allan Eitzen, 230; Nancy Freeman, 178-179; Brian Fujimori, 184-185; Manuel Garcia, 42-43; Jack Graber, 204-205; Griesbach & Martucci, 60-61; Jeffrey Gunion, 180-181; John Steven Gurney, 62-63; Randy Hamblin, 112-113, 318-319; Pamela Harrelson, 130-131; Dianne Teske Harris, 26-27; Kevin Hawkes, 30-31, 306-307; Mitch Heinze, 106-107; Cary Henrie, 182-183; Terry Herman, 1, 5, 12; Oscar Hernandez, 24-25, 260-261; Catherine Huerta, 120-121; Richard Hull, 22-23; Susan Huls, 233; Michael Ingle, 56-57, 386-387, 389, 390, 391, 392-393, 394-395; Ramona Jablonski, 114-115; Jakesevic and Lamut, 176-177; Shannon Jeffries, 190-191, 270-271; W.B. Johnson, 28-29, 36-37; Mark Kaplan, 186; Greg King, 214-215; Shannon Kriegshauser, 144-145; Dave LaFleur, 308-309; Barbara Lambase, 172-173, 320-321; Kathy Lengill, 206-207; Todd Leonardo, 58-59; Barry Maguire, 336-337; Mary Jo Mazzella, 166-167; Alan Mazzatti, 64-65; Sudi McCollum, 118-119; Francesca Moore, 338-339; Marjorie Muns, 66-67; Sal Murdocca, 132-133; Tom Nachreiner, 49; Randy Nelson, 68-69, 162; Carol Newson, 202-203; Nancy Nimoy, 236-237; Joseph Novach, 156-157; William O'Donnell, 217; Erik Olsen, 274-275; Edward Parker, 210-211, 230-231, 310-311; Bob Pepper, 262-263; Donna Perrone, 382-383; Bonnie Rasmussen, 74-75; Mike Reed, 108-109; William Rieser, 124-125; Robert Roper, 342-343; Robert Sauber, 32-33; John Schilling, 86-87; Fred Schrier, 324-325; Max Seabaugh, 92-95; Dorothea Sierra, 140-141; Michael Sours, 186-187; Randy South, 234-235, 282-283; Ken Spengler, 38-39; Gerardo Suzan, 80-81; Susan Swan, 21-213, 218-219; Glen Tarnowski, 222-223; Joseph Taylor, 136-137, 227; Kat Thacker, 40-41; Mary Thelen, 238-239; Gary Torrisi, 168-169; Elizabeth Traynor, 110-111; John Turrano, 44-45, 47; Jenny Vainisi, 100-103, 224-225, 302-303; Randy Verougstraete, 16-17; Carolyn Vibbert, 228-229; Pam Wall, 314-315; Mei Wang, 18-19; David Watts, 150-151, 152-153; David Wehrstein, 304-305; David Wenzel, 82-83; Kris Wiltse, 158-159; Gary Yealdhall, 264-265.

Tech Art by TCA Graphics, Inc.

PHOTOGRAPHY

All photographs are by the McGraw-Hill School Division (MHSD) except as noted below.

i: r. © Artville. iv: l. © Artville. m. © Artville. v: r. © Artville. vi: l. © Artville; violin, © Artville; drumsticks, © Artville; vii: flute, © Artville. **Unit 1** 10: Photofest. 11: l. Photofest; r. Daryl Pitt/Retna Ltd. 18: Superstock. 20: Jeff Sealik/Outline. 26: The Phillips Collection, Washington, D.C. 30: Martin Fox for MHSD. 33: UPI/Bettmann Newsphotos. 36-37: FPG. 41: Ken Karp for MHSD. 42: Gordon Photographic Ltd. 50: l. © 1998 Smithsonian Institution; r. Steve Velasquez/National Musueum of American History. 51: Teodoro Vidal Collection/National Museum of American History. 52: t. Rick Vargas/Smithsonian Institution. b. Martin Koenig/Center for Traditional Music and Dance. 53: Alex Viega/Center for Traditional Music and Dance. **Unit 2** 68-69. Jim Powell Studio for MHSD. 70 Archive Photos. 80-81: Ken Karp for MHSD. 85: Ron Scherl/Bettmann Newsphotos. 90: Jack Vartogian. 90-91: Dallas & John Heaton Westlight. 91: r. Shanghai Museum. 100-101: Ken Karp for MHSD. 101: r. Motion Picture and Television Photo Archive. 103: De Croce Studio. **Unit 3** 116: t. Culver Pictures. 116-117: b. Karen Meyers for MHSD; bkgnd. Ken Karp for MHSD. 120: Mark Phillbrick for MHSD. 123: David Heald © The Solomon R. Guggenheim Foundation, NY./ Canal, 1963, Helen Frankenthaler. Purchased with the aid of funds from the National Endowment for the Arts, Washington, D.C.; matching gift, Evelyn Sharp, 1976. 124: Ken Karp for MHSD. 125:

Anne Nielsen for MHSD. 126: The Granger Collection. 127: The New York Public Library. 129: Ken Karp for MHSD. 130: A. R. Linden/U.S. Marine Band. 131: UPI/ Bettmann Newsphotos. 134: David Lavender. 134-135: Wesley Bocxe/Photo Researchers, Inc.; bkgnd. Ken Karp for MHSD. 138: Michael Yamashita/Westlight. 139: Marka/International Stock. 141: *Baile en Tehuankpec* by Diego Rivera, Los Angeles Country Museum of Art. Gift of Mr. & Mrs. Milton W. Lipper, for the Milton W. Lipper Estate. 142-143: Ken Karp for MHSD. 144-145: Bill Waltzer for MHSD. 150: b. Anna Lee Walter/courtesy Chronicle Books; m. Jim Powell Studio for MHSD. 151: Mark A. Philbrick for MHSD. **Unit 4** 143-155: Bill Waltzer for MHSD. 160-161: Bill Waltzer for MHSD. 162: t. Brissand-Figaro/Gamma Liaison; m.l. Faria Castro Haraldo/ Gamma Liaison; m.r. Olivier Pighetti/Gamma Liaison; b. Krzystof Wojcik/Gamma Liaison. 163: l. Brissand-Figaro/Gamma Liaison, r. Peter Frey/Image Bank. 169: Iraq Museum. 170: t. Jack Vartoogian; b. Tim Bauer/Retna Ltd. 171: t.l. Mertan Simpson Gallery; b.l. Collection of Virgil Young; LP Music Group. 174:Bill Waltzer for MHSD. 175 Caroline Davies/Liaison International. 177: Maerten van Heenskerck, *Anna Codde;* Rijksmuseum, Amsterdam. 179: Gordon Parks/Life Magazine/ © Time Inc. 160-161: Bruce Caines for MHSD. 186: Paul Natkin/ Outline. 188: inset David G. Hauser; bkgnd. Bill Waltzer for MHSD. 189: Joe Viesti. 193: Bill Waltzer for MHSD. 194: FPG; m.r. Photoworld/FPG. 195: r. FPG; b.r. Ken Karp for MHSD. 198: Frank Driggs/Archive Photos. 199: The Bettmann Archive. 200: Ken Karp for MHSD. 201: San Francisco Craft & Folk Art Museum. **Unit 5** 213: Derek Smith for MHSD. 214-215: Bill Waltzer for MHSD. 216: b. Harry Heleotis. 220: Bill Waltzer for MHSD. 221-222: Bill Waltzer for MHSD. 223: Jim Stratford for MHSD. 226: Archive Photos. 228: *Down by the Riverside* by Daniel Pressley, 1966/DMA Photographers, Schomberg Center for Research in Black Culture, Art & Artifacts Division, NYPL, Astor, Lenox, & Tilden Foundation. 232: *Boy Playing Flute* by Judith Leyster, Statens Kontsmuseer, Stockholm, Sweden. 247: Marcia Keegan/Stock Market; Royal-Athena Galleries. **Unit 6** 250-251: b. Lois Ellen Frank/Westlight; Kevin Kolcyznksi for MHSD. 256: t.l. NASA/Peter Arnold. 257: t.l. NASA/Peter Arnold, t.r. NASA. 265: Jim Powell Studio for MHSD. 257: Jack Kenner for MHSD. 268: American Museum, Bath England/Superstock. 272: Mayna Treanor Avent, *Off Franklin*/Tennessee State Museum. 273: Ken Karp for MHSD. 274-275: Bill Waltzer for MHSD. 277: © 1993 The Estate of Keith Haring. 278: m. Owen Franken/Stock Boston; b. Ken Karp for MHSD; t. Murray Alcosser/ Image Bank. 278-279: M. David Frazier/Stock market. 279: t. Frank Siteman/Stock Boston; r., m. Lynton Gardiner; b. Ken Karp for MHSD. 280: l. George Ancona/International Stock; r. Robert Frerck/Odyssey Productions; 281: b. Roland & Sabrina Michaud/Woodfin Camp & Associates, Inc.; t. Owen Seumptewa for MHSD. 286-287, 289: Bill Waltzer for MHSD. 292: I. Granger Collection. 292-293: r. Americana Stock/Archive Photos. 294: H. Armstrong Roberts. 295: Bob Daemmrich/Stock Boston. **Celebrations** 296: Ken Regan/Camera 5. 300: t. S. Dooley/Liaison International. 312: t. Hot Shots; b. Luc A. Couturier/Départ. 322-323: Ken Karp for MHSD. 328-329: Nancy Palubniak. 332: I. David A. Harvey/Woodfin Camp & Associates, Inc; r. Richard Shiell/Earth Scenes. 339: Roberta Barnes/Gamma-Liaison. 340-341: Steve Gottlieb Photography. 303: inset The Bettmann Archive. **Music Library** 382-383: t. Karen Meytes for MHSD; b. Superstock. 384-385: t.l. Angelo Hornak Photograph Library, London; t.r. Dresden/Meissen Antique Import Corporation of America. 385: t.l. MMB Music; b.l. © 1985 Steve J. Sherman; r. The Ballet Shop, New York/A. Royzman. 396: t. The Bettmann Archive; m. Herb Snitzer Photography; b. Ken Karp for MHSD.

McGraw-Hill School Division thanks The Selmer Company, Inc., and its Ludwig/Musser Industries and Glaesel String Instrument Company subsidiaries for providing all instruments used in MHSD photographs in this music textbook series, with exceptions as follows: MHSD thanks Yamaha Corporation of America for French horn, euphonium, acoustic and electric guitars, soprano, alto, and bass recorders, piano, and vibraphone; MMB Music Inc., St. Louis, MO, for Studio 49 instruments; Rhythm Band Instruments, Fort Worth, TX, for resonator bells; Courtly Instruments, NY, for soprano and tenor recorder; Elderly Instruments, Lansing, MI, for autoharp, dulcimer, hammered dulcimer, mandolin, Celtic harp, whistles, and Andean flute.

CLASSIFIED INDEX

MUSICAL

NON-ENGLISH MUSIC

INDEX OF LITERATURE

POETRY

STORIES

INDEX OF LISTENING SELECTIONS

INTERVIEWS

INDEX OF SONGS AND SPEECH PIECES

Land of a Thousand Dances

Dance Hits Through the Decades

Arranged by Mark Brymer Script and Choreography by John Jacobson

Announcement: *(over school loudspeaker)* Attention! Attention! All students! I regret to announce the 4th grade field trip to the shopping mall for market research has been canceled… *(students moan)* Also, there will be no recess today due to bad weather someplace, somewhere…*(students moan loudest)* Sooooo….*(very excited)* we're cancelling everything and having a sock hop like you'll never forget! *(students cheer)*

At the Hop

Words and Music by Arthur Singer,
John Madara and David White

Ba ba ba ba, ba ba ba ba, ba ba ba ba,

ba ba ba ba, at the hop. 1. Well, you can

rock it, you can roll it, do the stomp and e - ven stroll it at the
swing it, you can groove it, you can real - ly start to move it at the

hop. When the rec-ords start a - spin-nin', you ca-
hop. Where the jock-ey is the smooth-est and the

lyp-so and you chick-en at the hop.   Do the
mu-sic is the cool-est at the hop.   All the

dance sen-sa - tions that are sweep-in' the   na - tion at the
cats and chicks__ can__ get their__ kicks____   at the

hop. }
hop. }   Let's go!   Let's go to the hop!

Let's go to the hop!   Let's go to the hop!

Let's go to the hop!   Come   on,   let's go to the hop!

1.   2.

2. Well, you can   Ba ba ba ba, Ba ba

ba ba, Ba ba ba ba, Ba ba ba ba, at the hop!

DJ: Hello Baby!! *(no response)*

DJ: I said....Hello Baaaaby!

All: *(shout)* Hello Baaaaby!

DJ: Now that's more like it! Welcome boys and girls, lads and lasses, moms and dads, teeny boppers and bobby soxers to the Land of a Thousand Dances! I'm DJ Howlin' Mac and in the Land of a Thousand Dances we're dancin' on the rooftops! We're dancin' on the ceiling and we're definitely....Dancin' in the Streets!

Dancing in the Street

Words and Music by Marvin Gaye,
Ivy Hunter and William Stevenson

Call - ing out__ a - round__ the world, "Are you

read - y for a brand new beat?" Sum-mer's here_ and the

time is right for danc - ing____ in the streets.

They're danc - ing in Chi - ca - go,__

down in New Or - leans,_ up in New York Cit -

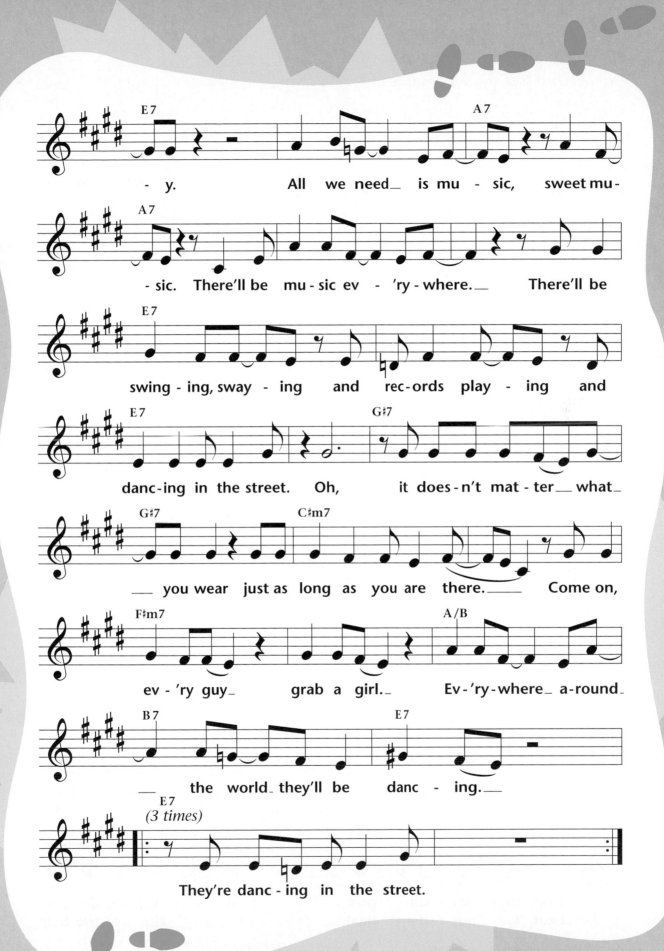

Kid 1: *(like a rap to student dancing)* What's up?… What ya doin' there? Just the way you're movin' is giving me a scare!

Kid 2: *(like a rap)* When I hear the music I just got to move my feet! Can't sit still 'cause I've really got the beat!

Kid 3: *(Shouting like leading a cheer)* Who's got the beat?

All: *(shouting)* We've got the beat!

Kid 4: *(Shouting like leading a cheer)* Who's got the beat?

All: *(shouting)* We've got the beat! LET'S GO!!!!

We Got the Beat

Words and Music by
Charlotte Caffey

1. See the peo-ple walk-ing down the street;   fall in line just watch-
2. See the kids just get-ting out   of school.   They can't wait to hang_

- ing all their feet._ They don't know where_ they want to go, but they're
__ out and be cool._ Hang a-round 'til quar - ter af - ter 12. That's____

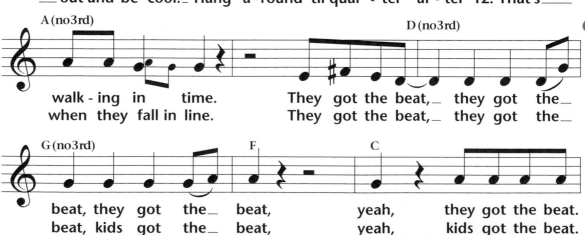

walk - ing in   time.   They got the beat,_ they got   the_
when they fall in line.   They got the beat,_ they got   the_

beat, they got   the_ beat,   yeah,   they got the beat.
beat, kids got   the_ beat,   yeah,   kids got the beat.

DJ: Line up everyone! It's time to do the Locomotion with me! *(All cheer)*

The Loco-Motion

Words and Music by
Gerry Goffin and Carole King

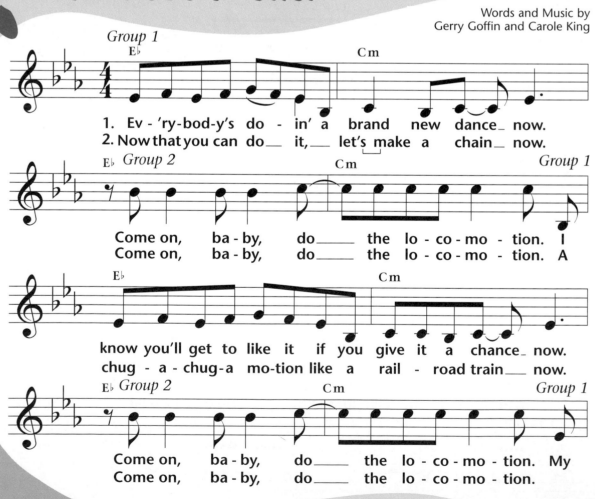

1. Ev-'ry-bod-y's do - in' a brand new dance now.
2. Now that you can do it, let's make a chain now.

Come on, ba-by, do the lo-co-mo-tion. I
Come on, ba-by, do the lo-co-mo-tion. A

know you'll get to like it if you give it a chance now.
chug - a-chug-a mo-tion like a rail - road train now.

Come on, ba-by, do the lo-co-mo-tion. My
Come on, ba-by, do the lo-co-mo-tion.

DJ: Okay kids are ya ready to romp?
Let me introduce you to the Bristol Stomp.

Bristol Stomp

Words and Music by
Kal Mann and David Appell

The kids in Bris-tol are sharp as a pis-tol
when they do the Bris-tol Stomp. Real-ly sum-pin' when the
joint is jump-in' when they do the Bris-tol Stomp.

1. The sounds are spin-in'___ ev-'ry Fri-day night.___
2. It start-ed in Bris-tol___ at a D. J. hop.___

The kids start danc-in'___ an' they do it right.
They hol-ler and whis-tle,___ nev-er wan-na stop.

One dance is spe-cial,___ it's a cra-zy sight to
We po-ny and twist-ed,___ and we rocked with dad-dy

Kid 5: Hey everybody let's go! I heard that the real fun is Down at the Twist and Shout!

Down at the Twist and Shout

Words and Music by
Mary Chapin Carpenter

Refrain

Sat-ur-day night_ and the moon is out._ I wan-na

head on o - ver to the Twist and Shout, find a two-step part - ner and a

ca - jun beat, when it lifts me up,_ I'm gon-na find my feet

out in the mid-dle of a big dance floor. When I

hear that fid - dle, wan - na beg for more. Wan - na

dance to a band from a Loui-si - an'__ to-night._

DJ: Hold on boppers! No need to run!
Stay right here and have your fun!
I've got a number that will wear you out!
Come on everybody let's Twist and Shout!

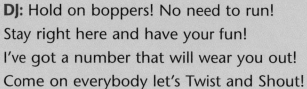

Twist and Shout

Words and Music by
Bert Russell and Phil Medley

Well, shake it up ba - by, now.
(Shake it up ba -

- by.) Twist and   shout.___
(Twist and   shout.)___

Come on, come on, come on,   ba - by now.___
(Come on ba -

- by,) Come on and work it on   out.___
(work it on out.)___

Announcement: *(like the beginning)* Attention! Attention! The sock hop for today is just about over. Your reports on the influence of the Bristol Stomp on modern civilization are due Friday! *(students moan)*

DJ: Don't worry kids, I still have a little time. And lucky for you I have one more little rhyme! *(students cheer)*

DJ: When you're down, feeling out, and you don't like your chances, take a trip to the Land of a Thousand Dances! *(students cheer louder)*

Land of a Thousand Dances

Words and Music by Chris Kenner

You got-ta know how to po - ny___ like

Bo - ny Mar - o - nie, Mashed Po - ta - to,

do the Al - li - ga - tor. Put your

hands on your hips, let your back - bone slip.

Do the Wa - tu - si like my lit - tle Lu - cy.

ACKNOWLEDGMENTS

Grateful acknowledgment is given to the following authors, composers, and publishers.

At The Hop
Words and Music by Arthur Singer, John Madara and David White
Copyright © 1957 (Renewed) by Arc Music Corporation (BMI) and Six Continents Music Publishing, Inc. (BMI)
All Rights Controlled by Arc Music Corporation (BMI)
International Copyright Secured   All Rights Reserved
Used by Permission

Bristol Stomp
Words and Music by Kal Mann and Dave Appell
Copyright © 1961 Kalmann Music, Inc.
Copyright Renewed
All Rights Controlled and Administered by Spirit Two Music, Inc. (ASCAP)
International Copyright Secured   All Rights Reserved

Dancing In The Street
Words and Music by Marvin Gaye, Ivy Hunter and William Stevenson
© 1964 (Renewed 1992) FCG MUSIC, NMG MUSIC, MGIII MUSIC, JOBETE MUSIC CO., INC. and STONE AGATE MUSIC
All Rights Controlled and Administered by EMI APRIL MUSIC INC. and EMI BLACKWOOD MUSIC INC. on behalf of JOBETE MUSIC CO., INC. and STONE AGATE MUSIC (A Division of JOBETE MUSIC CO., INC.)
All Rights Reserved   International Copyright Secured   Used by Permission

Down At The Twist And Shout
Words and Music by Mary Chapin Carpenter
© 1990 EMI APRIL MUSIC INC. and GETAREALJOB MUSIC
All Rights Controlled and Administered by EMI APRIL MUSIC INC.
All Rights Reserved   International Copyright Secured   Used by Permission

Land Of A Thousand Dances
Words and Music by Chris Kenner
© 1963, 1970 (Renewed 1991) EMI LONGITUDE MUSIC
All Rights Reserved   International Copyright Secured   Used by Permission

The Loco-Motion
Words and Music by Gerry Goffin and Carole King
© 1962 (Renewed 1990) SCREEN GEMS-EMI MUSIC INC.
All Rights Reserved   International Copyright Secured   Used by Permission

Twist And Shout
Words and Music by Bert Russell and Phil Medley
Copyright © 1960, 1964 Sony/ATV Songs LLC, Unichappell Music Inc. and Sloopy II Music
Copyright Renewed
All Rights on behalf of Sony/ATV Songs LLC Administered by Sony/ATV Music Publishing, 8 Music Square West, Nashville, TN 37203
International Copyright Secured   All Rights Reserved

We Got The Beat
Words and Music by Charlotte Caffey
Copyright © 1981 by BMG Songs, Inc.
International Copyright Secured   All Rights Reserved

Illustrations by Mitch Mortimer

PRONUNCIATION KEY
Simplified International Phonetic Alphabet

VOWELS

ɑ	father	æ	cat
e	ape	ε	pet
i	bee	ι	it
o	obey	ɔ	paw
u	moon	ʊ	put
ʌ	up	ə	ago

SPECIAL SOUNDS

β say *b* without touching lips together; *Spanish* nueve, haba

ç hue; *German* ich

ð the, *Spanish* todo

ņ sound n as individual syllable

ö form [o] with lips and say [e]; *French* adieu, *German* schön

œ form [ɔ] with lips and say [ε]; *French* coeur, *German* plötzlich

ſ flipped r; butter

r̄ rolled r; *Spanish* perro

ɬ click tongue on the ridge behind teeth; *Zulu* ngcwele

ü form [u] with lips and say [i]; *French* tu, *German* grün

ü̆ form [ʊ] with lips and say [ι]

x blow strong current of air with back of tongue up; *German* Bach, *Hebrew* Hanukkah, *Spanish* bajo

ʒ pleasure

' glottal stop, as in the exclamation "uh oh!" [ʌ 'o]

~ nasalized vowel, such as French bon [bõ]

˥ end consonants *k*, *p*, and *t* without puff of air, such as sky (no puff of air after *k*), as opposed to *kite* (puff of air after *k*)

OTHER CONSONANTS PRONOUNCED SIMILAR TO ENGLISH

ch	cheese	ny	onion, *Spanish* niño
g	go	sh	shine
ng	sing	ts	boats

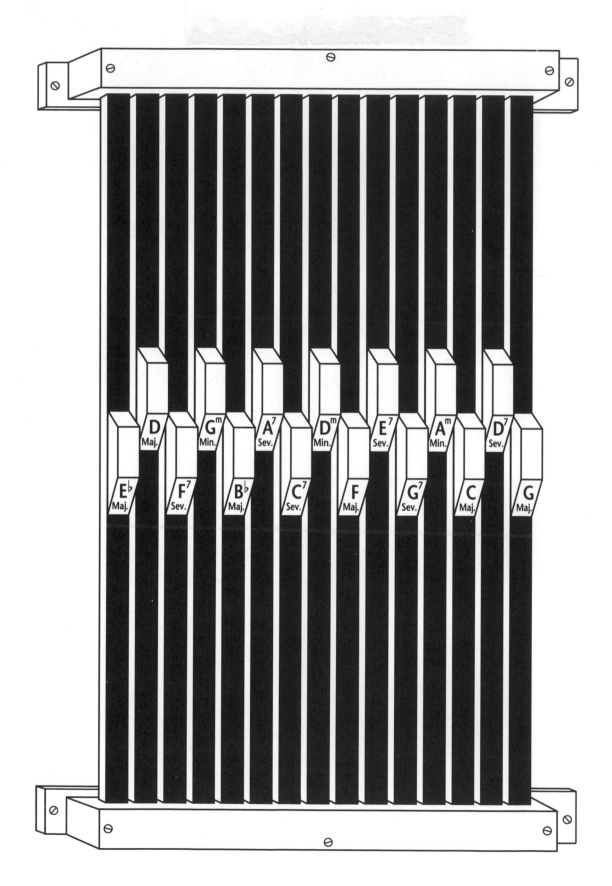